2010 and Beyond

A Vision of America's Transportation Future

2010 and Beyond

A Vision of America's Transportation Future

Hudson Institute
2004

2010 and Beyond: A Vision of America's Transportation Future

ISBN 1-55813-144-2

Printed in the United States of America.

For information about obtaining additional copies of this or other Hudson Institute publications, contact:

Hudson Institute Fulfillment Center
P.O. Box 1020
Noblesville, IN 46061
Toll free: 888-554-1325
Fax: 317-913-2392

Or, visit Hudson's online bookstore at http://www.hudson.org

For media and speaking engagement purposes, contact Hudson Institute at 202-223-7770 or email info@hudson.org.

Table of Contents

Foreword

In the 1950s the Eisenhower administration embarked on a program that literally changed the face of America. The interstate highway system was built, catapulting the nation into the modern era of transportation. This revolutionary development enhanced economic growth, added to personal mobility, reduced transactional business expenses, and offered housing opportunities undreamed of until this point in U.S. history. For half a century the nation lived on this legacy.

Now the roads are congested, waiting time for truckers at ports has increased exponentially, and what was once an American dream—rapid and reliable highway travel—has been converted for many into an American nightmare. It is time to revisit the issue of national transportation.

In this book, which emanated from what is arguably the most comprehensive study of transportation in a generation, Hudson Institute calls for revolutionary changes in the financing, technology, and management of the nation's surface transportation system. This study contends that changes are essential if the American economy is to progress without major impediments. Since these changes are likely to take a generation to work their way fully through the nation's surface transportation system, the time to begin is now.

The most serious financial challenge involves the nation's roadways, where existing methods of funding highways and streets seem to have broken down. The American Association of State Highway and Transportation Officials (AASHTO) estimates that $5.3 trillion will be needed during the first quarter of the twenty-first century to prevent further deterioration of the nation's highways, and this estimate does not include the similar shortfalls in spending for transit, rail, and freight needs. In order to overcome the effects of past underspending and keep pace with growing transportation demand, new investment is necessary. But the present federal motor vehicle fuel tax and appropriations from state and local government budgets are projected to meet less than two-thirds of these needs.

It is our contention that the solution to this funding shortfall is to end the traditional practice of regarding highway access as "free." Instead, motorists should be charged reasonable user fees for using the roads based on miles traveled, the kind of vehicles driven, the amount of pollution generated, and the level of traffic demand in effect when trips are made. New technology now makes it feasible to enable the nation's existing highways to collect user fees to generate revenue without affecting traffic flow. The goal is to deliver highway access to motorist "customers" through the marketplace in a manner similar to that which governs the allocation of other goods and services. Highway user fees should be accompanied by "money-back performance guarantees" so that each motorist can make meaningful tradeoffs between travel time savings and how much is paid to use highway lanes.

New technology offers many potential improvements to the surface transportation system. Equally important from the perspective of this book are the many ways that technology can help smooth the flow of people and goods in travel time and cost savings.

For example, technology already available or being developed can greatly reduce the incidence of motor vehicle accidents on crowded highways, as well as limiting the personal injuries and property loss from crashes. (In 2003, 42,000 lives were lost in highway fatalities in the United States, with an estimated cost of $230 billion.) "Smart cars" and "smart highways" could reduce the increasing financial burden that such events impose on American society and minimize the travel time delays. The same technology can also work around the clock to optimize vehicle spacing, speeds, and routings so that any number of highway lane miles can move more vehicles in less time.

Perhaps most significantly, we foresee effective technology helping to break down the artificial barriers among surface transportation modes so that people and goods move expeditiously door-to-door through a properly integrated system. But superior technology is not enough to make the difference by itself. More important is how the use of technology is managed to produce desirable results. That is why the study's conclusion stresses the need for transportation system managers to change their focus from traditional engineering-oriented performance measures like vehicle-miles-of-travel to customer-oriented measures that emphasize reduced door-to-door travel time, greater reliability, and smoother interfaces among various transportation modes. With improved customer service as their primary goal, transportation managers will find new uses for technology as it becomes available and new ways to have different technologies work together.

Perhaps the study's most ambitious concept is a proposal to convert what is now a disconnected group of surface transportation modes into a fully integrated "system" that travelers perceive as seamless and transparent. The key for accomplishing this goal is to have the national, user-fee-supported highway network become a major funding source for all surface transportation activity, not just for roadways. This can include using user-fee revenues to support a large network of freight railroad tracks so that more goods can be moved by rail, easing the impact of trucks on the nation's highways. The same approach can be applied to public transit in large metropolitan regions in order to avoid clogging highways with single-occupancy vehicles.

The use of cross-subsidization is a necessary step in our opinion, but one that has its risks. There are obviously huge institutional, administrative, and public acceptance hurdles that could not be explicitly considered in this book. Issues related to the sharing of road revenue with transit services in the same corridor, for example, are vastly different from what is involved in using nationwide road revenue for selected investments in the freight system.

It should also be noted that an extended transition period is needed to move from the present gas tax to road pricing and cross subsidies. We realize as well that despite the best efforts of the government and the private sector, petroleum fuels are likely to dominate the transportation market for some time to come, and notwithstanding the many issues associated with the gas tax, it does offer low transactional costs and is roughly related to usage.

Hudson Institute's visionary approach to creating an integrated surface transportation system poses major new financial, technological and management challenges. But we regard it as a step in maintaining national economic competitiveness in a world economy which increasingly puts a premium on moving people and goods efficiently.

As we see it, just as the Eisenhower administration had the vision to see transportation as a catalyst for economic growth in the 1950s, the new century requires an integrated transportation system consonant with the demands of the twenty-first century. We now have the technology that is necessary to make that happen; all we need is the will to make it a reality.

H.I.L.

Policy Recommendations

Policy #1: Transportation Finance

Context

- Our nation's transportation network provides mobility for both people and goods.
- Transportation efficiencies represent a major factor in achieving economic competitiveness in the global market.
- Failure to invest in our nation's surface transportation systems and infrastructure will result in significant negative consequences to our quality of life and the nation's economic vitality.
- Traffic volumes have grown 80 percent in the last 20 years and will grow 50 percent more in the next 20 years.
- Cambridge Systematics estimates the cost to maintain the current transportation system to be $4.4 trillion between 2000 and 2025, or $1 trillion more than is currently available.
- Cambridge Systematics estimates that the cost to improve the current transportation system will be $5.3 trillion between 2000 and 2025, or a $2 trillion gap with available funds.
- Transit ridership is up 24 percent in the last six years, with 9.7 billion trips in 2001.
- It is estimated that it would take $43.9 billion per year to improve the current physical condition of our nation's transit system.
- Current New Starts projects number 78, with a total value of $47 billion, vying for just about $1.2 billion per year in funding.
- There are another 150 projects in the development stage that would compete for New Starts funding in the near future.
- Funding for homeland security measures is insufficient to protect national transportation assets in an adequate manner.

Policy Recommendation

Transportation investments must be funded from a comprehensive set of revenue sources that are sustainable and reflective of consumer choice.

Strategies

1. The United States Congress should adopt funding strategies that represent "net new" revenue sources for transportation investment.

2. The Congress should encourage and expand High Occupancy Toll (HOT) lanes and the use of user fees by giving the states broad authority to implement these strategies on state corridors as well as interstate freeways.
3. Congress should create new opportunities for transportation agencies and properties to enhance revenue through consumer choice for mobility and mode.
4. The United States should begin to develop the strategies necessary to transition to a Vehicle Miles Traveled (VMT) based revenue system to be implemented in the 2015 timeframe.

Policy Issue #2: Mobility Management

Context

- Our nation's transportation system is made up of transportation modes that operate individually with unrelated performance measures.
- Funding for transportation is largely mode-specific.
- The public is unable to make mobility decisions based on time, value, and cost because of the disparate manner in which the modes operate.
- The transportation system lacks a robust technology backbone that will allow further achievements in efficiency and effectiveness.

Policy Recommendation

The United States must establish a transportation system where all modes operate as one in a Mobility Management environment.

Strategies

1. It is our hope that Congress shall enact legislation giving transportation agencies broad authority and flexibility to employ funding in ways to create truly multi-modal transportation solutions to our nation's mobility needs.
2. Congress should enact legislation that removes barriers to technology deployment, thus advancing technology's role in creating the Mobility Management system.
3. Congress should remove organizational barriers at the federal level, allowing transportation modes to advance toward a seamless transportation system. These barriers include onerous environmental legislation, funding mechanisms, administrative procedures, and other impediments that serve to separate the modes and create inequality.

Policy Issue #3: Technology Deployment

Context

- Fatalities on our nation's highways exceeded 42,000 in 2003.
- In spite of significant gains in seat belt usage, air bags, and other safety equipment in vehicles, the fatality rate continues to be approximately 1.5 per 100 million vehicle miles traveled.
- Our nation expends $230 billion per year on crash related costs.
- Operational inefficiencies on our nation's surface transportation system resulted in an annual user cost of $69.5 billion in lost productivity in 2001 for time spent on congested roads.
- There were 5.7 billion gallons of wasted fuel due to congestion in 2001.
- Technology advancements such as the crashless vehicle and other systems are available for deployment, but liability issues and other institutional/policy related barriers prevent their use.

Policy Recommendation

The United States must advance the rapid deployment of technology in all aspects of its transportation system to achieve optimal safety, security, and operational benefits into the future.

Strategies

1. Congress should require the U.S. DOT to accelerate the integration of in-vehicle technologies for all modes and systems to achieve required safety and operational goals.
2. Congress should establish regulatory reform on insurance, tort liability, and anti-trust issues.
3. Standards and protocols should be adopted to address security and privacy issues as well as environmental integrity.
4. Congress should provide state transportation agencies and properties with broad authority to implement key technology components in their infrastructure.

Policy Issue #4: Freight Systems

Context

Freight growth (in billions of ton-miles) between now and 2020 will increase as follows:

- ➢ Truck – 64 percent
- ➢ Rail – 49 percent
- ➢ Barge – 15 percent
- ➢ Air – over 100 percent

- Truck freight movements are impacted by the same issues of congestion and capacity as are the passenger modes of travel.
- Marginal changes in transportation cost for goods movement in both the domestic and international markets are critical to the economic vitality of our nation.
- Lack of investments in port infrastructure, transfer facilities, and intermodal centers is resulting in freight inefficiencies and capacity issues.
- Investments in freight infrastructure are not separately funded and have no dedicated revenue stream.
- Rail infrastructure is in need of significant investment. In order to maintain and operate current rail systems it would take an estimated investment of $8.5 billion per year in new funding.
- Freight facilities, especially ports, are vulnerable to terrorist threats, with only 5 percent of the containers coming into U.S. ports subject to careful screening.

Policy Recommendation

Establish freight transportation systems, including highway, rail, ports, river, and air, as critical interrelated components contributing to our nation's role in the global economy.

Strategies

1. Congress should establish the National Strategic Freight Investment Program with dedicated revenues and a management system to accommodate needed freight investments in the future.
2. Congress should provide needed authority for the governance of freight investment to the U.S. DOT.
3. Congress should establish the Innovations Program for State and Local Freight Transportation to provide incentives for local and regional investments in freight systems impacting our nation's freight movement.

Part I

Transportation Finance

by
Lance R. Grenzeback

Chapter 1

Current Outlook for Transportation Finance

Hudson Institute, the American Association of State Highway and Transportation Officials (AASHTO), and the American Public Transportation Association (APTA) are concerned that transportation revenues are not adequate to support a productive and cost-effective twenty-first century transportation system. The concern is well-founded.

The Federal Highway Administration (FHWA) estimates that revenues in 2004 were $21 billion short of the level of expenditure needed to maintain the nation's roadway system and $15 billion short of the level needed to maintain the nation's transit systems.[1] And the FHWA's estimates are conservative. AASHTO's most recent "need to maintain" estimates show that revenues in 2004 were $37 billion short for roadways and $19 billion short for transit.[2]

If revenues were increased by these amounts, they would be sufficient only to maintain the current physical condition of pavements, bridges, and transit infrastructure. They would not be adequate to improve the performance and economic productivity of the nation's transportation systems.[3] Population, economic activity, and demand for transportation are increasing more rapidly than roadway capacity and transit service. Without additional investment, highway congestion will increase and transit services will deteriorate. The FHWA estimates that revenues in 2004 were $52 billion short of the level of expenditure needed to improve the performance of the nation's roadways and $21 billion short for transit. AASHTO's "need to improve" estimates show that revenues were $71 billion short for roadways and $29 billion short for transit.

The recent recession and delays in reauthorization of the federal surface transportation programs have forced states and the federal government to cut back on transportation improvements in the short term. This will exacerbate highway congestion and accelerate the deterioration of transit services, driving up costs in the long term.

The challenge of increasing investment in highways and transit to the levels the nation needs will get tougher during the period ahead, especially beyond 2010. When the federal government made the commitment to build the Interstate Highway System and provide states and localities with capital assistance for highways and transit, a decision was made to fund the programs on a pay-as-you-go basis through the Highway Trust Fund, which was to be funded with dedicated user fees, primarily motor fuel taxes. Today's federal highway assistance program is supported entirely by the Highway Trust Fund. Federal transit assistance also depends heavily on revenues from the Highway Trust Fund's Mass Transit Account. To meet the nation's growing needs and sustain the purchasing power of the program, Congress has periodically increased the motor fuel taxes that support the Highway Trust Fund. Gasoline taxes were increased by 4.0 cents under President Eisenhower, 5.1 cents under President Reagan, 5.0 cents under President Bush, Sr., and 4.3 cents under President Clinton.

Although the issue is still under debate, it appears unlikely that the pending reauthorization of the federal surface transportation programs will increase motor fuel taxes. However, spending on highways and transit will expand in the coming years because of strong bipartisan support in Congress for transportation projects. By 2009 obligations for highways are expected to grow from $33.6 billion to approximately $40 billion annually, and transit from $7.3 billion to as much as $10 billion. But the resources in the Highway Trust Fund will increase only to $35 billion annually for highways and to $5 billion annually for transit. This will create a significant funding gap.

When federal policy-makers consider options for reauthorization, they must address two challenges: first, how to generate revenues sufficient to close the gap between the highway and transit funding levels achieved under SAFETEA and the levels that can be sustained by the Highway Trust Fund; and second, how to boost federal funding beyond 2010 to a level that meets the nation's highway and transit capital investment needs.

Hudson Institute, working in partnership with AASHTO and APTA, commissioned Cambridge Systematics to identify revenue strategies that will fund transportation projects and programs into the twenty-first century. The goals are to develop strategies that increase the total amount of revenue available for transportation system maintenance and improvement and make the transportation system more responsive to customers. At a minimum, the strategies should produce sufficient revenue to meet the FHWA's "need to maintain" target and, ideally, strategies that will provide policy-makers with the option of investing in projects up to the AASHTO "need to improve" target. These solutions also should provide transportation system users and providers—automobile drivers, transit riders, freight shippers, carriers, and agencies—with clearer links between the prices they pay and the services they receive.

Five criteria were defined to assess current revenue sources and future strategies for generating additional transportation revenues. These criteria are:

1. **Yield and Reliability** – How much money does the revenue strategy generate and how reliable is the yield over time?
2. **Economic Efficiency** – Does the revenue strategy provide clear pricing signals that encourage transportation users and providers to use the transportation system in ways that minimize wasteful and unproductive travel and maximize economic growth?
3. **Social Equity** – Does the revenue strategy unfairly restrict access to basic transportation services or impose an unfair financial burden on users based on their ability to pay?
4. **Administrative Effectiveness** – Does the revenue strategy allow for cost-effective and hassle-free collection of revenues while minimizing evasion?
5. **Public Acceptance** – Will a majority of voters, system users, and transportation providers support the revenue strategy?

The report first describes the current sources of transportation revenue. These are compared to the anticipated costs of maintaining and improving the highway and transit systems. The current revenue sources are then evaluated against the five criteria. The conclusions of that assessment are used to develop a set of short-term revenue strategies that could be implemented between now and 2015. These short-term strategies are in turn assessed against the five criteria. The conclusions of that assessment set the stage for development of long-term revenue strategies that could be implemented beginning in 2015 to meet the needs of the nation's transportation system well into the twenty-first century.

The short- and long-term strategies are matched to the reauthorization cycles of federal surface transportation legislation. The short-term strategies are intended for implementation over the current and next reauthorization cycles. The long-term strategies are targeted for the two reauthorization cycles following 2015. Figure 1-1 shows the timeframes for the two sets of strategies.

Figure 1-1: Timeframes for Short- and Long-Term Strategies

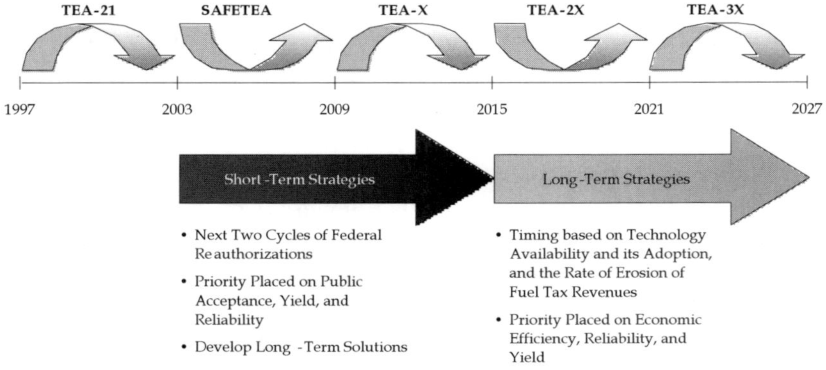

Source: Cambridge Systematics, Inc.

The report looks at revenue strategies that support the major surface transportation modes: highways, transit, passenger rail, and the public elements of freight rail (e.g., investments in highway-rail grade crossings). The report quantifies the needs of both the highway and transit systems because these have been well-documented by the major transportation agencies, associations, and stakeholders and submitted to the most rigorous peer review. Less attention is given to the passenger- and freight-rail systems. Estimates of the costs to maintain and improve the passenger- and freight-rail systems exist, but the data and methodologies are not as fully developed and the public sector's role in these systems is less clear.

The report examines highway and transit revenue sources, but focuses on highway revenue sources because they are the dominant sources of revenue for public investment in transportation. Transit farebox revenues and local-option sales taxes dedicated to transit generate considerable revenue for the nation's transit systems, but they do not have the capacity to generate enough new revenue to fill the large shortfalls identified in this report.

Therefore, the short- and long-term strategies proposed in the report look primarily to highway revenue sources because they are and will continue to be the major sources of public revenue for transportation.

The report's recommendations and the underlying analyses deal with revenues, not expenditures. The report does not suggest how best to allocate revenues among competing transportation interests—between modes (drive alone, carpool, transit, etc.), between urban and rural areas, or between passenger and freight systems—nor does the report address the impact of the revenue strategies on land use and development patterns. The focus of the report is on how to make the transportation revenue pie larger and more predictable, not on how to slice it up. The report is intended to begin a national discussion on how to generate transportation revenue in the twenty-first century. It must be paired with a national discussion on how to invest in transportation in the twenty-first century.

Outlook for Transportation Revenues

Revenue Sources

For the purposes of this chapter, all transportation revenue sources are assigned to one of four revenue categories: direct user fees, indirect user fees, specialized taxes, or general taxes. The categories are designed to distinguish between revenue sources such as user fees, which send a price signal to transportation users and correspond to the marginal or average cost of using a particular transportation service or facility, and general taxes such as income taxes, which tax society at large and provide little or no price signal. The four categories are:

1. **Direct User Fees** – Direct user fees are fees that are charged directly to the traveler or shipper. Examples include tolls, parking charges, transit fares, and airport passenger facility charges. This category includes both marginal- and average-cost revenue sources. An example of a marginal-cost revenue source is a toll that is based on (and perhaps varies with) peak demand; an example of an average-cost revenue source is a transit fare based on average demand over a year or longer period.
2. **Indirect User Fees** – Indirect user fees are fees that are charged indirectly to the traveler or shipper. They are most commonly applied to vehicles in the form of motor fuel taxes, vehicle registration fees, excise taxes, and taxes on replacement parts such as tires. These revenue sources are almost all average-cost user fees. They differ significantly from direct user fees because they send a

weaker price signal, one that does not reflect clearly the amount of benefit a user receives. The motor fuel tax is the largest of these sources and is relatively invisible to the average motorist, who may see the cost of fuel fluctuate by 25 to 50 percent within any given year. Also included in this category are value-capture techniques, such as development impact fees and special assessment districts, where the costs for expanding the capacity of transportation infrastructure are charged back to developers and businesses located in special assessment districts.[4]

3. **Specialized Taxes** – Specialized revenue sources include local-option sales taxes, lease revenues, and improvement district levies. They are typically applied to consumers, landowners, businesses, and homeowners. These sources are distinct from user fees because they are applied to non-transportation consumption and activity. The largest and most rapidly growing source of specialized tax revenue is state and local option sales taxes. Specialized taxes have no influence on travel demand and mode choice because the cost to the taxpayer is independent of the benefits the individual taxpayer receives from the transportation system. The distinguishing feature of specialized taxes, compared to general taxes, is the assurance given to the voters, who must approve them, that the money will be spent on transportation only. In many cases, ballot measures specify exactly which transportation improvements will be funded by specialized taxes. These taxes are often levied through ballot referenda, some of which may require super-majorities, and therefore reflect a strong statement of local support. In many cases, these referenda are an outgrowth of local initiatives to resolve congestion that has become unacceptable because of inadequate transportation revenues from traditional sources such as motor fuel taxes and vehicle registration taxes.
4. **General Taxes** – General tax revenue sources for transportation include income, property, sales, and ad valorem taxes. These taxes are based on ability to pay and send no price signals that would influence an individual's decision to use transportation more efficiently. General taxes treat transportation as a public good that benefits all society and are analogous to paying for national defense through income taxes.

The categories are summarized in Table 1-1. The first column lists the four categories and provides examples of the taxes or fees in each category.

The second column describes how the tax or fee is applied—whether to the trip maker, the trip buyer, the vehicle, etc. The third column in the table lists the most likely direct payers for each category. For example, transit fares, a type of direct user fee, are typically paid by the individual transit rider.

In a majority of cases, transportation fees and taxes accrue to those who should absorb the burden. However, some payers pass the cost of the fee or tax on to others, who may be upstream or downstream of the transaction. For example, sales taxes are usually paid by consumers, but in highly competitive retail markets, deep discounts on products and services may force retailers to absorb some of the tax. In overheated housing markets, development impact fees are often passed from developers to homebuyers. But in tight labor markets where housing is scarce, commuters may demand that employers cover some of the cost and inconvenience of long or congested commutes.

Table 1-1: Structure of Transportation Funding
Four Categories of Revenue Sources

Type Tax or Fee	Applied To	Payer
Direct User Fees		**Drivers and Passengers**
Transit fares, tolls, parking charges	Trip maker or trip	Single occupant vehicle (SOV) drivers
Passenger facility charges	buyer	and carpoolers
Access and service or use fees		Transit riders
Transportation services taxes		Shippers, carriers, and receivers
Indirect User Fees		**Drivers and Passengers**
Motor fuel taxes (MFT)	Vehicle	SOVs and carpools
Vehicle registration taxes, excise taxes		Transit riders
Replacement parts taxes (e.g., tires)		New development
Development impact fees		
Specialized Taxes		**Property Owner and Consumers**
Local option sales taxes	Property	Consumers
Leases	Consumption	Land owners
Improvement district levies	Infrastructure	Businesses
		Homeowners
General Taxes		**Tax Payers**
Income taxes	Society	Homeowners
Property taxes	Consumption	Businesses
Sales and ad valorem taxes		Consumers

Source: Cambridge Systematics, Inc.

Revenue Allocation by Mode

Table 1-2 shows the current allocation of annual U.S. transportation revenues as expenditures by mode and source.[5] The figures include revenues from all levels of government: federal, state and local. The expenditures are shown in billions of dollars for the year 2000. Of the $153.9

billion spent by the public sector on transportation, $117.2 billion or 76 percent was spent on highways, and $34.3 billion or 23 percent on transit. Passenger rail and public spending on freight rail (typically for improvement of highway-rail grade crossings) accounted for about one percent of transportation expenditures.

Indirect user fees, primarily motor fuel taxes, generated $81.6 billion, over half of all transportation revenues. Indirect user fees made up $75.6 billion or 64 percent of the $117.2 billion expended on highways and $5.8 billion or 17 percent of the $34.3 billion expended on transit. The indirect user fees allocated to transit and rail come primarily from the Highway Trust Fund. Figure 1-2 shows the relative size of expenditures on highways, transit, and rail and the portions derived from indirect user fees.

Table 1-2: Allocation of Current Annual Transportation Revenues by Mode, 2000 *(Billions of Dollars)*

			Rail			
Type Tax or Fee	Highway	Transit	Passenger	Freight	Total	Share
Direct User Fees	$ 5.3	$ 8.1	$1.3	$0	$ 14.70	10%
Indirect User Fees	$ 75.6	$ 5.8	$0	$0.2	$ 81.60	53%
Specialized Taxes	$ 11.7	$14.3	$0.8	$0	$ 26.8	17%
General Taxes	$ 24.6	$ 6.1	$0.1	$0.02	$ 30.8	20%
Total	$117.20	$34.3	$2.2	$0.22	$153.9	100%
Share	76%	23%	1%	<1%	100%	

Source: Cambridge Systematics based on FHWA and AASHTO data.

Figure 1-2: Current Expenditures by Mode and Portion Funded by Indirect User Fees, 2000 *Motor Tax Revenues*

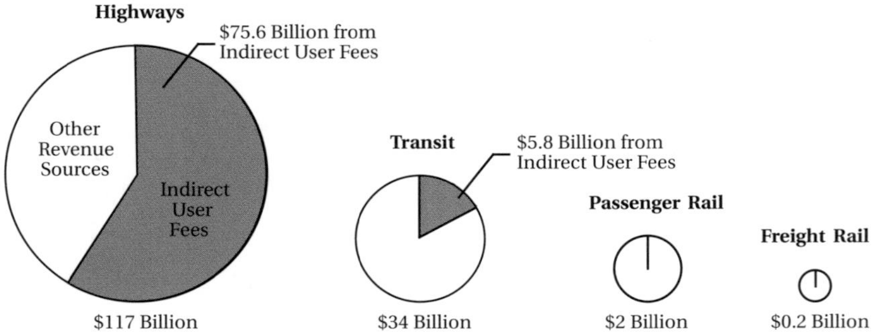

Source: Cambridge Systematics based on FHWA and AASHTO data.

Revenue Forecasts

This section describes the current revenue outlooks for highways and transit. For each mode, the report describes the current and projected annual revenues for the period 2000 to 2025; the assumptions underlying the forecasts; and then the cumulative revenues for 2005 through 2025.

Highway Revenues

Annual revenues allocated to highways from all levels of government totaled $117 billion in 2000. Annual highway revenues are forecast to grow to $134 billion in 2015 and to as much as $147 billion in 2025. However, annual highway revenues may be as low as $131 billion in 2025 because of uncertainty about the yield of motor fuel taxes. Revenue from motor fuel taxes accounted for $55 billion or 47 percent of all highway revenues and 64.5 percent of indirect highway user fees in 2000. Figure 1-3 shows the two forecasts of annual highway revenues.

Figure 1-3: Annual Highway Revenues, 2000-2025 *Base Case Forecasts*

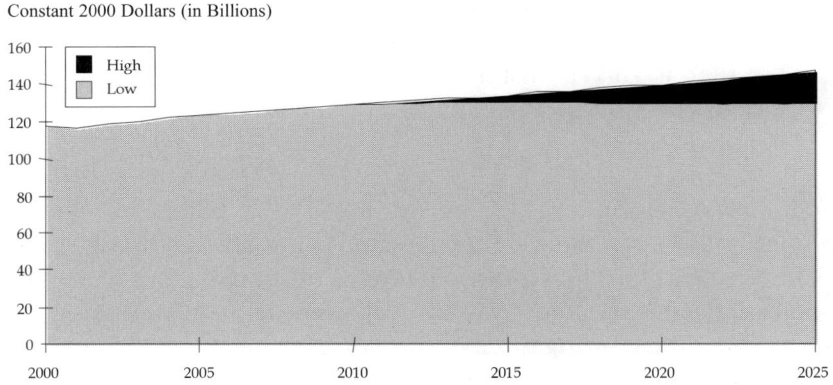

Source: Cambridge Systematics based on FHWA and AASHTO data.

The key assumptions behind the annual forecasts are as follows:

- Federal motor fuel tax remains constant; it is not increased or indexed to inflation. However, federal motor fuel tax revenues grow because total vehicle-miles-of-travel (VMT) are projected to grow by 2.26 percent annually, tracking population and economic growth.[6]

- State motor fuel tax revenues increase annually at 2.26 percent because of VMT growth. In addition, three states (Florida, Maine, and Wisconsin) that currently index their motor fuel tax rate to the consumer price index (CPI) continue to do so.
- Other federal vehicle tax revenues grow at the same rate as the United States gross domestic product (GDP). The GDP growth rate was 2.9 percent in 2001 and increased to a projected 5.4 percent in 2004. The forecasts assume that the GDP growth rate declines from 5.4 percent in 2005 to 4.9 percent by 2010 and remains at 4.9 percent through 2025, the end of the forecast period. These rates are consistent with historical trends, projections prepared by the Congressional Budget Office (CBO), and the Administration's budget forecasts to 2014.
- State vehicle taxes grow at the 10-year historical growth rate of 3.9 percent annually, slightly lower than the 20-year historical rate.
- Special purpose taxes such as local option taxes grow at the GDP rate. The GDP rate is slightly lower than in the 10-year historical growth rate of special purpose taxes, but is realistic in light of current state and local budget constraints.
- General taxes allocated to transportation grow at 3.2 percent annually or 0.7 percent over inflation, which is consistent with the 10- and 20-year historical rates.
- Toll revenues grow at 6.0 percent annually, also consistent with historical trends.

The lower, less optimistic forecast yields $131 billion in highway revenues by 2015, but the yield then remains virtually flat through 2025. This forecast assumes that growth in VMT is offset in the out-years by a 25 percent decline in motor fuel tax revenues because of increasing fuel efficiency and the growing number of vehicles using untaxed fuels (e.g., electric, hydrogen, natural gas, etc.). The high forecast assumes some erosion of motor fuel tax revenues because of increasing fuel efficiency, but the effect is modest.[7] The second forecast, based on a recent Transportation Research Board study, provides a realistic lower bound to future annual highway revenues.[8]

Figure 1-4 shows the cumulative revenue from all highway funding sources for the period 2005 to 2025. Cumulative revenue is calculated by summing the annual revenue forecast for each year from 2005 to 2025, equivalent to the area under the revenue curve. The cumulative highway revenue for the high forecast is $3.4 trillion; for the low forecast, $3.0

trillion. The difference of $100 billion represents revenue that may be lost to increasing fuel efficiency and untaxed fuels.

Figure 1-4: Cumulative Highway Revenues, 2000-2025 *Base Case Forecasts*

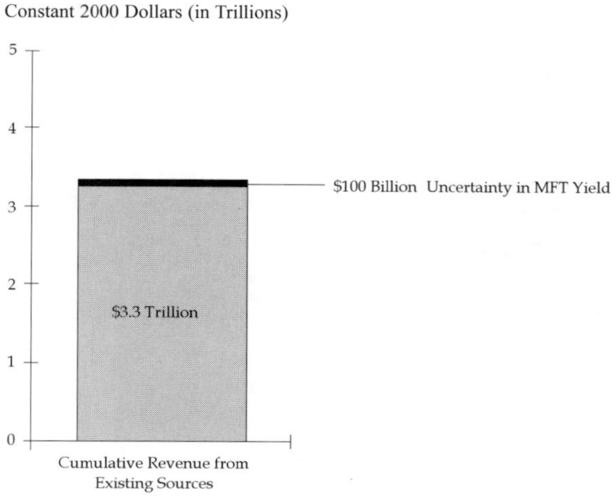

Source: Cambridge Systematics based on FHWA and AASHTO data.

Transit Revenues

Annual transit revenues from all levels of government totaled $31 billion in 2000. Annual transit revenues are forecast to grow to $39 billion in 2015 and to as much as $47 billion in 2025. However, annual transit revenues may be as little as $45 billion in 2025 because of uncertainty about the yield of motor fuel taxes, which accounted for $5 billion or about 16 percent of all transit revenues in 2000. Figure 1-5 shows the high and low forecasts for annual transit revenues. By 2025, the potential loss of annual transit revenues due to fuel efficiency effects could reach 3.5 percent of total revenues.

The critical assumptions used in forecasting transit revenues are:

- Consistent with the highway assumptions, federal motor fuel taxes directed to transit grow at 2.26 percent annually, tracking the growth in highway VMT. The tax is not increased or indexed to inflation. The transit share of the federal motor fuel tax is 2.86 cents per gallon. In 2000, the federal motor fuel tax generated $4.26 billion for transit, a yield of $1.49 billion per penny of per-gallon tax.

Figure 1-5: Annual Transit Revenues, 2000-2025 *Base Case Forecasts*

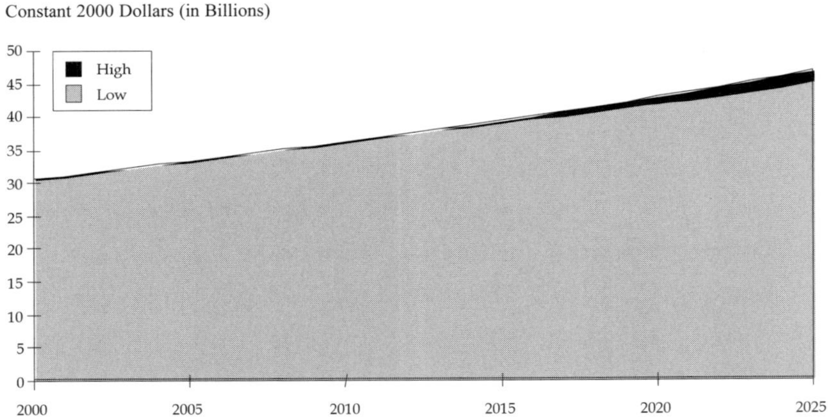

Source: Cambridge Systematics based on FHWA and AASHTO data.

- State and local motor fuel taxes directed to transit also grow at 2.26 annual. These taxes generated $0.5 billion for transit in 2000. (Revenues in the three states that index their motor fuel tax rate to the CPI were not included in the transit forecast, since these revenues are largely dedicated to highway programs.)
- Operating revenues from passenger fares grow at 1.6 percent annually and are inflated using the CPI projections from the Congressional Budget Office. Passenger fares were estimated at $7.81 billion in 2000. Other operating revenues increase annually using the GDP growth rate projections from the Congressional Budget Office. Other operating revenues were $2.0 billion in 2000.
- Specialized taxes increase annually at the GDP growth rate projections developed by the Congressional Budget Office. Specialized taxes, primarily local option sales taxes, generated $6.86 billion in 2000.
- General taxes grow at 4.83 percent per year, consistent with the 10-year historical rate.[9] This funding source generated $9.65 billion for transit in 2000.

Figure 1-6 shows the cumulative revenue from all transit funding sources for the period 2005 to 2025. As with highways, cumulative revenue is calculated by summing the annual revenue forecast for each year from 2005 to 2025, equivalent to the area under the revenue curve. The cumulative transit revenue for the high forecast is about \$844 billion; for the low forecast, \$834 trillion. The difference of almost \$11 billion represents motor fuel tax revenue that may be lost to increasing fuel efficiency and untaxed fuels; but because transit is less dependent on motor fuel taxes than highways, the impact of increased fuel efficiency and untaxed fuels is smaller, reducing cumulative revenues by only 1.3 percent.

Figure 1-6: Cumulative Transit Revenues, 2000-2025 *Base Case Forecasts*

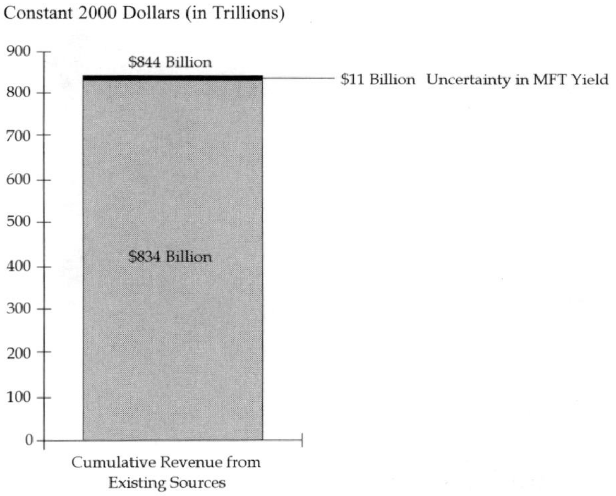

Source: Cambridge Systematics based on FHWA and AASHTO data.

Total Highway and Transit Revenues

Annual highway and transit revenues from all levels of government totaled \$148 billion in 2000. Annual revenues are forecast to grow to \$174 billion in 2015 and to as much as \$194 billion in 2025. Annual revenues may be as little as \$175 billion in 2025 because of uncertainty about the yield of motor fuel taxes, which accounted for \$60 billion or about 40 percent of all revenues in 2000. Figure 1-7 presents the high and low forecasts for the combined annual highway and transit revenues.

Finally, Figure 1-8 shows the cumulative revenues from all highway and transit funding sources for the years 2005 through 2025. As with the component highway and transit forecasts, cumulative revenue is calculated by summing the annual revenue forecast for each year from 2005 to 2025, equivalent to the area under the revenue curve.

The cumulative revenue for the high forecast is $3.6 trillion; for the low forecast, $3.5 trillion. The difference of $131 billion represents motor fuel tax revenue that may be lost to increasing fuel efficiency and untaxed fuels. This represents 3.7 percent of all revenues collected between 2005 and 2025.

Figure 1-7: Annual Highway and Transit Revenues, 2000-2025 *Base Case Forecasts*

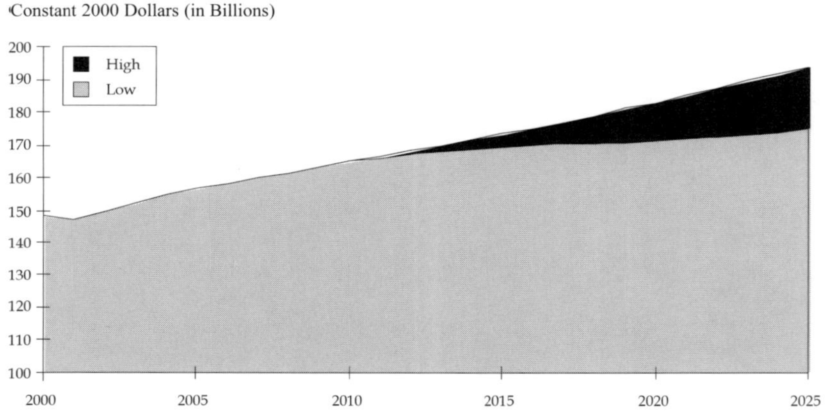

Source: Cambridge Systematics based on FHWA and AASHTO data.

Figure 1-8: Cumulative Highway and Transit Revenues, 2000-2025 *Base Case Forecasts*

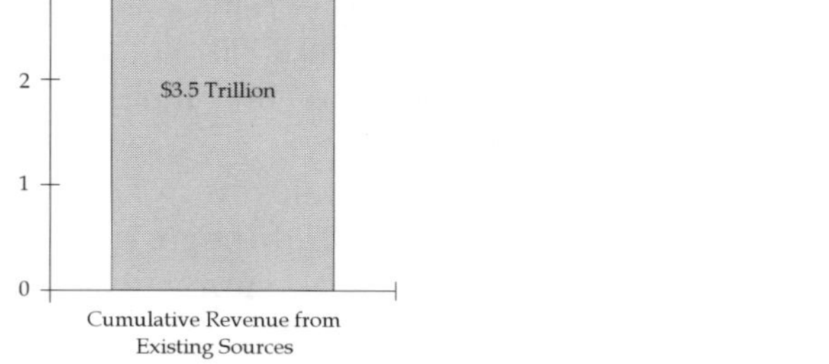

Source: Cambridge Systematics based on FHWA and AASHTO data.

Needs Forecasts and Gaps

This section describes the expenditures needed to maintain and improve the nation's highway and transit systems. For each mode, the report describes current and projected annual needs for the period 2000 to 2025; the assumptions underlying the forecasts; and then the cumulative needs for 2005 through 2025. These are compared to the annual and cumulative revenues to determine the shortfalls and gaps.

Highway Needs and Revenue Gaps

There are four estimates of highway needs: two are estimates of the expenditures needed to maintain the nation's roadways; two are estimates of the expenditures needed to improve the performance and economic productivity of the roadways. The needs are estimated in constant 2000 dollars. The needs scenarios, beginning with the lowest and most conservative, are as follows.

"Need to Maintain" Estimates:

- **FHWA Condition and Performance (C&P) Cost to Maintain** – The FHWA *C&P Report* to Congress estimates that the minimum amount of capital investment needed to maintain the highway system is $76 billion annually. The FHWA *C&P Report* does not include operations, maintenance, administration, and other non-capital costs (O&M costs) for highways. O&M highway costs were estimated to be approximately $57 billion in 2000 and, based on growth rates over the last 10 and 20 years, will increase at a rate of 1.6 percent above inflation annually. When highway O&M costs are added to the capital requirements, the total FHWA "need to maintain" estimate is $133 billion in 2000 and grows to $161 billion in 2025.
- **AASHTO Cost to Maintain** – AASHTO's *Bottom Line Report,* using slightly different analytical assumptions, estimates that the minimum amount of capital investment needed to maintain the highway system is $92 billion annually. Adding O&M costs brings the total AASHTO "need to maintain" estimate to $149 billion annually in 2000. These annual needs will grow to $177 billion in 2025.

"Need to Improve" Estimates:

- **FHWA C&P Cost to Improve** – The FHWA *C&P Report* estimates that $164 billion of highway capital improvements must be made annually to improve the highway system. Only those highway projects that have a benefit/cost ratio of 1.0 or higher as measured by FHWA's Highway Economic Requirements System (HERS) are considered for funding in the FHWA's estimate. Adding O&M costs brings the total FHWA "cost to improve" estimate to $192 billion annually in 2025.

- **AASHTO Cost to Improve** – The AASHTO's *Bottom Line Report,* again using slightly different analytical assumptions than the FHWA *C&P Report,* estimates the capital investment needed to improve the highway system at $120 billion annually. Adding O&M costs brings the total AASHTO "cost to improve" estimate for highways to $183 billion annually in 2000. In 2025, needs will rise to $211 billion annually.

Figure 1-9 compares the four estimates of annual highway needs to the forecast of annual highway revenues for the period 2000 to 2025. Annual highway revenues fail to meet even the annual needs for the lowest and most conservative "need to maintain" forecast.

Figure 1-9: Annual Highway Needs Compared to Annual Highway Revenues, 2000-2025 *Base Case Forecasts*

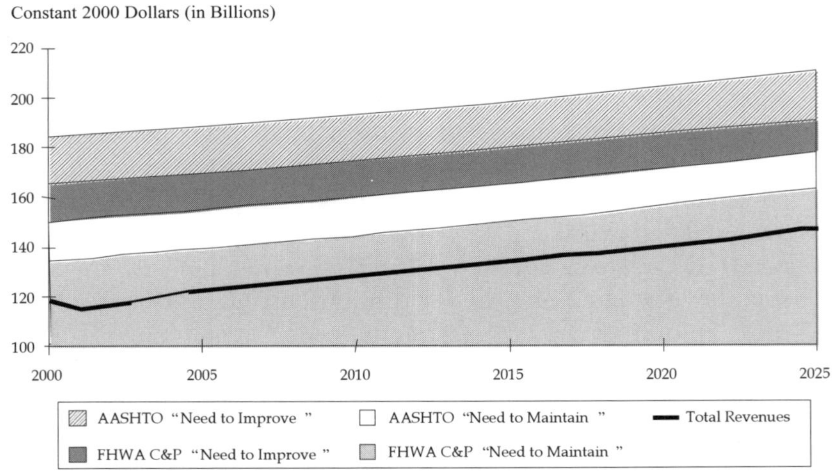

Source: Cambridge Systematics based on FHWA and AASHTO data.

Figure 1-10 compares cumulative highway needs to cumulative highway revenues for 2005 through 2025. The gap between estimated needs and expected revenues—which ranges from a low of almost $400 billion to a high of almost $1.6 trillion—is the challenge facing transportation financing in the twenty-first century.

Figure 1-10: Cumulative Highway Needs Compared to Cumulative Highway Revenues, 2005-2025 *Base Case Forecasts*

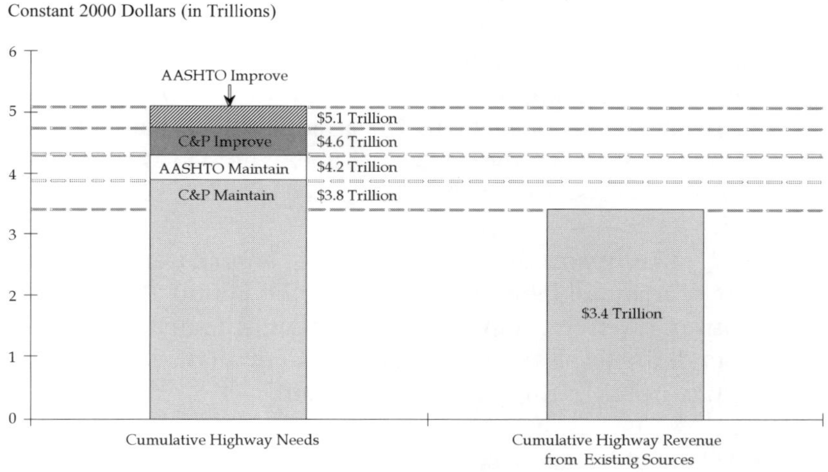

Source: Cambridge Systematics based on FHWA and AASHTO data.

Transit Needs and Revenue Gaps

There also are four estimates of transit needs: two are estimates of the expenditures needed to maintain the nation's transit systems; two are estimates of the expenditures needed to improve the performance and economic productivity of transit systems. The needs are estimated in constant 2000 dollars. The needs scenarios, again beginning with the lowest and most conservative, are as follows.

"Need to Maintain" Estimates:

- **FHWA Condition and Performance (C&P) Cost to Maintain** – The FHWA *C&P Report* to Congress estimates the minimum amount of capital investment needed to maintain the nation's transit systems at $35 billion annually, increasing to $45 billion in 2025, driven by population and economic growth.
- **AASHTO Cost to Maintain** – AASHTO's *Bottom Line Report,* using slightly different analytical assumptions, estimates the minimum

amount of capital investment needed to maintain the transit systems at $39 billion annually, increasing to $49 billion in 2025.

"Need to Improve" Estimates:

- **FHWA C&P Cost to Improve** – The FHWA *C&P Report* estimates the expenditures needed to improve the performance and economic productivity of the nation's transit systems at $41 billion in 2000 and $50 billion annually in 2025.
- **AASHTO Cost to Improve** – The AASHTO's *Bottom Line Report,* again using slightly different analytical assumptions than the FHWA *C&P Report,* estimates the capital investment needed to improve the nation's transit systems at $49 billion in 2000 and $59 billion in 2025.

Figure 1-11 compares the four estimates of annual transit needs to the forecast of annual highway revenues for the period 2000 to 2025. Unlike highway revenues, annual transit revenues match and exceed annual expenditure levels after 2015; however, cumulative revenues do not catch up to needs during the analysis period.

Figure 1-11: Annual Transit Needs Compared to Annual Transit Revenues, 2000-2025 *Base Case Forecasts*

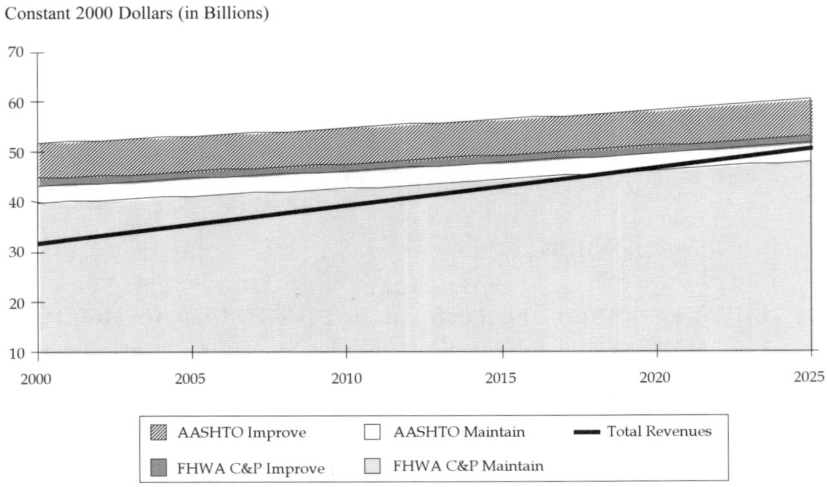

Source: Cambridge Systematics based on FHWA and AASHTO data.

Figure 1-12 compares cumulative transit needs to cumulative transit revenues for 2005 through 2025. The gap between estimated needs and expected revenues ranges from a low of $13 billion to a high of almost $309 billion.

Figure 1-12: Cumulative Transit Needs Compared to Cumulative Transit Revenues, 2000-2025 *Base Case Forecasts*

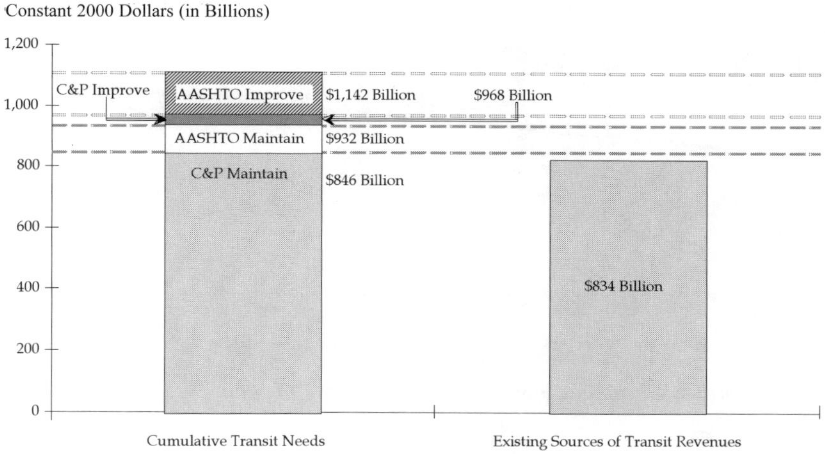

Source: Cambridge Systematics based on FHWA and AASHTO data.

Total Highway and Transit Needs and Revenue Gaps

Figure 1-13 shows the combined annual highway and transit needs for 2000 to 2025. They are as follows:

- Total FHWA "cost to maintain" is $168 billion in 2000 and $205 billion in 2025.
- Total AASHTO "cost to maintain" is $188 billion annually in 2000 and $226 billion in 2025.
- Total FHWA "cost to improve" is $205 billion annually in 2000 and $242 billion annually in 2025.
- Total AASHTO "cost to improve" estimate is $234 billion in 2000 and $270 billion in 2025.

The combined annual highway and transit revenues are not sufficient to meet the FHWA's "need to maintain" target.

Figure 1-13: Annual Highway and Transit Needs Compared to Annual Highway and Transit Revenues, 2000-2025
Base Case Forecasts

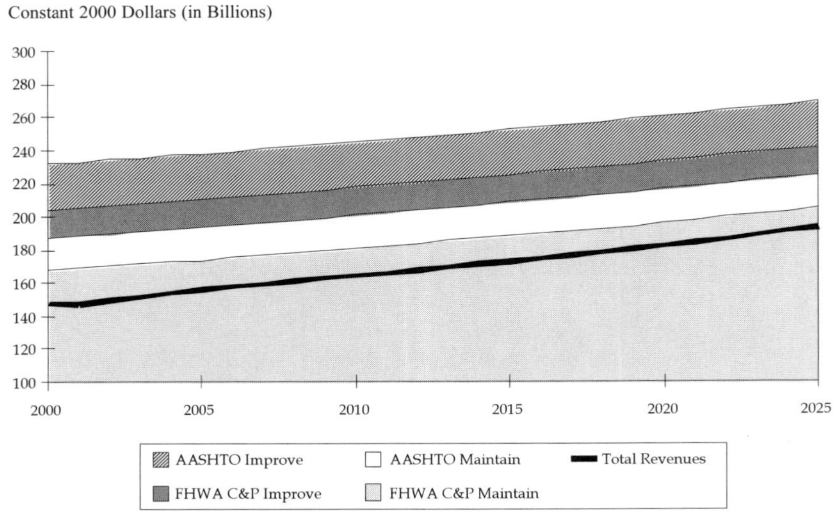

Source: Cambridge Systematics based on FHWA and AASHTO data.

Figure 1-14: Cumulative Highway and Transit Needs Compared to Cumulative Highway and Transit Revenues, 2005-2025
Base Case Forecasts

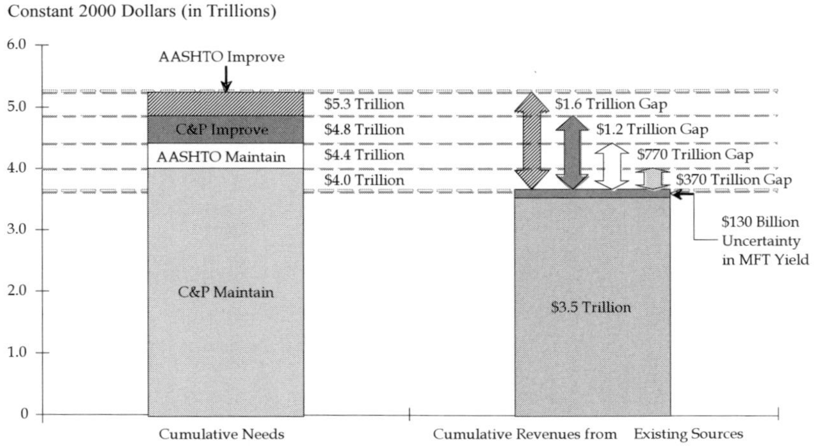

Source: Cambridge Systematics based on FHWA and AASHTO data.

Finally, Figure 1-14 compares cumulative highway and transit needs to cumulative highway and transit revenues. Cumulative needs and revenues are calculated by summing the needs and revenue estimates for each year from 2005 to 2025. The gap between estimated needs and expected revenues ranges from a low of almost $400 billion to a high of almost $1.6 trillion.

In summary, current and projected transportation revenues fail to meet even the most conservative estimates of the expenditures needed to maintain roads, bridges, and transit infrastructure. They fail dramatically to meet the expenditure levels needed to improve the performance of the highway and transit systems.

Transportation Performance Outlook

No systematic forecasts show how the performance of the nation's highway and transit systems will deteriorate given the revenue shortfalls and gaps forecast for the nation's highway and transit systems, but some sense of the future can be gained from recent trend data. Figure 1-15 shows the relative increase in vehicle-miles-of-travel (VMT) compared to the increase in lane-miles of roadway from 1980 to 2002. The index year is 1980. The figure shows that VMT have grown almost 90 percent while lane-miles of roadway have grown only two percent. With

Figure 1-15: Vehicle-Miles-of-Travel Index Compared to Lane-Mile Index, 1980-2002

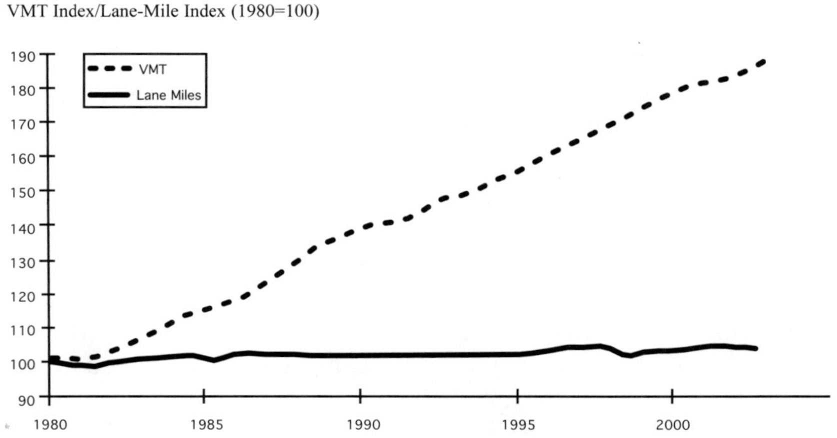

Source: Federal Highway Administration

larger amounts of highway revenue committed to maintaining existing roads and current expenditures failing to meet "need to maintain" targets, lane-miles of roadway are unlikely to catch up to demand in the near future.

Figure 1-16 shows the increase in annual highway congestion costs from 1982 to 2001. Consistent with the growth of VMT shown in the previous figure, this figure shows a tenfold increase in congestion costs accruing to drivers in the 75 urban areas reported by the Texas Transportation Institute in its Urban Mobility Report. Congestion in large urban areas accounts for over half of all urban congestion costs, but the rate of increase of congestion costs in medium and small urban areas has been very high.

Figure 1-16: Annual Highway Congestion Costs, 1982-2001

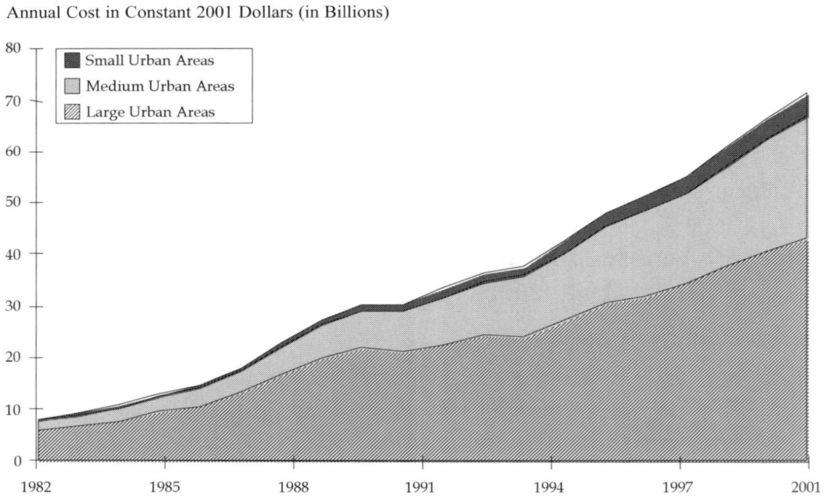

Source: Texas Transportation Institute.

State departments of transportation submit counts of current traffic volumes and estimates of future traffic to the FHWA's Highway Performance Monitoring System (HPMS). Figure 1-17 shows traffic conditions on major U.S. roadways in 1998. Congestion is indicated by level of service, measured in terms of roadway traffic volume compared to roadway traffic capacity. Level of service is rated from A (free flowing) to F (intensely congested).

Figure 1-17 Traffic Conditions on Major U.S. Roadways, 1998

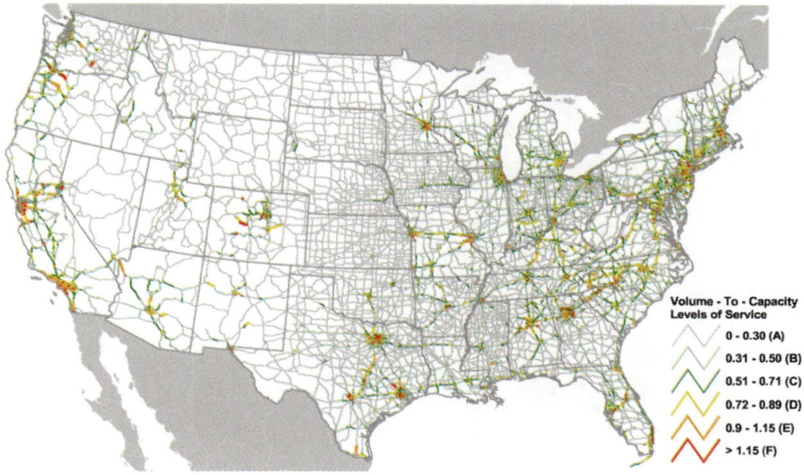

Source: Federal Highway Administration Freight Analysis Framework.

Figure 1-18 shows the estimated levels of service on major U.S. roadways in 2020. These are straight-line estimates that do not account for future changes in travel behavior and therefore may overstate future travel and congestion. Nevertheless, the level-of-service patterns show the potential for intense and widespread increases in congestion, especially in major metropolitan areas and along the most intensively used intercity highways.

Assessment of Existing Revenue Sources

An assessment of the current revenue system provides useful insights into the deficiencies of the revenue sources and opportunities to make short-term corrections. The assessment is made using the five criteria described in the introduction to this chapter.

1. **Yield and Reliability** – Motor fuel taxes, the linchpin of transportation revenues, have had mixed success in providing sufficient, reliable revenues over the past 65 years. Figure 1-19 shows the pattern of federal motor fuel tax rates and revenues from 1935 to 2002. Volatile swings and shortfalls in both rates and revenues have been the rule. Motor fuel tax rates, shown on the right-side

Figure 1-18 Estimated Levels of Service on Major U.S. Roadways, 1935-2002

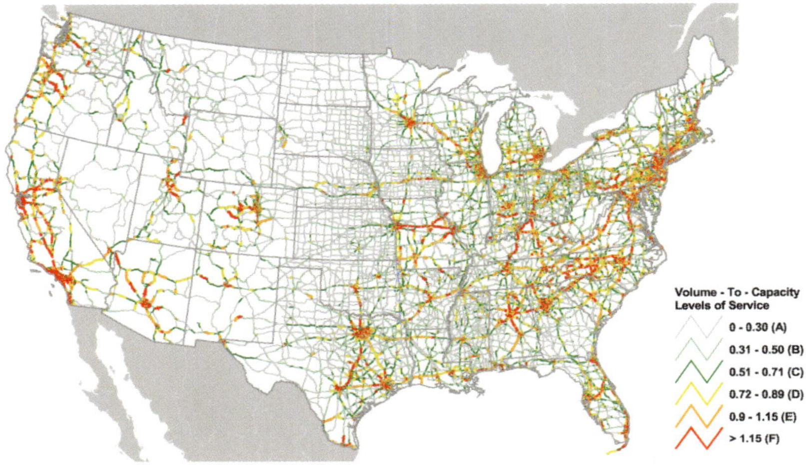

Source: Federal Highway Administration Freight Analysis Framework.

Figure 1-19: Historical Trends in Federal Fuel Tax Rates and Revenues, 1935-2002

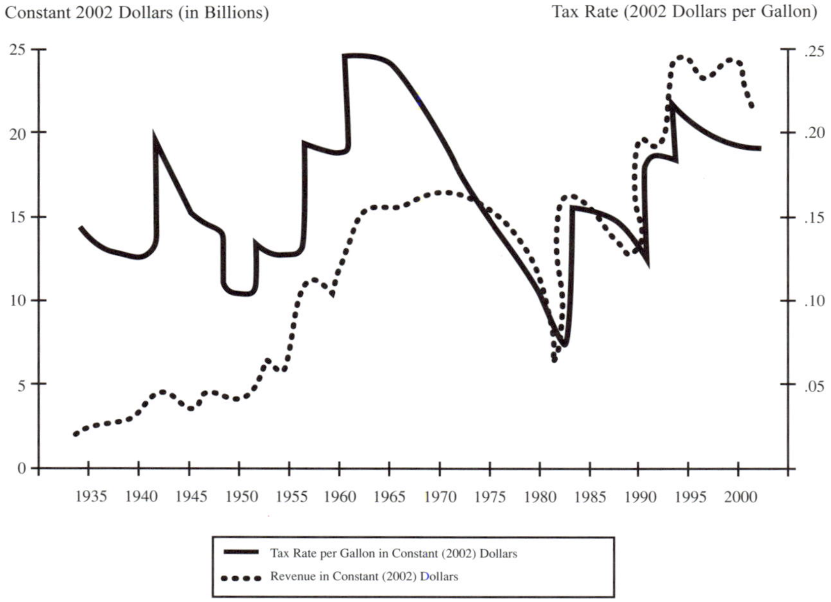

Source: Robert Puentes and Ryan Prince, "Fueling Transportation Finance: A Primer on the Gas Tax," The Brookings Institution Series on Transportation Reform, March 2003.

scale, are not much higher today than they were in the 1930s when the motor fuel tax was introduced. Motor fuel tax revenues, shown on the left-side scale, have grown significantly: from $2 billion in 1935 to $20 billion in 2001 when measured in constant 2000 dollars. However, motor fuel tax revenues have not kept pace with inflation in the past five years. And the yield from motor fuel taxes is expected to decline by $2 billion to $5 billion per year after 2015, driven by the sale of more fuel-efficient engines, tax exemptions for alternative fuels, and the introduction of hydrogen-, natural gas-, and electric-powered vehicles. At current tax rates, motor fuel tax revenues are not sufficient to meet future highway and transit needs, but fuel tax rates could be increased to generate a significant share of the additional revenues needed between now and 2015.

2. **Economic Efficiency** – While motor fuel taxes and the other indirect user charges are technically user charges, they send relatively modest pricing signals to most motorists. The lack of a strong linkage between the amount paid at the pump and the benefits derived from using a roadway at a particular time and place make this a flawed means of improving economic efficiency.
3. **Equity** – Motor fuel taxes are moderately regressive for lower-income vehicle owners because large, low-fuel-mileage vehicles are owned disproportionately by lower-income households, and the poor spend a greater share of their income on fuel taxes and registration fees than do rich households. Specialized transportation taxes such as local-option sales taxes also are considered somewhat regressive because they tax moderate- and lower-income individuals who do not drive.
4. **Administrative Effectiveness** – Motor fuel taxes and vehicle registration are not widely evaded and do not cost a great deal to collect. Fuel taxes are collected from distributors, not retailers. With only 1,200 fuel distributors to audit, the motor fuel tax is a relative easy tax to administer and enforce. Nevertheless, researchers have reported up to 15 percent evasion on diesel fuel taxes (due to its availability as home heating oil), and some jurisdictions that charge supplemental motor vehicle excise taxes report significant evasion.
5. **Public Acceptance** – Federal and state motor fuel taxes have gained widespread public acceptance as user fees that support the construction and maintenance of highways. The best measure

of their popularity is their continued use over 65 years. Nevertheless, resistance to increasing or indexing fuel taxes is strong today, despite rather muted public reactions to routine price fluctuations of 50 percent or more in fuel prices. Only Florida, Maine, and Wisconsin index their gas tax to the consumer price index.

Chapter 2

Strategies for Twenty-First Century Transportation Finance

Short-Term Strategies

This section explores three short-term strategies for increasing the yield and reliability of transportation revenues. The three strategies are: indexing the federal motor fuel tax to inflation; increasing the number of highways on which user fees are collected; and issuing tax credit bonds backed by general fund revenues. The three strategies increase the yield and reliability of transportation revenues but avoid aggressive changes and wholesale substitutions of new fees and taxes for existing fees and taxes. These short-term corrections could be implemented over the two federal surface transportation legislation reauthorization cycles between now and 2015.

Indexing Fuel Taxes

The first strategy is to index the federal motor fuel taxes to the increasing cost of building, maintaining, and operating transportation infrastructure.[10] This strategy has been recommended by the House Committee on Transportation and Infrastructure. Their proposal would index the federal motor fuel tax backwards from 2005 to 1995, then increase the motor fuel tax annually thereafter based on the CPI. This proposal would effectively add five cents per gallon at the time of enactment. The revenue impact, shown in Figure 2-1, would be to increase annual revenues, approaching the FHWA "need to maintain" level by the year 2025. This strategy would not generate sufficient annual revenues to match the AASHTO "need to maintain" nor the FHWA or AASHTO "need to improve" levels. This strategy would only reach the FHWA "need to maintain" level if increasing fuel efficiency does not significantly erode motor fuel tax revenues beginning in the year 2010. If fuel efficiencies were to increase, total revenues would fall about $20 billion short of the

FHWA "need to maintain" by 2015 and then drop away, leaving roughly $30 billion in unfunded annual needs by 2025.

Figure 2-1: Annual Highway and Transit Needs Compared to Annual Revenues, 2000 to 2025 ***Indexed Federal Motor Fuel Tax (MFT) Strategy***

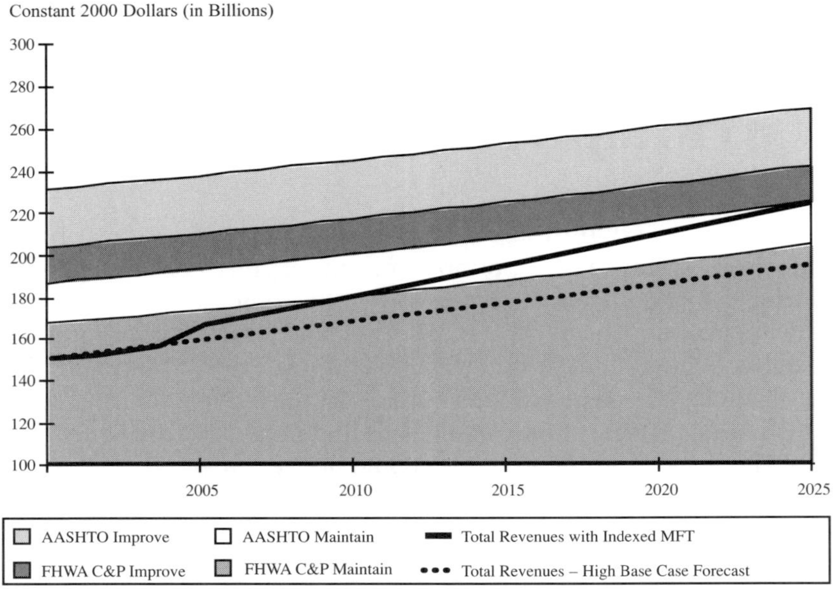

Source: Cambridge Systematics based on FHWA and AASHTO data.

Figure 2-2 compares cumulative highway and transit needs to the cumulative revenues generated by indexing the federal motor fuel tax. Indexing the federal motor fuel tax would generate an additional $352 billion over the next 20 years, closing the gap between current revenues and the FHWA "need to maintain." This would ensure the continued maintenance of the highway and transit systems, but would not provide enough revenue to improve the performance of the transportation systems.

Expanding Collection of User Fees

The second strategy is to expand the collection of user fees. Toll road revenue has increased at about six percent per year over the last decade.[11] Increased need for revenue, increased federal flexibility for collection of user fees, and increased automation have spurred interest in user fees, particularly to meet highway needs in high-growth areas. User

Figure 2-2: Cumulative Highway and Transit Needs Compared to Cumulative Revenues, *Indexed Federal Motor Fuel Tax (MFT) Strategy*

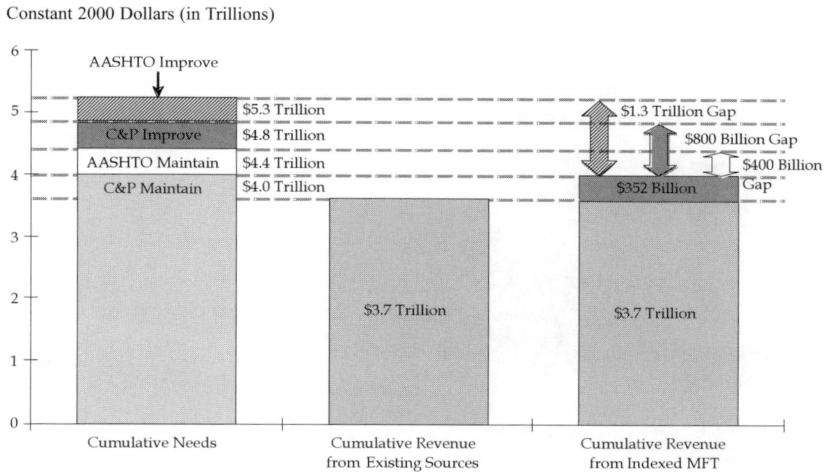

Source: Cambridge Systematics based on FHWA and AASHTO data.

fees represent a source of revenue that can supplement other revenues available to states and fund transportation investments. The largest potential for such user fees is on high-volume, high-cost routes, which are primarily Interstate routes. New legislation, proposed as part of the reauthorization of the federal surface transportation programs, will encourage more aggressive implementation of user fees on Interstates.[12] Finally, automated user fee collection technology is improving rapidly, which greatly enhances collection efficiency and the ability to collect user fees that vary by time of day.

This short-term strategy proposes expanded collection of user fees and implementation of high-occupancy vehicle/toll (HOT) lanes. It assumes that as a result of expanded use of toll roads, user fee revenues grow faster than their historical growth rate of 6.0 percent per year. Under this strategy, revenues from traditional tolling grow at 6.0 percent per year in 2004, then increase gradually to a growth rate of 7.5 percent per year in 2020. The strategy also assumes development of additional HOT lanes, creating a 3,500-mile network as proposed by Poole and Orski.[13] The strategy assumes that implementation of such a national HOT-lane network begins in 2005 and is mostly complete by 2020.

Expanded collection of user fees would increase annual highway revenues modestly as shown in Figure 2-3. The revenues would not be sufficient to close the gap between annual revenues and annual "need to maintain" expenditures, nor would expanded collection of user fees generate sufficient annual revenues to achieve the "need to improve" levels.

Figure 2-3: Annual Highway and Transit Needs Compared to Annual Revenues, *Expanded Tolling and HOT Lanes Strategy*

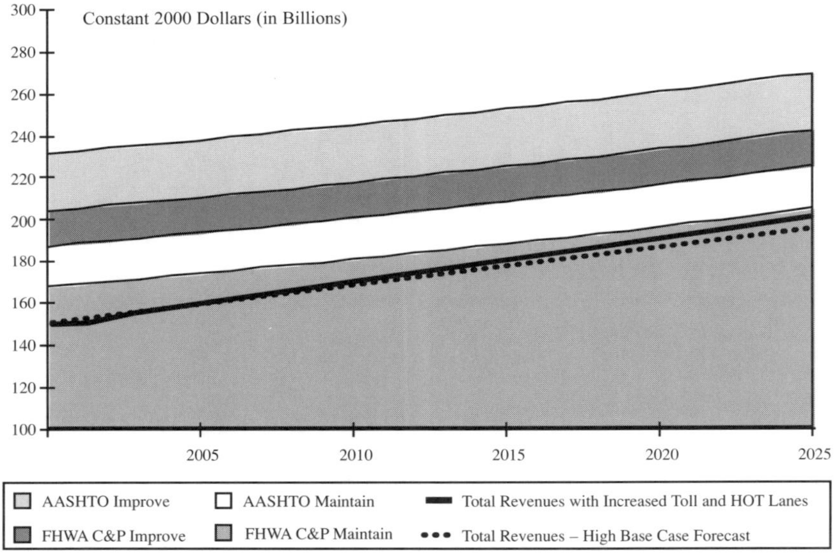

Source: Cambridge Systematics based on FHWA and AASHTO data.

Figure 2-4 compares the cumulative revenues generated by increased collection of user fees—including implementation of HOT lanes—to the four cumulative needs estimates. Increased collection of user fees would generate an additional $67 billion over current revenues. An additional $250 billion would be needed to reach the FHWA "need to maintain" level and upwards of $1.6 trillion to achieve the AASHTO "need to improve" level.

Issuing Tax Credit Bonds

Since 1994, innovative finance techniques have been applied to transportation investments to expedite project delivery and expand sources of revenue. These financing mechanisms have made it easier to invest private capital in public transportation projects. The Bush Administration's SAFETEA proposal includes enhancements to these

Figure 2-4: Cumulative Highway and Transit Needs Compared to Cumulative Revenues, 2005-2025 *Expanded Tolling and HOT Lanes Strategy*

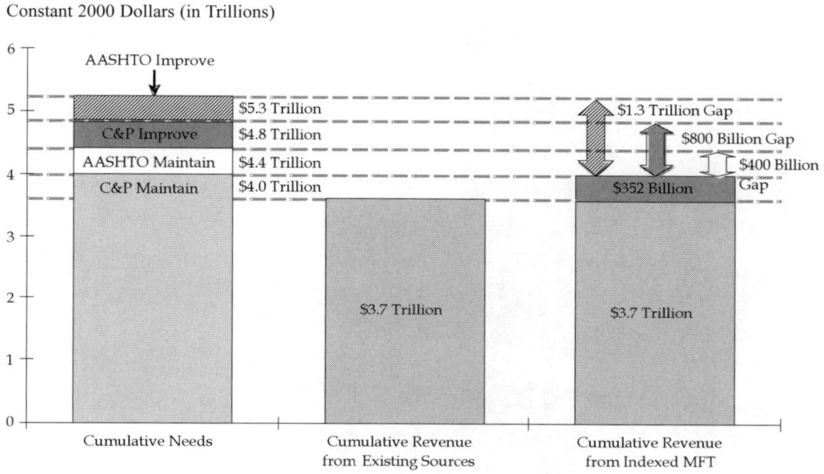

Source: Cambridge Systematics based on FHWA and AASHTO data.

innovative finance mechanisms and allows the use of private activity bonds to finance transportation projects. However, none of the existing or proposed innovative finance mechanisms bring net new revenues to transportation.

AASHTO has proposed issuance of tax credit bonds to expand the amount of revenue available to the surface transportation program in the short term.[14] AASHTO's proposal envisions the sale of up to $80 billion of tax-credit bonds. About $20 billion of the proceeds would be set aside and invested in a sinking fund to pay back the principal of the bonds, leaving $60 billion of revenue for investment in transportation projects. The cost of the tax credits, estimated at a total of $47 billion over the course of the program, are assumed to come from the general fund, not from transportation revenues, thus bringing new revenues to transportation.

The annual revenue impacts of a tax-credit bond program are shown in Figure 2-5. The analysis assumes that revenues from tax-credit bonds are a one-time infusion of general revenues and that the $60 billion is disbursed over a 10-year period from 2005 to 2015. The revenue from the tax-credit bonds would increase annual highway revenues between $13 billion and $26 billion per year over a 10-year period. The revenues would not be sufficient to close the gap between annual revenues and annual "need to maintain" expenditures, nor would tax-credit bonding generate sufficient annual revenues to achieve the "need to improve" levels.

Figure 2-5: Annual Highway and Transit Needs Compared to Annual Revenues, 2000-2025 *Tax Credit Bonds Strategy*

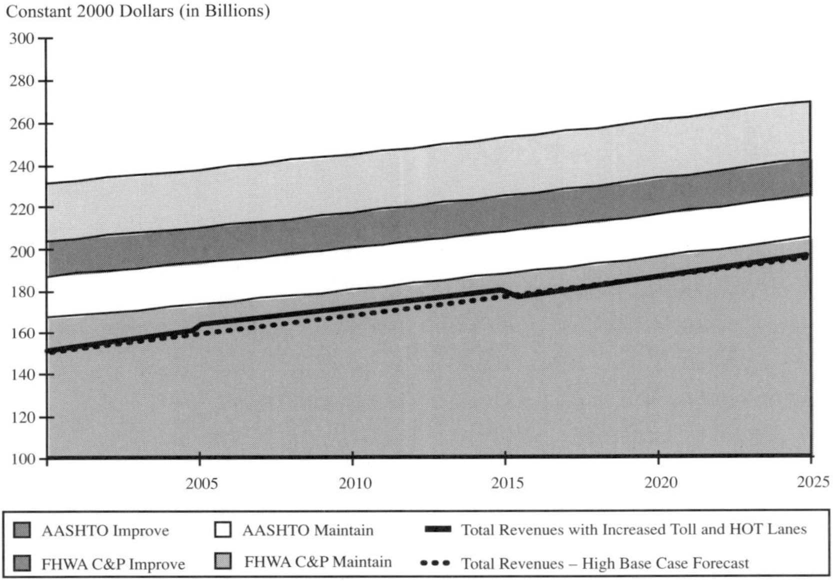

Source: Cambridge Systematics based on FHWA and AASHTO data.

Figure 2-6 compares the cumulative revenues generated by tax-credit bonds to the four cumulative needs estimates. Tax-credit bonds would generate an additional $47 billion over current revenues. An additional $260 billion would be needed to meet the FHWA "need to maintain" level and about $1.6 trillion to meet the AASHTO "need to improve" target.

While not new sources of funding, several short-term financing options would help accelerate project construction at the state and local levels over the next five to 10 years. In the highway field these include the use of GARVEE Bonds, TIFIA financing, state infrastructure banks (SIB), tax-exempt bonds, design-build contracts, and public-private partnerships. In the transit field these include the use of tax-exempt bonds, TIFIA financing, design-build-operate-maintain contracts, public-private partnerships, passage of local option sales or property tax measures, and sale

Figure 2-6: Cumulative Highway and Transit Needs Compared to Cumulative Revenues, 2005-2025 *Tax Credit Bonds Strategy*

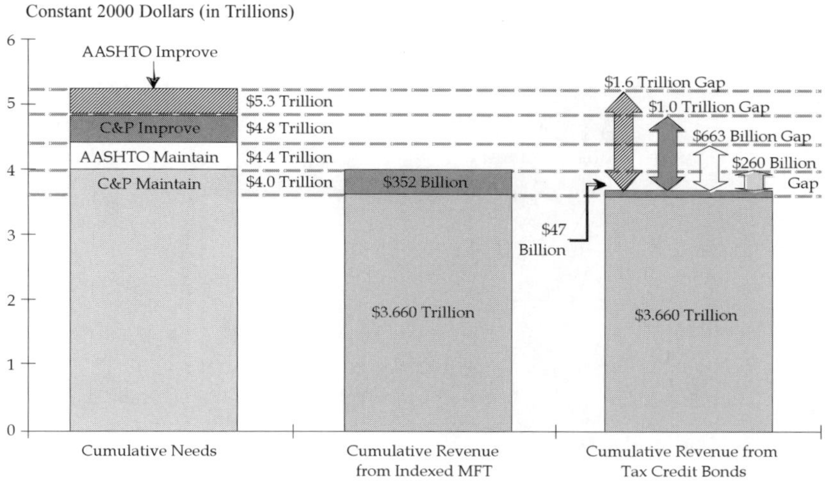

Source: Cambridge Systematics based on FHWA and AASHTO data.

and leaseback proposals. In addition, proposed federal legislation would authorize $15 billion in private-activity bonds for highways and transit programs. This provision would make transportation-related, public-private partnerships eligible to use tax-exempt debt, lowering the cost of project finance. By accelerating project construction, these financing techniques can lower total project costs, reducing carrying costs and avoiding future inflation; and they can increase total project benefits by reducing congestion and delay earlier rather than later.

Figure 2-7 compares the cumulative revenues generated by all three short-term strategies with the four cumulative needs estimates. None of the three corrections would close the funding gap, but all would provide critically needed revenues in the short term. More important, they are established revenue sources: the mechanisms for increasing and administering these fees and taxes are in place, and their fiscal impacts on individuals, businesses, and government are well understood.

Other Conventional Sources

Other conventional sources of highway revenues include vehicle registration fees and special taxes. Vehicle registration fees provide states with more revenue—about $25 billion more annually—than state motor fuel taxes. Revenues from vehicle registration fees are projected to

Figure 2-7: Cumulative Cumulative Needs Compared to Cumulative Revenues, 2005-2025 *All Three Short-Term Strategies*

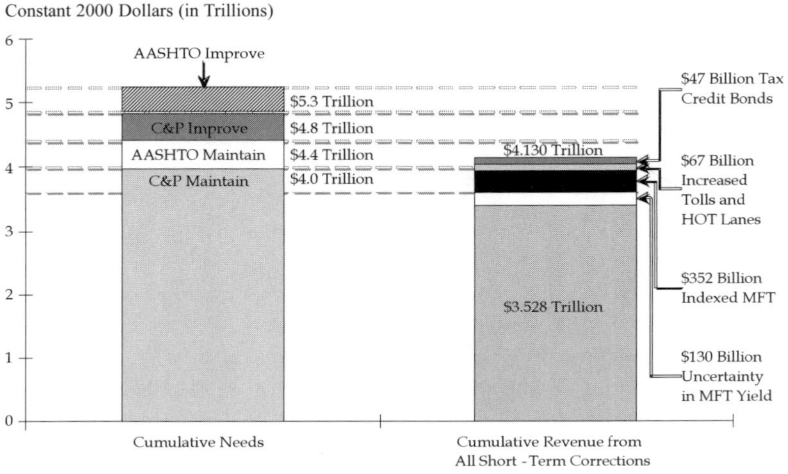

Source: Cambridge Systematics based on FHWA and AASHTO data.

grow at the same rate as GDP. Counties in many states have aggressively adopted special taxes dedicated to transportation projects. For this analysis, revenues from special taxes also are assumed to grow at the rate of the GDP. Other conventional sources such as value-capture assessment, truck fees, and tire taxes make a contribution to highway revenues, but their tax bases are too small to generate significant additional revenues regardless of how aggressively they are indexed or expanded.[15]

Freight and Intermodal Rail Revenues

Section Two of this book and other studies suggest increasing or expanding freight-transportation user fees. Proposed sources of increased revenues for publicly funded freight improvements include the following:

- **Gateway/hub user fees** would impose cargo access fees at freight gateways or hubs of national significance. The potential yield from this source cannot be estimated at this time.[16]
- **Value-added tax on freight** would provide a yield of about $10 billion a year.[17]
- **VMT (or weight-based VMT) charges applied to freight vehicles** would be a variant of conventional weight-distance taxes that

have been used by some states. The potential yield has not been estimated at this time.

- **National vehicle registration fees and excise-sales taxes**, modeled after the current federal excise tax on new large trucks, could be applied to classes of trucks.[18]
- **Infrastructure banks and tax-credit bonds for freight and intermodal improvement projects** have been proposed by AASHTO and by the consortium of states and railroads that make up the Mid-Atlantic Rail Operations (MAROps) program.[19,20]

Several congressional bills propose the use of finance corporations or banks issuing tax credit bonds for intermodal freight projects. To the extent that these banks and bonds are funded from general revenue sources, they would bring new revenues to transportation.

Assessment of Short-Term Strategies

The strengths and weaknesses of the proposed short-term strategies are as follows:

- **Yield and Reliability** – The cumulative yield of the three strategies over 25 years is $471 billion of additional revenue, or a 13 percent increase in total revenues compared to what can be expected from current revenue sources. In the short term, the proposal to index the federal motor fuel tax backwards from 2005 to 1995 would effectively add five cents per gallon at the time of enactment and increase annual revenues by roughly $7 billion annually immediately. In the mid term (2010 through 2015), indexing the federal motor fuel tax would improve the reliability of transportation revenues by ensuring that motor fuel tax revenues keep pace with costs.
- **Economic Efficiency** – More implementation of user fees, especially in the most congested urban corridors, would increase the share of revenues generated from direct user charges. This would send stronger price signals to drivers and could help reduce congestion at peak periods by making off-peak travel and transit more economically attractive. Indexing motor fuel taxes, which would raise the price of fuel at the pump, would influence travel decisions, but the magnitude of the proposed increases is modest, well within the envelope of anticipated gas price increases and fluctuations and well short of European motor fuel tax rates. The

overall pricing effect of indexing motor fuel taxes is expected to be modest. Tax credit bonding would reduce the price signal by diverting general funds into transportation, but the effects would be marginal.

- **Equity** – Collection of user fees on roadways has often been cited as creating privileges in what may be considered the largest remaining common social experience left in America. Rich or poor, drivers of all income levels are stuck in traffic. Nevertheless, paying more for faster travel increases costs for those that can most afford to pay, thus tilting toward more equity in highway pricing. Moreover, data from some Southern California toll roads and HOT lanes show that usage is fairly constant across demographic groups, suggesting that collection of user fees generates travel benefits for some lower-income drivers.
- **Administrative Effectiveness** – Indexing the current motor fuel tax is straightforward and should not stimulate more evasion than does the present motor fuel tax. Collection of user fees, however, relies on significant investment in equipment, billing systems, enforcement costs, and physical infrastructure to control ingress and egress.
- **Public Acceptance** – Indexing fuel taxes presents significant political challenges; only three states have successfully indexed their motor fuel taxes. Developing toll roads and HOT lanes often involves expanding roadways in developed urban corridors where community opposition and environmental concerns can slow construction and increase costs. Public acceptance of the short-term correction strategies will likely hinge on the level of public frustration with congestion, which increases delays and makes travel times highly unpredictable. It also will hinge on the transportation community's ability to reduce transportation bottlenecks and choke points through targeted capital improvements and better transportation operations management.

Long-Term Strategies

The short-term strategies provide only modest increases in the total amount of revenue available for transportation system maintenance and improvement. They do not meet the FHWA "need to maintain" level of investment and fall well short of the AASHTO "need to improve" target. The strategies strengthen somewhat the links between the prices that transportation users pay and the services they receive, but not enough to make the transportation system significantly more responsive to customers. New long-term transportation revenue strategies are needed to address these goals. This section explores mileage-based strategies for increasing the yield and reliability of transportation revenues and making transportation systems more responsive to customers.

Mileage-Based Revenues

A mileage-based transportation revenue system would have two elements: a base fee and a service fee. All users of the highway system would be charged a base fee. This fee would reflect the average cost of providing the basic unit of service—a vehicle-mile-of-travel (VMT). The VMT base rate would be comparable to the base rate charged by utilities for delivering a cubic foot of water or a kilowatt hour of electricity. The fee would be based on the total demand across the entire service population regardless of when and where the unit of service is demanded. It would reflect the average cost to build, maintain, and operate a mile of roadway.

The VMT base fee would be applied to the total VMT accrued by each vehicle each year. For the purposes of this analysis, each user would be charged the same VMT base fee for a mile of travel, regardless of the type of fuel used, the propulsion system in the vehicle, the vehicle's fuel mileage, or the value of the vehicle. (In a fully developed strategy, different base fees might be assigned to different classes of vehicles. For example, a higher base fee might be assigned to heavy trucks to reflect their impact on pavement costs and a lower fee to hybrid-fuel vehicles.)

If highway users are to use roadway capacity efficiently, the VMT price also should reflect the marginal cost, not just the average cost. This requires adding a second fee—a local-option VMT service fee—that would take into account the demand for any given segment of roadway. This VMT service fee would send a price signal to the user that reflects the cost of a providing roadway capacity during periods of peak demand. This would ensure that the higher cost of building sufficient capacity in congested corridors is passed on to the users who derive the greatest value from using a congested roadway. Service fees also would stimulate some users to divert their trip to a less congested route, a less congested time, or to transit, thus removing some of the need to build additional capacity. Local-option VMT service fees would be established by state or local jurisdictions and could be applied to a metropolitan region or specific roadways. It is anticipated that the revenues would accrue to state or local jurisdictions and would be invested in highway or transit improvements as determined locally.

Two VMT strategies were analyzed: one with a VMT base fee only; the other with a VMT base fee and a local-option VMT service fee. As a starting point, both strategies assume that the federal motor fuel tax is indexed as proposed under the short-term strategies, and both strategies assume that implementation of VMT fees begins about 2015.

The first strategy replaces motor fuel taxes with a VMT base fee in a revenue-neutral swap. The VMT base fee required to make the swap in 2015 would be 1.89 cents per VMT. (The average vehicle owner spent $6,990[21] to own and operate a car 11,976 miles[22] in 2000, the equivalent of $0.58 per mile. Of this amount, about $0.11 per mile was spent on fuel and oil and $0.019 per mile on federal and state motor fuel taxes.) The strategy assumes that the VMT base fee is indexed to CPI projections from the Congressional Budget Office after 2015 to ensure that revenues keep up with inflation.

The second strategy replaces motor fuel taxes with a VMT base fee and a local-option VMT service fee. The VMT base fee is 1.89 cents per VMT in 2015 and the local-option VMT service fee is 10 cents per VMT. Both are indexed to CPI projections after 2015. (A fee of 10 cents per VMT is at the mid-range of current toll road and HOT-lane prices.) The strategy assumes that the local-option VMT service fee is gradually phased into the top 75 cities covered by The 2003 Urban Mobility Report prepared by the Texas Transportation Institute.[23] Urban VMT in these cities accounts for 45 percent of the nationwide urban VMT. According to the report, 34 percent of the VMT in these cities is accrued under congested conditions. The percent of congested VMT in these areas is assumed to increase at 0.5 percent per year, the historical trend reported in the FHWA C&P Report. The VMT service fee is applied to five percent of congested urban VMT in the 75 cities in 2015, ramping up to 50 percent by 2025.

Figure 2-8 compares the annual revenues generated by the two VMT strategies to the four estimates of highway and transit needs. Both strategies would significantly increase annual revenues. Annual revenues are higher approaching 2025 than the motor fuel tax revenues they replace because VMT-based revenues increase apace with VMT as population and the economy grow. Sometime shortly after the year 2025, the annual revenues approach the AASHTO "need to improve" amount of $270 billion annually. Depending on the objectives of federal, state, and local policy-makers, the VMT base rate, the local-option VMT service fee, or both could be adjusted downward after 2025 or set at lower rates initially. The latter approach would reduce the cost to motorists but delay improvements to the highway and transit systems. The choice of

Figure 2-8: Annual Highway and Transit Needs Compared to Annual Revenues, 2000-2025 *VMT Base Fee and VMT Service Fee Strategy*

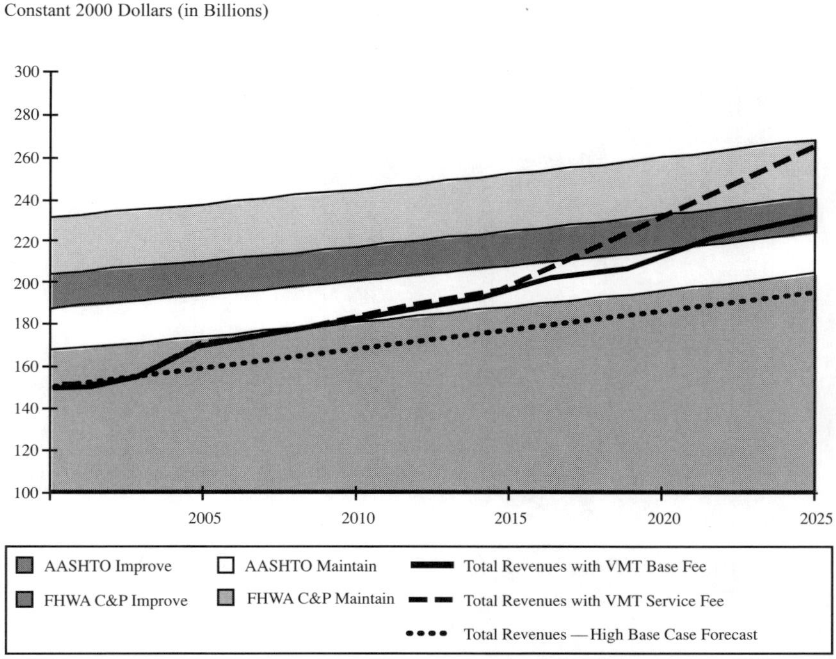

Source: Cambridge Systematics based on FHWA and AASHTO data.

VMT rates—beyond the direct substitution of a VMT base rate for current motor fuel taxes—is properly a subject for national and local policymakers, but this first approximation indicates that a two-tier mileage-based fee is capable of generating sufficient revenues to begin to close the gap between annual revenues and annual needs.

Figure 2-9 compares the cumulative revenues generated by a mileage-based revenue system implemented after 2015 to the four cumulative needs estimates. Implementation of a VMT base fee would generate $4.1 trillion between 2005 and 2025. This would meet the FHWA "need to maintain" target and begin to close the gap to the AASHTO "need to maintain" target of $4.4 trillion. A local-option VMT service fee would generate an additional $147 billion, pushing cumulative revenues over the period within $70 billion of the AASHTO "need to maintain" target. Neither strategy generates enough cumulative revenue by 2025 to

Figure 2-9: Cumulative Highway and Transit Needs Compared to Cumulative Revenues, 2000-2025 *VMT Base Fee and VMT Service Fee Strategy*

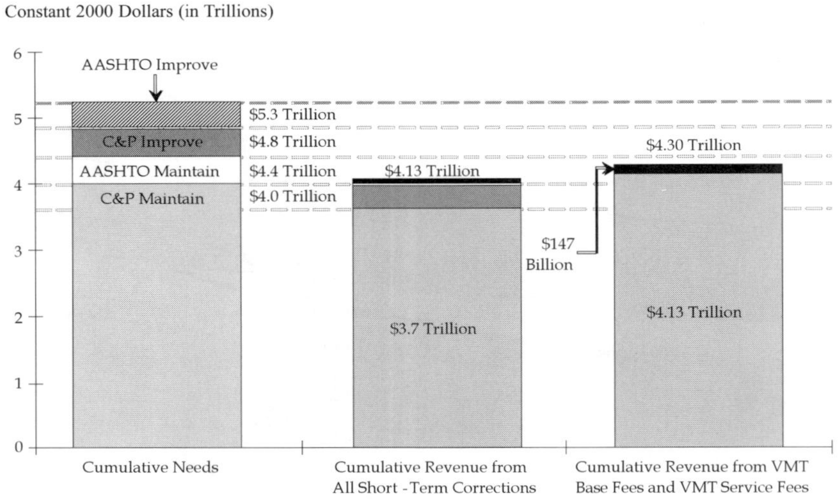

Source: Cambridge Systematics based on FHWA and AASHTO data.

improve the performance of the highway and transit systems, but an indexed VMT-base revenue system should generate enough revenue in the following decade to give policy-makers the option of investing in projects up to AASHTO's "need to improve" target.

Evaluation of Long-Term Strategies

The strengths and weaknesses of the proposed long-term strategies are as follows:

- **Yield and Reliability** – The two-tier VMT strategy closes the gap between highway and transit needs and revenues over time. Revenues will track the costs of constructing and maintaining highway and transit systems because the VMT base fee and local-option VMT service fee are indexed.
- **Economic Efficiency** – The VMT fees send stronger price signals than any of the current revenue sources, with the exception of variable user fees. By more accurately pricing highway transportation costs, transportation agencies and private investors will have a clearer sense of how much travelers are willing to pay for highway and transit services and where they should invest.

- **Equity** – Implementation of a VMT base fee as a revenue neutral swap for motor fuel taxes should not shift the burden of funding transportation among users. Nevertheless, VMT service fees have the potential to impose a higher financial burden on low-income households who cannot afford to live close to their jobs and other major destinations. Despite extensive discussions of the effects of pricing in transportation planning, finance, and economics literature, the empirical land use impacts of a shift to mileage-based transportation fees—and their equity effects on the location of businesses, households, and socioeconomic groups—are only partially understood. These impacts will require careful attention.
- **Administrative Effectiveness** – The task of collecting user fees from millions of vehicle owners will present the greatest challenge in shifting from a motor-fuel-tax-based revenue system to a VMT-based revenue system. However, the technology needed to implement this proposal will be available and is described in chapters 7 and 8 of this book.
- **Public Acceptance** – Implementation of a VMT-based revenue system presents many challenges, not least of which are privacy concerns and the overall increase in the amount paid by most users for access to transportation.

Recommendations

Current transportation revenues are barely sufficient to maintain the condition of the nation's highway and transit systems through 2015 and insufficient to add capacity, maintain performance, and address congestion into the 21st century. To address the transportation revenue shortfall, two major initiatives are recommended:

1. In the short term—between 2005 and 2015—index and increase the existing federal motor fuel tax and expand the implementation of user fees to avoid falling further behind in maintaining the nation's highway and transit systems; and
2. In the long term—2015 and beyond—implement mileage-based transportation fees to increase revenue and improve the economic efficiency of the transportation system.

In the short term, indexing and increasing the existing federal motor fuel tax is the most effective strategy for generating additional transportation revenues. Development and implementation of a mileage-based revenue program will take at least two reauthorization cycles. New investment cannot be postponed until a new revenue system has been fully developed and proven. Deferring investment in the transportation system will simply aggravate congestion and mortgage the future to higher transportation system repair and replacement costs.

Indexing and increasing the existing federal motor fuel tax will meet, at least partially, immediate transportation needs and respond to public concern about congestion and delay. The federal motor fuel tax is the only major tax that is not indexed structurally to inflation. While increasing fuel taxes will not be popular, a number of states have shown that motor fuel taxes can be indexed successfully. Paired with expanded implementation of user fees and short-term innovative finance supports such as tax-credit bond financing, increasing motor fuel tax revenues will stabilize transportation revenues through 2015. Maintaining and extending the motor fuel tax system will leverage the existing and very effective tax collection and enforcement system developed over the last 50 years.

Beyond 2015 there is substantial risk that the yield and reliability of motor fuel tax revenue—even indexed and increased—will deteriorate. To respond to this long-term problem, mileage-based transportation fees should be implemented to increase revenue and improve the economic efficiency of the transportation system.

A two-tier mileage-based fee system is recommended. A vehicle-miles-of-travel (VMT) base fee should be applied to all mileage accrued by a vehicle each year; and a local-option VMT service fee should be applied to the portion of that mileage accrued in congested metropolitan highway networks and on high-demand facilities (e.g., toll roads and congested urban arterials).

The VMT base fee should be applied nationally and should be explained as maintaining the condition of the transportation system by replacing current fuel-tax revenues. The VMT service fee should be made a local option (e.g., state, region, or city) that can be tailored to local highway and transit needs and explained as addressing capacity needs and performance.

A range of implementation scenarios should be explored. These should include a "low-tech" (or transitional) scenario in which VMT base-fee payments are determined by tamper-proof odometer or hub-odometer readings and VMT service-fee payments are determined by location (e.g., residence or registration jurisdiction) and pay-as-you-go user fee tags (e.g., EZPass model, time-of-day value-pricing lanes, etc.).

The implementation scenarios should also cover a "high-tech" scenario in which both VMT base-fee payments and VMT service-fee payments are determined by "smart vehicle" GPS/GIS calculations. Both implementation scenarios are sufficiently plausible given today's technology that development and initial implementation of a mileage-based fee system is considered feasible.

A mileage-based transportation fee system will yield sustainable and reliable revenues that will track the growth of the economy. They will generate predictable streams of revenue needed to sustain and cost-effectively finance major capital improvements. Mileage-based fees will better link the pricing of service to transportation system performance, helping to ensure that investments are economically efficient and respond to consumer and community needs. To the extent that revenues from mileage-based fees can replace more regressive local sales taxes and support local transportation options, they also will maintain reasonable equity in transportation system access and cost.

Implementation of mileage-based taxes will require development of a new administrative system to control collection costs and assure enforcement. It is reasonable to expect that computer and telecommunications technology can be harnessed to the task. A mileage-based fee system will be a departure from the familiar and established system of motor fuel taxes; however, the approach maintains the continuity of the user-pays principle and will gain public acceptance if it effectively and flexibly addresses the public's need for improved transportation performance and responsiveness to customer needs.

Deployment of a mileage-based transportation revenue system should be targeted for the period 2015 to 2025; however, development should begin now. Planning and initial implementation of a mileage-based fee system will require several decades of work to:

- Build political consensus
- Design and test administrative systems
- Integrate technology into the vehicle fleet
- Address issues of privacy, security, and robustness
- Understand and adjust to land use and travel pattern changes
- Educate the public to a major cultural change

Delaying implementation will result in continuing deterioration of system performance, structural condition, and customer satisfaction, burdening the economy with less productive transportation.

As illustrated in the hypothetical diagram in Figure 2-10, implementation of these recommendations will increase the revenue available for transportation and, through greater application of direct user fees, provide transportation system users and providers—automobile drivers, transit riders, freight shippers, carriers, and agencies—with clearer links between the prices they pay and the services they receive.

Figure 2-10: Short- and Long-Term Transition of the Transportation Funding Portfolio

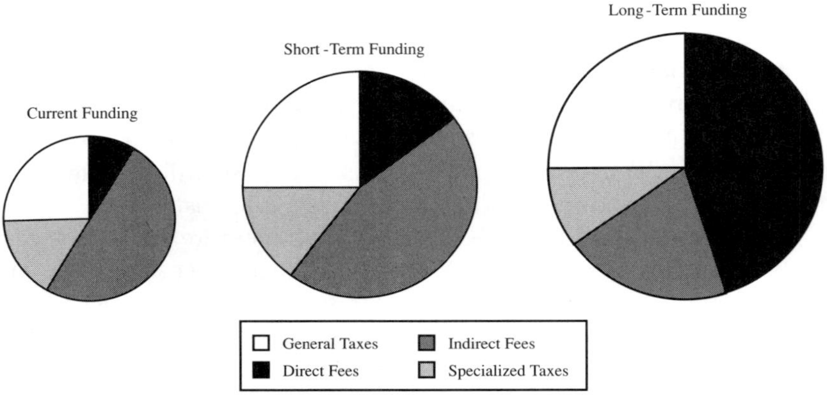

Source: Cambridge Systematics

Part II

Freight Transportation

by
Sergio J. Ostria

Chapter 3

Freight and the Economy

As illustrated in Figure 3-1, trucking is the dominant mode of domestic freight transportation in the United States. In 2000, trucking accounted for 78 percent of the nation's intra- and intercity freight tonnage, 60 percent of total ton-mileage, and 88 percent of our total freight bill (all exclusive of pipelines).[24] The picture changes, however, when one focuses on just intercity freight movements. According to BTS, in 1990, rail accounted for almost 40 percent of intercity ton-mileage. By 2000, rail's share had grown to 47 percent. During that same period, the trucking share of intercity ton-mileage also grew from 28 to 33 percent, while water's share fell from about 32 percent to 19 percent.[25]

Figure 3-1: U.S. Domestic Freight Movement (2000)

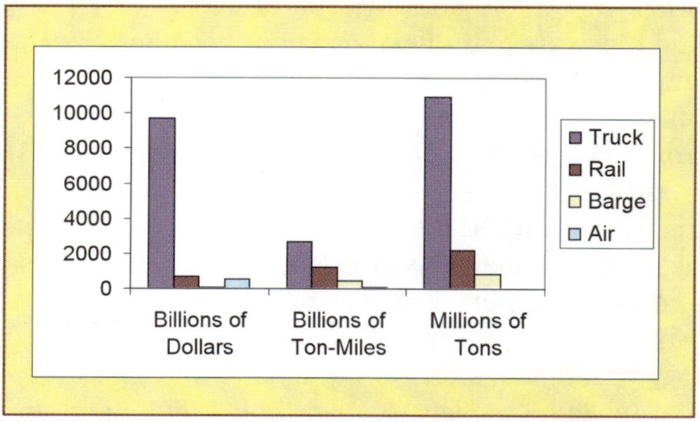

Source: ASSHTO, Freight-Rail Bottom Line Report

In the past, policy-makers, government agency practitioners, carriers, and even shippers viewed our freight system from this type of modal perspective, and focused analyses and decisions on mode-specific considerations. The advent of intermodalism, which has been enabled by technology, has changed this perspective to a more holistic viewpoint that is blurring the lines between specific modes. Today, shippers, carriers, forwarders, and integrators are reshaping freight networks. The modal industries are evolving from "carriers" to "supply-chain managers." Shippers are delegating carrier selection to third-party logistics (3-PLs) firms. Government is focusing on system performance, rather than facility design and mode-specific capacity issues. Overall, the trend is toward market integration, and efficiency and reliability are defined by the performance of the overall system.

There are a number of drivers generating this change. The most significant are changes in the structure of our economy and technological innovation:

- ➢ ***Changing economic structure.*** Between 1970 and 1999, the share of U.S. Gross Domestic Product (GDP) that is attributable to international trade increased from approximately 11 to 30 percent. During this period, the services sector of our economy increased significantly and manufacturing became relatively less of a driver in our economy. These changes have had a profound effect on our freight system. First, relatively more finished products are being transported, meaning that carrier flexibility and reliability are becoming more and more important. Second, the connectivity between our trade gateways (ports and border crossings) and inland highways and rail systems has become critical to the performance of the freight system. Modes depend more on one another to meet the demands of customers.
- ➢ ***Technology.*** Technological innovation has enabled: 1) the shift from push to pull logistics which led to a focus on supply-chain management and the advent of 3-PLs and 4-PLs (i.e., specialists in total logistics management), and 2) significant decreases in logistics costs as shippers have consolidated distribution centers and substituted more transportation for costly inventory. Today, technology is enabling shifts to consolidated logistics based on new carrier business models to meet time-definite and door-to-door needs of shippers (e.g., mode-neutral service products). In the future, technology may enable the development of freight villages and city logistics practices, further reshaping networks and service paradigms.

Even though our freight system has proven to be highly adaptable, there is growing concern on the part of government and industry about the future performance of our freight transportation system, its ability to foster continued economic growth, and its effects on the environment, public safety, and other social issues (see table 3-1). Growing congestion on critical highway segments, increases in delay at freight terminals and border crossings, rail infrastructure downsizing, insufficient dock or near-dock loading facilities at our ports, and the effects of potential new security requirements are examples of the types of factors that affect the productivity of our freight system. When coupled with our inability to quickly increase the capacity of the system, these factors could have significant adverse effects on our future standard of living.

Table 3-1: Freight Transportation Externalities

- Air quality
  - Diesel exhaust is a primary source of PM and air toxic contaminants which are deemed as major health threats, especially to children.
  - Diesel exhaust is a primary source of NOx emissions, a precursor to ozone.
- Community livability and environmental justice
  - Location of many freight facilities may lead to a disproportionate impact on minority and economically disadvantaged communities.
- Transportation safety
  - In 2002, 434,000 large trucks were involved in traffic crashes in the U.S.; 4,542 were involved in fatal crashes. A total of 4,897 people died and 130,000 were injured.
- Homeland security
  - The vulnerability of the freight system, especially given globalization, is a major cause for concern when it comes to terrorism.

This section provides information on the issues that determine the balance between the demand for freight transportation and its supply (as characterized by capacity), so that decision-makers can answer the following question:

What can government (at all levels) do to ensure an efficient and reliable freight system that fosters economic productivity and growth while minimizing unwanted externalities?

First, a review of the role of freight transportation in our economy is presented. Second, an assessment of the capacity challenges facing users of the freight system is provided. Third, a future demand scenario is constructed against which future supply considerations can be evaluated. Fourth, past and current policy initiatives to improve the performance of our freight system are reviewed. Finally, approaches for mitigating the imbalance between supply and demand are investigated from a policy perspective.

Carriage of goods is the movement of the inputs and outputs of all the production and distribution processes—manufacturing, farming, mining, and the wholesale and retail trades. Freight carriage is important in the economy in two ways. Taken by itself as an economic activity, goods movement is a major industrial sector. But the carriage of the inputs and outputs of the other sectors is a critical input to all the production and distribution processes in the economy. As such, the cost and quality of freight movement affect the productivity of the entire economy.

The importance of freight movement as an industrial sector is seen in Table 3-2, which shows total value of for-hire freight at about $560 billion, almost 5.4 percent of GDP. If we add in an estimated $100 billion for private carriage of freight (a low estimate), the total dollar figure is around $660 billion and the share of GDP is almost 6.4 percent.

Table 3-2: U.S. Business Logistics System Costs, 2002

2002	Billions of Current US$	% of GDP
Trucking (intercity & local)	462	4.41%
Rail	37	0.35%
Water (domestic & int'l.)	27	0.26%
Air (domestic & int'l.)	27	0.26%
Oil Pipelines	9	0.09%
Total	562	5.37%
2002 Nominal GDP	*10,470*	

Source: Cass/ProLogis 14th Annual State of Logistics Report, 6/2/03

As these numbers show, movement of goods is a non-trivial share of the national economy. For American consumers, however, the significant impact of freight carriage is felt through its effect on productivity and, hence, on the standard of living. An increase in productivity reflects more efficient use of the labor, capital, materials, and so forth that are available to society at any given time. Production can always be increased if more resources can be found, but the supply of resources at any particular time is always limited. Productivity gains allow us to enjoy more or better goods and services with the resources we have available. As depicted in Figure 3-2, growth in our per capita GDP tends to rise and fall in conjunction with growth in labor productivity.

Figure 3-2: Productivity and Economic Performance

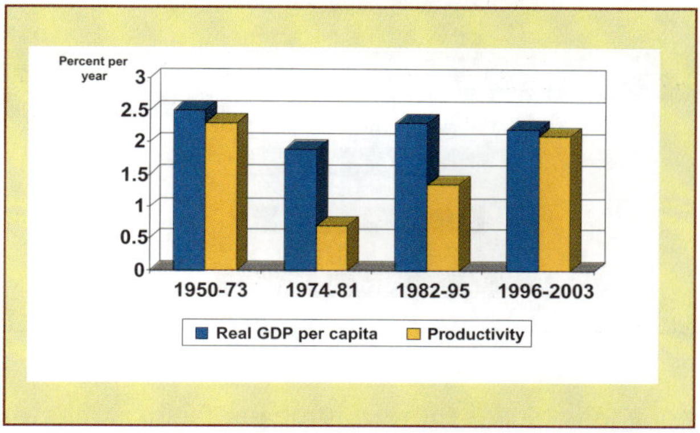

Source: Congressional Budget Office, Commerce Department

Freight Transportation and Economic Productivity

The performance of the goods-movement system affects economic productivity in several ways. Changes in the cost of freight movement and the quality of freight movement both affect the amount of freight transport that firms buy and the ways in which they use freight transport. At the most basic level, a drop in the cost of goods movement means firms will buy more goods movement. This will most likely take the form of shipping products longer distances and obtaining inputs, materials, and intermediate products from longer distances. This increases the market that can be served from a given facility and gives access to lower-cost inputs and, perhaps, to a wider spectrum of choices of inputs. Figure 3-3 traces the links from an improvement in freight-transport to a higher standard of living.

Improvements in the quality of transportation take the form of reduced transit times and greater reliability of delivery times. Both of these effects, and especially the second, affect the way in which firms design their logistics systems. Lower transit times increase the "reach" of facilities such as factories and distribution centers; if these facilities can be more widely spaced, placed farther apart from each other, a given market area can be served with fewer facilities. Since fewer facilities for

Figure 3-3: Transportation and the Economy

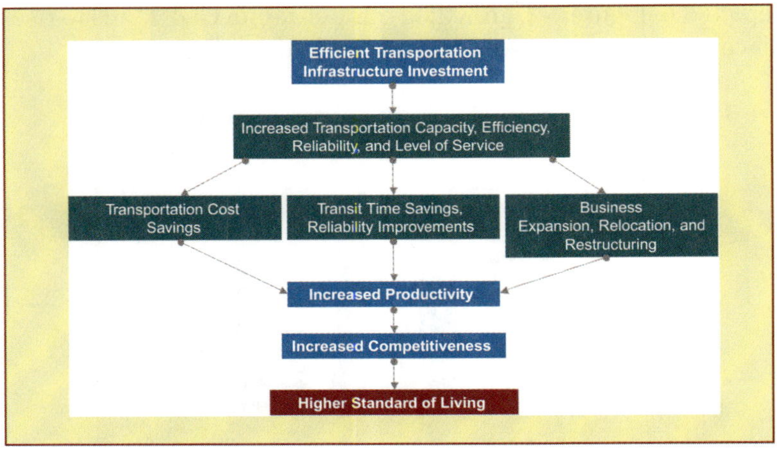

a given flow of goods means more volume per facility, operating costs as well as investment costs may be reduced. Thus, when firms consider their logistics arrangements and the design of their distribution systems, they will take account of improved freight transport to develop lower-cost systems.

As described in Figure 3-4, increased reliability has a further effect. It allows firms to reduce the total investment in inventory required to support a given volume of sales. The greater the reliability of the system, the less the requirement for buffer stocks to guard against delivery failures. Again, firms will take advantage of this factor when they redesign or build new logistics systems, leading to overall reduction in logistics costs even while they buy more transport services to ship longer distances. Substitution of transportation for the other elements of logistics costs—principally inventory and warehouses—has been a marked feature of the U.S. economy over the last two decades as shown in Figure 3-5.[26]

Firms Responses to High-Quality Freight Transport

If we think of freight transport as a necessary input in the production of goods and services (e.g., manufacturers must move their product from a production site to a consumption site or market), then the benefits of freight improvements become clearer. First, as the cost of transportation falls, firms substitute more transportation for other inputs. Second, the result is that producers can now generate more output at the

Figure 3-4: How do firms react to improvements in freight transportation?

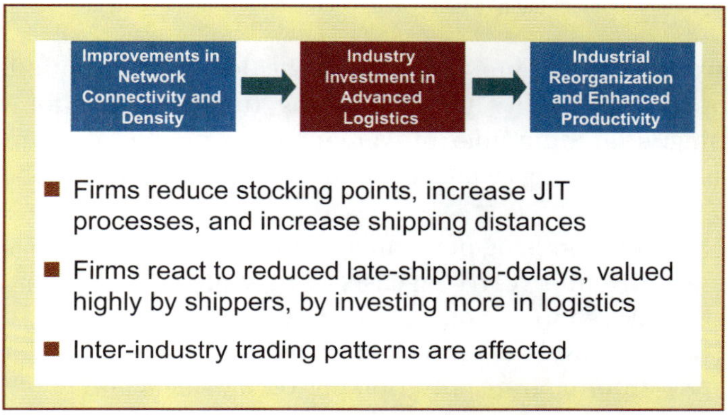

Figure 3-5: Shippers substitute transportation for inventory

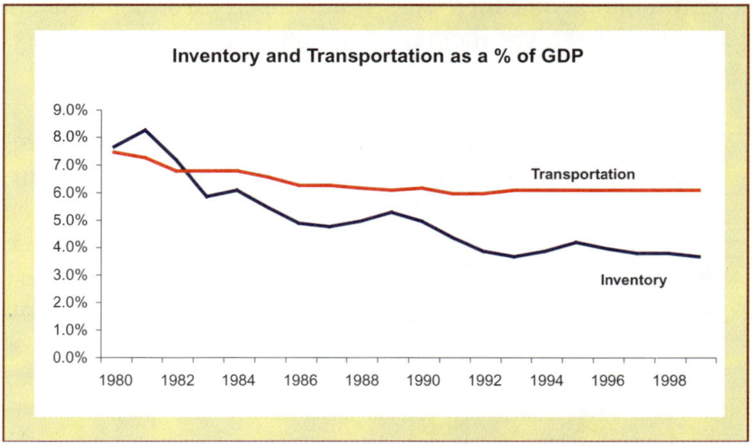

same level of cost. By definition this effect is an increase in economic productivity. The end results from the decrease in transportation cost are 1) an increase in the demand for transportation from the drop in the cost of transportation and 2) a long-term change in the structure of that demand as firms rely more on the efficiency and reliability of the freight system and less on the other components of logistics.

Below are three specific examples of how firms have restructured their logistics systems to take advantage of high-quality transportation and reduce costs.[27]

1. **Polaroid** – In the late 1980s, Polaroid decided to centralize its European inventories by substituting transportation for warehousing; a large number of warehouses were closed. Estimated annual gross savings were $6.9 million, broken down as follows:

   - ✓ Warehousing personnel - $2.5 million
   - ✓ Inventory carrying costs - $2.2 million
   - ✓ Warehouse rental costs - $1.0 million
   - ✓ Facilities and offices - $0.6 million
   - ✓ Internal transportation between dealers and subsidiaries - $0.5 million
   - ✓ Insurance premiums - $0.1 million

   Net annual savings were $6.3 million after subtracting $0.6 million per year for increased costs resulting from computer system maintenance and increased warehouse personnel at headquarters. A capital investment of $3.0 million for new computer equipment was required.

   Besides these savings that Polaroid could quantify, there were other gains that were not measured. Prior to centralizing inventory, 69 percent of orders could not be filled at the location that received them, so that items were backordered until they could be filled from other locations. This required significant internal transportation among dealers and subsidiaries to reposition inventory. Polaroid also achieved unspecified freight cost savings based on volume discounts for consolidated (truckload) shipments to centralized warehouses as well as reduced freight rates that reflected truck cost savings from reduction of border crossing inefficiencies.

2. **Dell Computer** – In 1996, Dell Computer launched its "online" store. Customers were able to choose their own computer configurations and receive 24-hour support online. When an online order is received, the configuration of the desired computer is immediately transmitted to the manufacturing group. Using a specification sheet, the order is broken down to individual com-

ponents. Components are either ordered for just-in-time (JIT) delivery on very short notice or drawn from relatively small stocks that are replenished on a JIT basis. The computer is assembled by a production team and then shifted to software loading where it is tested for between four to eight hours. The entire process from receipt of order to shipping requires about 36 hours. Dell would not be able to achieve this combination of rapid response and low level of inventory without a very high level of freight service from United Parcel Service (UPS) under a comprehensive contract covering all inbound movements of parts, in addition to a sophisticated, computer-based communications system.

The online store concept was a revolutionary precedent for the computer industry, which had been dominated by manufacturers with complex supply chains and relatively large inventories of parts and computers. By building to order and outsourcing most components, Dell gained a major cost advantage by greatly reducing parts inventories and virtually eliminating stocks of finished machines. Dell effectively became little more than an assembly and shipping company.

The JIT system for parts delivery allows Dell to reduce inventory of components from an industry norm of 75 to 100 days to 13 days. Suppliers are integrated into Dell's online ordering and procurement system, resulting in a span of fifteen minutes for most suppliers between receipt of order and shipment to Dell's assembly plant. Shippers of monitors, for example, receive an e-mail giving the day a customer's order is to be shipped, and the monitor is delivered on that day. Dell estimates that they save $30 per monitor by virtually eliminating inventory.

Dell's build-to-order approach is of particular significance in an industry characterized by continuous innovation and introduction of new products. Since prices of components decline rapidly in response to continuous innovation, Dell derives a cost advantage from the fact that most components are not bought until an order is received.

The Dell JIT system of procurement and online ordering typifies the virtual substitution of transportation and communications for inventory. It would not be possible without the availability of very high-quality freight transportation services.

3. **Ford Motor Company** – Ford presents another example of using communication and transportation improvements to establish closer links to the customer and eliminate inventory. The transportation-improvement stimulus came from cost and service gains realized from sharply increased use of rail service. Railroads went from moving very few new vehicles from assembly plants to a dominant share (over 80 percent) of this market. For example, in 1980 railroads handled 342,000 carloads of vehicles compared to 609,000 carloads in 1990. Since 1990 annual movements of finished vehicles have increased to nearly 900,000. This is a case in which shippers reorganized their logistics to exploit fully the financial advantages of a low-cost mode while improving service to customers.

   Several trends have favored increased use of rail movements of finished automobiles and light trucks in the United States:

- Domestic vehicle production has grown largely as a result of foreign transplants and resulting decreases in imports with a more recent shift to exports.
- The mixture of new vehicles shipped has changed in the direction of more light trucks, which tends to favor rail for shipments from factories because the cubic-space requirements of light trucks and sport utility recreational vehicles are better met by rail cars.
- North American assembly plants, with the exception of recent rail served expansions in Mexico, have remained relatively concentrated in the Midwest and southern Ontario at rail-competitive distances from major coastal markets.
  The Big Three did not respond to the service characteristics of rail shipment in any substantial way until 1997. Commencing in 1997, both Ford and GM announced sweeping changes in how new vehicles were to be distributed from assembly plants to domestic markets. Ford moved to implement a "regional mixing center" concept.

Ford created four national mixing centers in Chicago; Shelbyville, Kentucky; Kansas City, Missouri; and Fostoria, Ohio. Ford has an

> exclusive contract with Norfolk Southern (NS) Railway under which NS constructs and operates these sites. Each mixing center performs the function of a logistics distribution center by creating an assortment of vehicles that can be shipped in response to dealer orders in full rail cars or trucks to destination markets.
>
> The mixing centers replace a distribution system in which dealer orders for different lines of vehicles were accumulated at individual assembly plants until a sufficient quantity existed to fill an entire rail car (ten to twenty vehicles, depending on size) or truck (five to ten vehicles, depending on size) for shipment to the local market. Instead of waiting for sufficient dealer orders to fill rail cars and trucks with vehicles made at a particular plant, each assembly plant now makes daily shipments to the mixing centers. Each mixing center receives shipments from different assembly plants. Rail cars and trucks from assembly plants are unloaded at a mixing center and reloaded with a specific set of vehicles for destination markets, responding to orders by local area dealers. Vehicles will normally be held at the mixing center only as long as necessary for transloading. It is estimated that vehicles will be received at the mixing centers, unloaded, reloaded, and shipped within eight to 24 hours.
>
> The Ford distribution center concept has been adopted to achieve economies of transportation time by maximizing trainload and truckload movements of vehicles from all plants to the centers and from centers to local markets. The four Ford mixing centers handle over 3.2 million new vehicles per year. The mixing center concept also appears to have achieved substantial transportation cost savings for Ford.
>
> Through a major restructuring of its logistics operations and facilities, Ford was able both to reduce transportation costs and inventory costs while improving service to its customers.

The gains in logistics that are exemplified by the experiences of Polaroid, Dell Computers, and Ford are examples of how an efficient and reliable freight transportation system can lead to increases in economic productivity. In general, such gains may occur when a firm responds to a freight improvement, or, for whatever reason, analyzes its logistics arrangements and discovers that it is not taking full advantage of the freight transportation system's capabilities.

Either way, these productivity gains will not occur unless a firm's management perceives that the freight system is robust and reliable enough to support its plans. These gains certainly will not occur if a firm's managers perceive that the quality of the freight system (as defined by speed and reliability) is deteriorating or will deteriorate in the near future (see Table 3-3). In a nutshell, any degradation of the goods-movement system will seriously erode the profits firms now gain from successful inventory management. The success of these logistics operations depends on deliveries, mostly truck deliveries, hitting time windows, sometimes as narrow as 15 minutes, day in and day out. With any sustained decay in schedule reliability, the efficiency in these carefully designed systems would quickly disappear. In past interviews conducted by the author with both carriers and shippers, a recurrent theme was the damage that could be done by system failure or degradation. Any such loss of efficiency would have an impact on the economy well beyond lower profit margins for the companies directly affected. There would be a negative effect on productivity that would ripple through the whole economy, lowering our competitiveness and our standard of living. This is the importance of the link between the quality of the freight system and national productivity gains.

Examples of System Strain and Potential Degradation

At the most general level, degradation of freight-system performance would be felt all along supply and distribution chains and, accordingly, by all producers and importers of goods and all consumers of goods. It is useful to identify some specific parts and segments of the freight system where declines in performance would have especially strong effects and some characteristics of the logistics systems where those effects would be felt. The following are examples of some specific segments that are now showing some signs of strain from pressure on capacity.

➢ **Congestion in the Southern California Ports and Chicago** – Enormous volumes of inbound container traffic (almost 11 million Ton Equivalent Units, TEUs, in 2002) move through the ports of Los Angeles and Long Beach. Containers destined for the major consumption centers of the Midwest and the East largely move from Los Angeles to Chicago by intermodal rail, an efficient and

Table 3-3: Some Findings from Interviews with Shippers and Carriers

As part of FHWA's Freight Benefit-Cost Analysis Study, ICF Consulting conducted interviews with shippers and carriers. This is some of what those interviews showed.

Current service is good.

- On-time rates often over 95%

Firms frequently revisit their logistics arrangements.

- Of 13 shippers, 5 changed or were about to change logistics.

Firms concerned if highway conditions get worse.

Businesses revisit logistics under a variety of business pressures (cost and customer service).

- Freight-transport improvements affect the outcome of industry reorganizations.
- Shippers revisit logistics in response to business pressures.

low-cost movement. But congestion around the docks and along the roads from the docks to the rail terminals constantly threatens efficiency of the dock-to-rail move. Similarly in Chicago, the transfer of eastbound containers from western railroads to eastern carriers is made by drayage moves through highly congested urban roads. Congestion and inefficiency in urban drayage degrade the efficiency of the 2,000-mile move at either end of the trip.

- A starker example of the vulnerability of the Los Angeles and Long Beach ports was the west coast dock dispute in 2002. After a ten-day lockout of dockworkers, it took the system 23 days to get back to normal flows and eliminate the backlog. Goods with a cumulative value of $6.3 billion were held up. Some major importers had to take drastic steps to keep freight moving to their customers. Hewlett-Packard (HP), for example, resorted to air cargo to keep its commitments to customers. The fact that HP was able to turn to another mode (although a more costly one) highlights the flexibility of our freight system. But should the lockout have lasted longer, the increases in shipping costs likely would have limited HP's ability to turn to air cargo and maintain desired profit margins over the longer term.

Table 3-4: Top West Coast Ports by TEUs (in thousands), 2002

Los Angeles (CA)	6,105
Long Beach (CA)	6,105
Oakland (CA)	1,707
Tacoma (WA)	1,470
Vancouver (BC)	1,458
Seattle (WA)	1,438
Manzanillo (COL)	634
Anchorage (AK)	463
Portland (OR)	256
Fraser River (BC)	101
Ensenada (BCAL)	53

Source: AAPA

➢ Another important consideration that is brought to light by the ten-day lockout is the potential effect of a terrorist attack (or other major event) on one of our major ports. Should such an event lead to longer disruptions in port operations, the effects on shippers and our economy could be far-reaching. As depicted in Table 3-4, the Ports of Los Angeles and Long Beach, for example, handle the lion's share of container traffic into and out of the west coast of North America. If one of those ports became incapacitated for an extended period, the stress on the freight system (including other west coast ports, as well as the rail and highway facilities that connect to them) most likely would significantly reduce our west-coast freight system capacity, with concomitant effects on shippers and the U.S. economy.

- ➢ **Inland Waterways: The Mississippi** – The lock-and-dam system on the Mississippi River and its major tributaries is aging, and many observers believe its capacity is no longer sufficient for the traffic moving on the river. Some locks are heavily congested, with delays of well over six hours during peak-flow periods. The Mississippi and its principal tributaries, the Illinois and Ohio Rivers, are major highways for bulk traffic, especially coal and grain. The river system is the lowest-cost carrier of these commodities. Excessive delays on the river can add to shippers' costs, especially if they are forced to use more costly rail service. The river system is also a major factor in international competitiveness, as a large proportion of our grain exports goes down the Mississippi to New Orleans.
- ➢ **Border-Crossing Delays** – The great preponderance of NAFTA trade moves over our northern and southern borders in trucks. Partly because of customs procedures, and partly because of limited infrastructure at key crossing points, there is a significant potential for congestion and delay. Very long back-ups on the Ambassador Bridge are an ordinary occurrence for traffic inbound from Canada to Detroit. Since major auto-production facilities are clustered in both Michigan and western Ontario, congestion at the Detroit crossing can be a major source of inefficiency in the logistics systems of the automakers. This is the kind of cost that spreads quickly through the whole economic system, affecting both producers and consumers.
- ➢ The same issues arise at the southern border, especially at the Laredo crossing point. A combination of customs procedures, limited infrastructure, and periods of very heavy traffic flows leads to inefficiencies that ripple through the production and distribution of all traded goods. Laredo and Detroit are leading examples, but congestion and delay are issues at several other crossing points as well.
- ➢ A 2001 sample of seven U.S. ports of entry found average travel time for inbound crossings at 26.8 minutes, with a 95th percentile

time of over 70 minutes.[28] Efforts have been underway to help alleviate this problem. For example, the Bureau of Customs and Border Protection (CBP) has recently published new rules requiring advance electronic filing for inbound truck (and rail) traffic over both borders and for outbound traffic over the Mexican border. CBP is making efforts to streamline processes so heightened security requirements will not impede traffic flow, but this is a concern, nonetheless.

- **System-wide Highway Issues** – There is serious road congestion in our large metropolitan areas, and as depicted in Figure 3-6 congestion is getting worse. It has been estimated that the annual cost of congestion and delay in the 75 largest urban areas is about $70 billion.[29] Congestion is even spreading to major rural roadways. Just over 7,000 miles of rural arterial roads are classified as significantly or severely congested.[30] No change in policy will eliminate all highway congestion; that is impossible. But these data on congestion tell us that our economy is bearing costs that could be significantly reduced with effective policy responses.
- **Rail Capacity and Intermodal Movements** – A recent article from the Journal of Commerce states the following.

Figure 3-6: Highway traffic congestion has been getting worse in urban areas of all sizes.

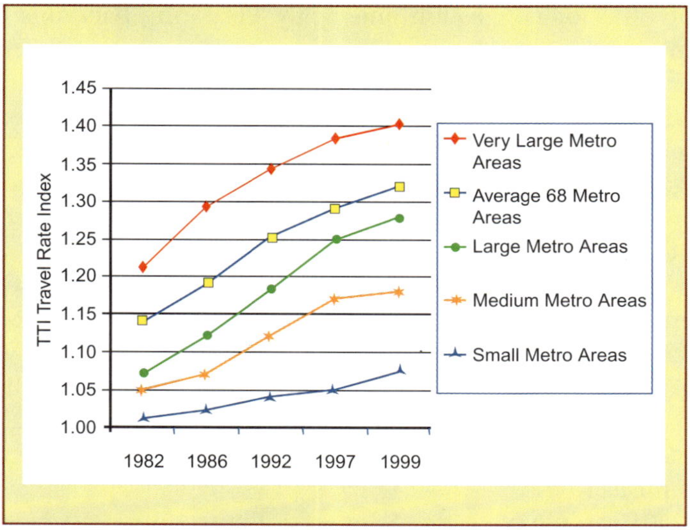

Source: FHWA

Box shortage crisis coming, says Pacer exec.
By BILL MONGELLUZZO - THE JOURNAL OF COMMERCE ONLINE.
7 April 2004
Journal of Commerce Online

LOS ANGELES - The president of a leading intermodal service provider warned that rail congestion in North America is squeezing the supply of containers, a situation that could reach crisis proportions during the peak shipping season.

"We will have the mother of all box shortages this fall," Jeff Brashares, president of Pacer Global Logistics' transportation division, told the Los Angeles Transportation Club Tuesday.

Congestion on the intermodal rail network stretches from Vancouver, Canada, to Los Angeles, Chicago and all the way to the east coast. This development is especially troubling because it began in the winter, traditionally the slowest period of the year for intermodal shipments.

Brashares noted that the Union Pacific Railroad is struggling with a crew and power shortage; Norfolk Southern Railway's ramps in the East are busier than they were during the peak season last October, and CSX Transportation is dealing with operational problems in the East.

Canadian shippers on Tuesday asked the government to help resolve growing congestion problems on the Canadian Pacific Railway that have left 10,000 TEUs sitting on the docks at the Port of Vancouver.

An unexpected flood of imports from Asia this winter caught the intermodal transportation industry by surprise. Ron Widdows, chief executive of APL Ltd. in Singapore, reported last month that vessels were leaving Asia fully loaded, something that normally doesn't happen until late summer.

Construction of new containers has also been hit by a shortage of steel caused in part by China's voracious appetite for raw materials. The intermodal congestion problem in the United

States is compounded by operational deficiencies on the rail networks.

The UP, for example, began to experience crew shortages one year ago when hundreds of crew took early retirement. The result: slower average train speeds and delays in returning rail cars and equipment to west coast ports.

Industry figures indicate that a decrease of just one mile per hour in the average network speed creates a need for an additional 250 double-stack rail cars and 300 locomotives to move the same volume of cargo. The UP this week is reporting delays of 24 to 48 hours out of Los Angeles and Chicago.

The UP hired 2,000 workers last year and is hiring 4,000 this year, with the first wave of trainees scheduled for certification in the spring. TTX, the U.S. railcar lessor, placed orders for 18,700 new intermodal platforms this year, the second consecutive year of substantial growth in equipment orders. TTX last year increased the double-stack rail car fleet by 14 percent.

The network congestion appears to be worsening, Brashares said, and soaring imports from Asia could push the system into crisis mode by the late summer peak shipping season.

Brashares called on shippers to demand a realistic assessment from their carriers of what they can and cannot do during the peak season.

The examples above highlight a number of important facts about our nation's freight transportation system. First and foremost, the multitude of transportation modes that comprise our freight system rely on each other. From the perspective of many shippers, the days of single-mode decision-making probably ended in the 1980s, in response to the effects of deregulation (such as the growth in intermodalism and truckload carriers). Consequently, a truly holistic, multimodal perspective must be brought to bear on decision-making on the policies, programs, and projects that affect the efficiency and reliability of our freight system. Second, and related to this, important capacity bottlenecks can affect efficiency and reliability, often with potentially significant effects on our nation's economic welfare. Third, and as will be discussed in the following chapters, each of the modes is confronting capacity constraints that will be difficult to resolve without vision, leadership, and coordinated decision-making from the public sector, at all levels.

Chapter 4

Freight Capacity and Performance Challenges

In 2000, the U.S. freight system (not including pipelines) moved well over 12 billion tons of goods worth roughly 10 trillion dollars. However, there is significant and growing concern on the part of both the private and public sectors about the future performance of our freight transportation system. Consider the following:

- ***Growing congestion on our highway system.*** The demand for highway travel has been growing at a fast rate. According to a recently released report from the General Accounting Office (GAO), peak-period highway congestion for passenger and commercial vehicles doubled from 1982 through 2000. From 1993 through 2001, truck traffic on urban highways increased more than twice as much as passenger traffic. This means that freight traffic is contributing to worsening congestion at a faster rate than passenger traffic, and as discussed in Chapter 5 of this book, there is no end in sight to the growth in freight traffic.[31]
- ***Our shrinking railway system.*** Before deregulation and the Staggers Rail Act of 1980, the U.S. rail industry was widely considered to have significant levels of excess capacity. From 1980 to 2001, however, Class I railroads consolidated from 22 carriers to 7 (four of which have 95 percent of Class-I revenue), the number of locomotives decreased by 29.7 percent, the number of freight cars decreased by 23 percent, and railroad employment decreased by 55.5 percent.[32] The amount of rail line has also contracted substantially since 1980, from 164,822 to only 142,633 in 2001, a decrease of 13.5 percent.
- ***Our constrained and inefficient port system.*** Globalization and growth in international trade are placing more demands on our ports. Between 1970 and 1999, trade's share of U.S. GDP increased

from 10.7 percent to 26.9 percent. As a result, our nation's ports and channels are becoming increasingly congested as ever greater amounts of freight are moved through a system with limited means for physical capacity expansion. From 1990 to 2000, tonnage at U.S. ports increased by 13.8 percent,[33] while capacity expanded only marginally. In fact, considerable resources were required merely to maintain physical capacity through efforts such as dredging.

- ***Our aging inland waterways.*** The U.S. inland waterways are critical for certain bulk commodities such as coal and grain. Investment in the infrastructure required to support these waterways, however, has not been adequate to maintain the system, and the median age of all lock chambers has been estimated at 35 years. Moreover, capacity of inland water channels has remained basically flat since 1970.
- ***Incredible growth in air cargo.*** At an annual growth rate of 5.1 percent from 1990 to 2000, air cargo is by far the fastest growing mode of freight transportation. (The exception would be intermodal rail if it were regarded as a separate mode.) Our aviation system already is characterized by frequent delays, traffic control safety concerns, and heightened security measures, and certain hubs are beginning to experience chronic problems.

As these points highlight, trends in freight movements cannot be understood outside of the context of capacity constraints. While these constraints are primarily infrastructure related (e.g., highways), they also include operational concerns, regulatory issues, and financial considerations. This chapter describes the capacity of the current freight system and likely trends over the next 20 years.

Highway Capacity Issues

Infrastructure

As of 2002, our nation's road network consisted of 8.3 million lane-miles. Local roads comprise around 66 percent of these lane-miles, leaving approximately 2.8 million lane-miles of interstates, arterials, and collectors to carry intercity freight traffic. While the overall number of lane-miles is impressive, growth in lane-miles has been scant over the last 20 years.

Figure 4-1 illustrates lane-mile growth from 1980 to 2002. Lane-miles of principal arterials grew by 30 percent while interstate lane-miles grew 17 percent. Total lane-miles across all roads, however, grew by a mere 5 percent over these 22 years, an annual growth rate of only 0.22 percent.

Figure 4-1: Trends in Lane-Miles of Roadway by Functional Class (1980-2002)

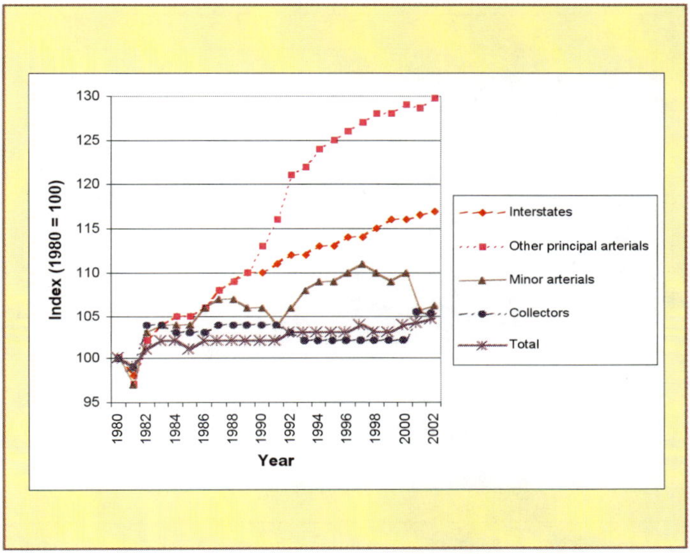

Source: FHWA

Traffic on this infrastructure has been growing at a much faster rate. Some of this growth comes from freight movements, but a large proportion is derived from a general increase in travel due to population and income growth. This has led to a significant increase in congestion over the past few decades.

Figure 4-2 depicts trends in intensity of usage as measured by the ratio of Vehicle Miles Traveled (VMT) to lane miles for various types of roads from 1980 to 2001. Usage has increased across all roads with the most dramatic increases on rural interstates (97 percent), followed by urban interstates (61 percent), rural arterials (52 percent), rural collectors (45 percent), urban arterials (38 percent), and urban collectors (27 percent).

These trends suggest that the ratio of volume to capacity is increasing at the greatest rate on interstates, the most important road segments for intercity trucking. While these metrics indicate trends that are useful when thinking about congestion, they are not direct measures of congestion in themselves. Volume-to-service flow ratios[34], however, indicate that there is considerable congestion on even the nation's rural interstates. For example, in 2001 7,225 miles of rural highways were classified as severely or significantly congested.[35]

Figure 4-2: Highway Traffic Density 1980 to 2001 (Vehicle Miles Traveled/Lane Miles)

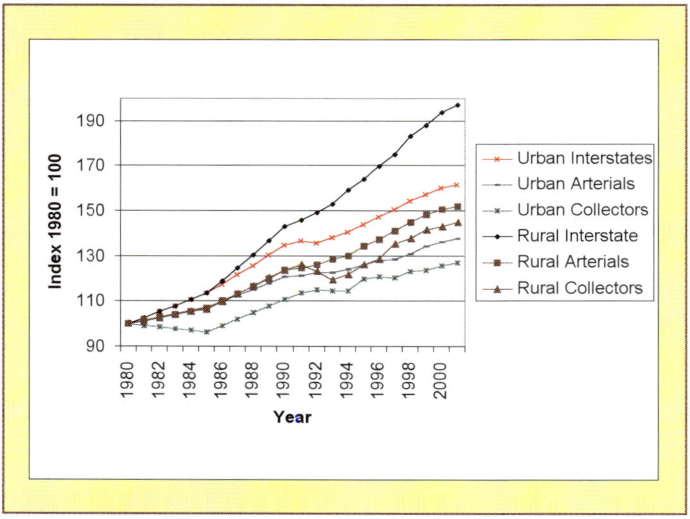

Source: FHWA

Even greater levels of congestion, naturally, characterize urban areas. Data from the Texas Transportation Institute (see figure 4-6) show increasing trends in congestion from 1982 to 2001 for different sized metropolitan areas. While all metro areas exhibit increasing congestion, the larger metro areas have the worst congestion. TTI estimates that in 2001, congestion in the top 75 U.S. urban areas cost the nation 69.5 billion dollars in terms of delay and fuel. This cost, however, does not adequately describe the full burden of congestion on highway freight movement.

Freight movements by trucks today are increasingly time sensitive. The ability of the trucking industry to delivery of goods in a reliable and time efficient manner is a key component of the mode's overall competitive position. Congestion increases transit times and decreases schedule reliability. Even in areas of persistent congestion, the extent of that congestion may vary widely from day to day depending on weather, accidents, or other events. Recent trends such as just-in-time delivery require reliability and performance, and unanticipated congestion comes at a great cost. For example, some recent evident suggests that unscheduled delays may cost shippers as much as $371 per hour.

Significant swings in the travel times of international trucking movements caused by border delays makes logistics planning difficult for shippers, intermediaries, and carriers. Such traffic bottlenecks could force costly redesigns to logistics systems, leading to decreases in productivity. Other findings from the recent border crossing study conducted by FHWA (referenced in Chapter 3 as well) include:[36]

- Time required for processing inbound commercial vehicles is significantly longer than for outbound vehicles;
- There was no single trend that accounted for the extent of delays across all ports-of-entry. Reasons varied by particular port-of-entry;
- Crossings varied greatly in their abilities to handle traffic volumes; and
- Studies of urban mobility reveal that delays on roadways are generally more predictable than at ports-of-entry.

Highway Capacity and Trucking Productivity Issues Not Related to Infrastructure

The effective capacity of the U.S. freight transportation system is also affected by operational and regulatory issues. Truck size and weight, hours of service, highway/road access restrictions, environmental regulations, and numerous other policy-driven considerations directly affect cargo payloads, trucking operation cycles, and route selection, for example. In addition, environmental laws and requirements and the amount of money available to public transportation agencies affect the ability to build needed facilities. Examples of some non-infrastructure-based capacity issues relevant to the trucking industry follow.[37]

- *Truck Size/Weight Regulations:* Congress, by statute, limits the allowable size and weight of trucks on the federal-aid highway system. Safety is the driving force behind these regulations, as many feel larger trucks, especially those known as Longer Combination Vehicles (LCVs), are potentially dangerous to the traveling public. Increased infrastructure costs are also a concern. The regulations, however, do act as a capacity constraint as they reduce the amount of goods that can be moved by trucks. The U.S. Department of Transportation's most recent Truck Size and Weight study concluded that use of LCVs would lead to productivity gains ranging from $10 billion to $40 billion per year.[38]

- *Hours of Service (HOS) Regulations:* The HOS regulations apply to motor carriers (operators of commercial motor vehicles, or CMVs) and CMV drivers, and regulate the number of hours that CMV drivers may drive, and the number of hours that CMV drivers may remain on duty before a period of rest is required. This has a palpable effect on how carriers operate.
- *Regulations Slowing Project Delivery/Capacity Improvements:* Environmental review processes for major federal-aid highway projects take an average of 5 years, 2 months, up from only 2 years in the 1970s.[39]
- *NAFTA Harmonization:* Differences in truck size and weight, emissions standards, insurance and liability rules still differ among the United States, Mexico, and Canada, thus reducing efficiency of truck freight movements. Other complications are due to anomalies, such as the U.S.'s unilateral move to block the provision in NAFTA allowing Mexican truckers to carry freight into and out of the United States.
- *Project Financing:* The pay-as-you-go financing strategies typically employed by State DOTs for highway projects are one reason that projects require 5 to 15 years to plan and 20 years to complete is not uncommon.[40] State Infrastructure Banks (SIBs), which are essentially revolving loan funds, are one financial mechanism designed to accelerate projects.
- *Homeland Security:* The events of September 11, 2001, elevated transportation security to an issue of critical importance. Industry experts and policymakers have highlighted the vulnerability of the nation's freight system to terrorist attack and proposed a variety of responses. Concerns have focused in particular on border crossings, freight moving through seaports, hazardous materials transport, potential contamination of food shipments, and the potential use of a truck trailer to deliver a weapon.
- The heightened focus on security since 9/11 has changed the operating environment for motor carriers. Long-haul truckers have reported difficulty in locating parking at night because informal roadside truck parking areas are now off-limits. Some have responded by stopping earlier for the night. The president of one of the major LTL carriers noted that his firm was feeling the cost effects of 9/11 in a variety of ways. For example, truck inspections, and the associated time lost, had increased by 150 percent.

As with the issues listed above, a number of market-driven factors affect the operating capacity and productivity of the trucking industry.41 For example, with average operating profit margins of five percent, the industry has little ability to absorb changes in fuel costs. While predictable and long-term price increases can be passed onto customers, where firms face unanticipated price increases and have long-term contract obligations to deliver freight, they may be unable to adjust their prices quickly enough to recapture these costs. It is not surprising that trucking firm bankruptcies are correlated with fuel price increases, as illustrated in Figure 4-3.

Likewise, insurance rates for the motor carrier industry have risen steeply over the last several years. The conditions causing rates to rise do not appear likely to be mitigated in the near future. Indeed, the low investment returns, increased risk of terrorism, and increased damage awards could cause further rate increases in the future. Additionally, competition in the trucking industry makes it difficult for carriers to pass these costs along to their customers in the form of higher prices. Insurance rate increases reduce the profitability and productivity of the motor carrier industry, and may force marginal companies out of business. Rising insurance rates were one of the factors cited by Consolidated Freightways as a cause of their recent bankruptcy.

Figure 4-3: Correlation of Trucking Firm Bankruptcies and Changes in the Price of Fuel

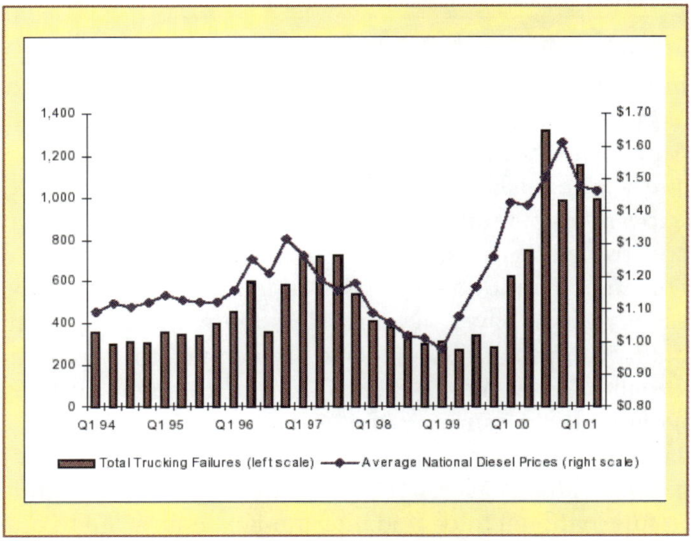

Source: A.G. Edwards & U.S. Department of Energy

Rail Capacity Issues

As discussed above, before deregulation and the Staggers Rail Act of 1980, the rail industry was widely considered to have much more capacity than was needed. But physical capacity (measured by the miles of rail line) has been steadily decreasing since deregulation (see Figure 4-4).

Figure 4-4: Miles of Rail Line in the United States (1980 - 2001)

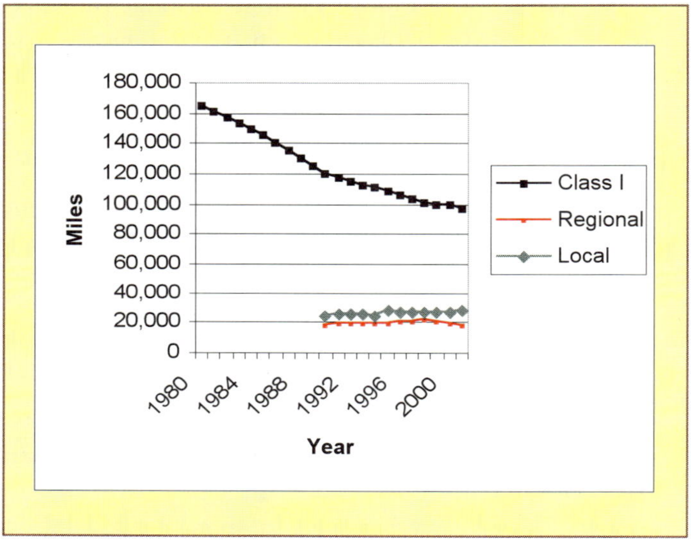

Although the reduction in capacity experienced since 1980 has led to increased productivity for the rail freight industry, there are signs that capacity levels are beginning to show signs of strain.

Figure 4-5 portrays growth in Class I rail traffic density, defined as revenue ton-miles per mile of track owned. The figure shows that density has almost tripled since 1980 and furthermore shows no signs of abatement. This trend cannot be increased indefinitely since moving greater volumes of goods over a shrinking network is unsustainable. Additionally, as the nation's rail system becomes more saturated with traffic, it will be even more sensitive to shocks, such as unanticipated levels of demand, infrastructure failures, or operational issues.

Rail mainline capacity, however, is not the only infrastructure related issue that the industry faces. The evolution of the rail system and new trends in international trade and intermodalism have led to other problems, such as:

Figure 4-5: Revenue Ton-Miles per Owned Mile of Track (in Millions: 1980 - 2001)

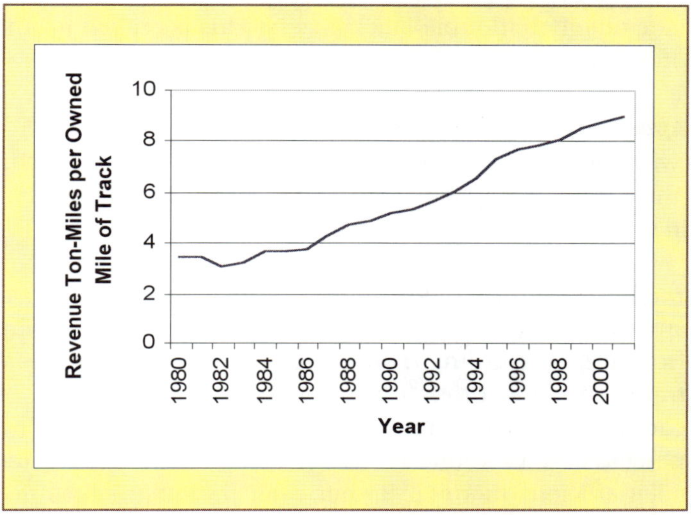

- ➢ *Highway Access from Terminals and Intermodal Terminal Capacity:* The evolution of rail infrastructure produced many terminals located in dense urban areas where little room for facility expansion exists. Higher capacity utilization rates necessitate additional access to these terminals, but providing this access is more difficult now than ever as land is scarcer and highway access routes are congested. In recent years, this situation has led to the development of rail terminals away from urban areas. These remote terminals, however, come with their own problems, as they often lack the road infrastructure needed for their efficient use. The development of this infrastructure would have a significant effect on intermodal freight capacity.
- ➢ *Deteriorating Bridges and Tunnels:* A significant part of our modern day rail infrastructure was constructed in the 1800s when rail was the preferred mode for East-West shipments and for connecting regional hubs. Much of this infrastructure, especially bridges and tunnels, is now in serious states of deterioration. Repairing this infrastructure will require a substantial investment over the next decade. These improvements, however, would yield benefits for years to come.

- *Height Clearances:* As intermodal freight grows, double-stack rail is becoming more commonplace, especially at large port facilities. The rail industry needs to invest and modernize in order to provide adequate double-stack access. This is crucial for the growth of intermodal rail.

Rail Capacity Issues Unrelated to Infrastructure

As with the trucking industry, a number of non-infrastructure issues affect the effective capacity of the railroads. Examples include the following:

- *Inefficient Carload Operations:* Carload service is movement of small shipments—one or a few cars in a shipment—in all-rail trips from origin to siding. These trips are made in a series of mixed trains running through a railroad's terminal network. Although carload service accounts for over 30 percent of carloadings and 40 percent of rail revenue, it has been handled, until fairly recently, in an inefficient manner. Rather than maintain schedules for the trains running between terminals, railroads pursued a strategy of holding trains until some tonnage level was reached. This resulted in lower labor costs per ton for line-haul movements but led to unreliable service and higher equipment costs because of poor utilization. Railroads are now moving to scheduled operations, which hold the potential of making this service both more reliable and profitable.[42]
- Labor Agreements and Short Lines: *All of the Class-I carriers have union crews and a variety of labor agreements that affect crew sizes and working practices. Over the past two or three decades, substantial progress has been made in removing inefficiencies from these agreements. Many industry observers, however, believe that there are still obstacles to efficiency in these agreements, especially regarding practices in local service—pick-up and drop-off of carload shipments. There are marked contrasts between the way local service is handled on big railroads and the way it is handled on short lines, the latter being free of union contracts. Some experts believe that the current mode of operation of local service is one of the biggest obstacles to achieving efficient carload operation.*[43]
- *Interchanges:* A great deal of traffic, especially carload traffic, moves on more than one Class-I railroad. While special arrangements are made for high-priority service (e.g., motor vehicles and

parts), the general pattern is that current practices for handling cars between railroads are slow and cumbersome, contributing both to unreliable service and inefficient use of equipment.

Water Freight Capacity Issues

The importance of our ports and harbors to an efficient and reliable freight system cannot be overstated. This is because the advent of globalization, with the concomitant increases in international trade, means that the efficiency and reliability of our ports now have a larger influence on the efficiency and reliability of our trucking and railroad industries, since these modes now function more as "one system" than ever before. Consequently, our ports have a growing influence on the nation's ability to minimize transportation costs and foster economic productivity.

The role that our port system plays in multimodal freight transportation can best be explained through examples of inefficiencies. Consider the following, which is borrowed from ICF's report to FHWA entitled *Evaluation of U.S. Commercial Motor Carrier Industry.*

Challenges and Opportunities.

Port facility delays are crucially important to trucking firms that pick up and deliver freight to ports. Port drayage firms operate in a highly competitive market, with many small firms and owner-operators competing to provide services. These firms typically use older equipment, charge low carriage rates, and operate on very slim profit margins. Delays at port facilities impose a cost on these firms in lost revenue and profits. The reduced efficiency of this critical link in the transportation system also imposes costs on the downstream customers of port drayage services.

Generally speaking, port facilities can impose long wait times on truckers with impunity since the ports do not bear the economic cost of the delay. Long wait times and congestion at port facilities are caused by a set of factors that are fairly distinct from the wait times encountered at other shipper facilities. These include lack of sufficient gates, limited hours of terminal operation, poor intermodal chassis maintenance, and vessel bunching.

The Maritime Administration recently conducted a survey of port facilities to determine which system elements of the intermodal transportation network were operating in an acceptable manner.[44] Unacceptable conditions were defined as those where "efficient and effective cargo movement cannot occur ... nor can additional cargo flows be easily handled". In the case of ports, gate hours of operation were deemed to be a problem at 38 percent of the largest container ports and 11 percent of all ports. Gate automation is a consistent problem at about half of all ports, both large and small.

- *Gate access - Ports often do not provide enough gates and only operate these gates during limited hours, creating lines to enter terminals that can back up for miles and wait times that can stretch into hours. Limited gate access can be attributed to several factors:*

 1. *Peaks in daily traffic are caused by the desire of firms for morning pickups and afternoon deliveries. Additionally, a mismatch between the hours of operation of marine terminals and those of the steamship lines and rail terminals exacerbates the need to move containers during peak hours.*
 2. *Rail terminals are typically open 24 hours a day, and steamship lines unload containers during hours when terminal gates are not open. Terminal gates are typically open during normal business hours, sometimes on a 9-5 schedule. Required breaks can cause gates to be closed during these hours as well. The need to move containers during these restricted hours to meet the pick-up and delivery schedules of customers causes congestion.*
 3. *Labor agreements often prevent expanding the hours of gate operation. In some case,s terminal operators can keep gates open longer by paying overtime to the required staff. Some labor contracts require a full crew be paid for an 8-hour shift, even if the gates are kept open for only a couple more hours. Terminal operators argue that restrictive labor practices make the cost of keeping gates open prohibitive. Unions tend to see restrictions on labor hours as one of the key benefits derived from negotiated labor contracts. The tense relationship between labor and management in marine*

terminal operations has made resolution of this issue difficult.

- *Chassis condition - The steamship lines own an overwhelming majority of the chassis used to haul containers. Some steamship lines do not properly maintain these chassis, and in some cases drivers are required to move chassis to repair facilities without compensation. When no roadworthy chassis are available, drivers may face the choice of waiting for a chassis to be repaired or using an existing one that may have mechanical defects. While the steamship lines are required by law to maintain safe chassis, the driver is most often the one who is punished through fines and tickets.*
- *A related problem is that ports frequently do not maintain enough space for chassis storage, resulting in chassis being stored in any available space. This creates traffic impediments within the terminal, further increasing wait times and congestion.*
- *Vessel bunching - Although port facilities are open seven days a week, the fixed schedules maintained by shipping lines can result in a number of vessels arriving at the same time. Vessel bunching causes vehicle congestion as trucks line up to load or unload cargo. The more efficient scheduling of vessel arrivals and departures may require a collaborative effort between port authorities. Shipping lines often have difficulty predicting the arrival dates of their vessels at particular ports since these often depend on uncertain arrival and departure dates from other ports.*

Infrastructure Deficiencies

As shown in Figure 4-6, port traffic has increased significantly over the last few decades. During this time, however, the physical capacity of our ports has not changed very much. With capacity becoming more constrained, disturbances create larger and larger shocks. For example, the recent collision of an offshore supply boat and a container vessel at the mouth of the Mississippi River's only channel deep enough for large oceangoing vessels created major bottlenecks delaying tankers and cargo ships at costs as high as $35,000 to $40,000 per vessel per day.[45]

Figure 4-6: Trends in U.S. Ports Container Traffic

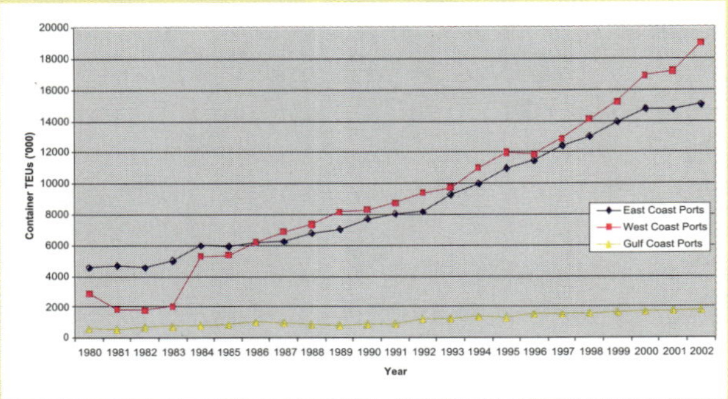

Note that according to a recent article in *The Washington Post*, Wal-Mart estimates it spent $15 billion on Chinese-made products in 2003. If Wal-Mart were a nation, it would be the fifth largest export market for China, ahead of Germany and Britain.

Source: American Association of Port Authorities www.aapa-ports.org

The following exemplify the infrastructure-oriented capacity issues that are affecting our water transportation system:

- *Dredging:* Not only is traffic growth into U.S. ports increasing, but industry consolidation and the ever-present drive for increased efficiency are leading to greater use of mega-containerships and traffic consolidation (hub-ports). This additional traffic necessitates wider and deeper channels. For example, the newest class of mega-containerships requires channels 50 to 53 feet deep, compared to historic standards in the 36-to-40-foot range. Although expansion dredging is an important issue, many of the nation's ports have not even been able to fulfill their maintenance dredging needs. For example, a 2001 U.S. DOT survey found that nearly 30 percent of all U.S. container ports reported unacceptable channel depths.[46] This could be particularly problematic should the Panama Canal be widened to accommodate post-Panamax vessels.
- *Land-Side Port Access:* Land-side access is a problem of increasing importance for U.S. ports and is becoming one of the primary

bottlenecks for the movement of goods from ships to the rest of the transportation system. Once vessels arrive at a port it makes little difference how efficient the rest of the port is if goods cannot be unloaded off a vessel promptly. In 2001, several of the top 15 U.S. deepwater ports reported unacceptable flow conditions on landside elements of the intermodal access system.[47] Compounding this problem is the fact that many ports do not have sufficient room to expand landside access, nor do they have the funds required to maintain this additional capacity even if it was acquired.

- *Congested Locks in Inland Waterways:* U.S. inland waterways are an important component of the nation's transportation system. These waterways transport approximately 20 percent of the nation's coal and 60 percent of the nation's grain movements.[48] Investment in the infrastructure required to support these waterways (e.g., locks) has not been adequate to maintain the system. In 1997, the U.S. Army Corps of Engineers reported that the median age of all lock chambers is 35 years.[49] This survey also concluded that locking delays have been increasing throughout the inland waterway system, and that delays averaged around six hours at the most congested locks and were sometimes much longer.

Water Capacity Issues Not Related to Infrastructure

There are also a number of regulatory and institutional issues that affect water transportation, of which the most influential are:

- *The Jones Act:* Originally known as the 1920 Merchant Marine Act, the Jones Act limits all waterborne trade between U.S. ports to U.S. flag vessels. Many critics of the Jones Act advocate its repeal since the Act inhibits capacity by reducing the available pool of transport vessels, raising the price of transportation and final cost of goods. A study by the International Trade Commission estimates that the Jones Act costs the nation $2.8 billion annually and its repeal would lead to reductions in relevant shipping prices by around 26 percent.[50]
- *Port Rate Competition:* Many U.S. ports charge users fees below their costs. This is partly due to subsidies from various levels of government, but also due to competition among ports where raising user fees would lead to losses of business. This creates an environment where individual ports may have excess capacity much of the time but are characterized by severe congestion during peak periods.

Air Cargo Capacity Issues

At an annual growth rate of 5.1 percent from 1990 to 2000, air cargo is by far the fastest growing mode of freight transportation (unless one counts intermodal rail as a separate mode). Available forecasts predict air cargo will continue to grow at rates of 4.0 percent to 5.2 percent through 2020. Growth at these rates will put considerable strain on an aviation system already characterized by frequent delays and traffic control safety concerns. To date, however, this growth in air cargo has yet to severely constrain the system as a whole, although certain hubs are beginning to experience chronic problems. About 16 percent of flight takeoffs and landings at LaGuardia Airport, for example, experience delays.[51]

The conditions at heavily trafficked airports such as LaGuardia suggest that air cargo may be beginning to strain the system. There are a number of issues involved in airport capacity expansion including terminal and runway expansion and need for additional landside connections for freight. Interrelated are freight and passenger conflicts and safety concerns such as the adequacy of the air traffic control system.

Non-infrastructure related air cargo capacity issues include regulations restricting the operations of non-U.S. carriers:

- *Economic Regulations:* Similar to the Jones Act in relation to water freight, air cargo also has regulations stating that foreign-flag carriers may not operate between U.S. points. These regulations, however, are not likely to receive the same scrutiny as the Jones Act, due in part to security concerns.
- *International Regulations:* Other international regulations, such as customs regulations, impact goods movements into the United States and the efficiency of those movements. For example, there are new Customs rules on electronic pre-filing for air cargo imports and exports (except to Canada). For long flights, import data must be filed well before landing. For flights less than four hours, import data must be filed before wheels-up.

Summary of Freight Transportation Capacity Issues

Table 4-1 summarizes the capacity challenges that characterize our current freight transportation system. Ensuring an efficient, reliable, and safe freight system will require concerted efforts from both government agencies and the private sector. There is ample evidence that the system is becoming increasingly strained, and disruptions in one part of the system can reverberate across the others and create bottlenecks that can adversely affect our national economy.

Of particular concern is the rapid growth in the demand for freight transportation that is expected for the future. The capacity of our current freight system and projected increases in demand suggest that the U.S. freight system could become severly strained. The next chapter presents information on the future demand for freight transportation.

Table 4-1: Summary of Capacity Issues by Mode

	Trucking	Rail	Waterways and Ports	Air Cargo
Infra-structure-based	• Urban bottlenecks • Congestion on rural highway corridors • Border crossing delays • Terminal specific congestion	• Mainline capacity • Deteriorating bridges and tunnels • Height clearances (e.g. double-stack access) • Highway access from terminals • Intermodal terminal capacity • Inefficient interchanges at rail hubs	• Land-side access • Channel depth (dredging) • Road and rail access to terminals • Congested locks and limited inland waterway infrastructure	• Airport capacity (major issue pre-9/11) • Landside connections • Air traffic control • Cargo/passenger conflicts
Regulatory- or Institutionally -based	• Truck size/weight regulations • Hours of Service (HOS) regulations • Regulations slowing project delivery/capacity improvements (e.g. EIS) • NAFTA harmonization • Driver retention • Project financing	• Organized labor • Scheduling challenges • Dedicated service vs. mixed • Steady decline in rail revenues on a ton-mile basis due to competition • Return on investment has fallen short of cost of capital, affecting railroads' ability to generate funds for infrastructure investment	• Lack of national/regional focus for port planning and development • Inefficient pricing due to port competition • Jones Act	• Landing rights restrictions • Cabotage restrictions (Open Skies) • Belly cargo safety concerns

Chapter 5

Expected Increases in Demand for Freight Transport

As depicted in Figure 5-1, with the exception of river barge and coastal/lake waterborne freight, during the ten years from 1990 to 2000 all modes of freight transportation experienced increases in demand (as measured by ton-miles). Intercity trucking grew at an annual rate of almost 4 percent, while intercity rail grew at about 3.6 percent per year. The demand for air cargo services grew at a whopping 5.2 percent per year.

Figure 5-1: Historic Growth Rates by Mode (Ton-Miles)

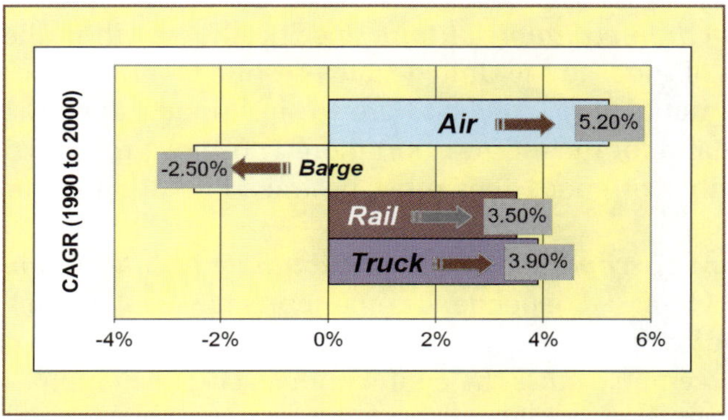

Source: Compiled by ICF Consulting using data from the Bureau of Transportation Statistics (BTS), U.S. Department of Transportation, and other sources.

To understand more clearly the severity of the capacity issues discussed in chapter 4 of this book, it is helpful to consider how the demand for freight transportation is expected to change in the future. Will trucking, for example, continue to grow at annual rates of 4 to 5 percent? If so, what does that mean from the perspective of system performance?

Likewise, will the demand for freight-rail continue to grow, and at what pace? Answers to questions such as these, with current capacity issues as a backdrop, facilitate policy analysis and decision-making on the part of government.

In a nutshell, numerous studies have been conducted to forecast growth in freight transportation demand. Although the results of those studies may differ, they all point to significant increases in demand—increases that are almost certainly sure to erode the performance of our current freight system unless something is done. This chapter presents information on the future demand for freight transportation in the United States and on the factors that affect that demand. We rely on previously developed freight demand forecasts to generate a plausible demand scenario for 2020. The goal is to demonstrate qualitatively how expected demand increases and existing capacity issues come together; and, in turn, how public policy can help to ensure that performance does not erode to levels that adversely affect our economy and living standards.

Demand Factors

Generally speaking, the factors driving the demand for freight transportation, in terms of both magnitude and structure, are as follows:

- ***Growth in economic output.*** Specifically, growth in the production of goods in the United States destined for both domestic and international markets and growth in imports directly affect the demand for freight transportation. Those two metrics define the number of goods that must be transported within the United States.
- ***Share of economic activity attributable to international trade.*** Our increased dependence on imports means that more finished goods move directly from our ports to distribution and consumption centers across the country, increasing the emphasis on carrier service flexibility and reliability and influencing the need for a leaner supply chain.
- ***Technology.*** In the past, technological innovation has enabled significant decreases in logistics costs as shippers have consolidated distribution centers and substituted more transportation for costly inventory. This substitution effect has contributed to the "warehouses-on-wheels" phenomenon.
- ***Carrier productivity.*** Carrier productivity directly affects demand. For example, unproductive practices imply that more

movements will be needed to carry a given amount of cargo from an origin to a destination. Carrier productivity is affected by regulation (such as the Hours of Service rules, truck size and weight limits, the Jones Act, etc.) and business practices (such as dedicated versus scheduled rail services).

The following subsections discuss expected trends in these factors, providing context for the demand forecasts that are presented later in this chapter.

Economic Growth

Given that freight transportation is all about moving goods, the state of our nation's economy is the primary determinant of the demand for freight movements. At the broadest level, both the production and consumption of goods and services determine the number of freight movements that are needed to support economic activity in the country.

Production affects freight demand both directly and indirectly. First, final goods that are manufactured in the United States must be transported to markets where end consumers can purchase them for consumption in the United States or where they can be exported for consumption in other nations. Second, inputs that are needed to produce goods must be transported to production sites from either other intermediate production facilities or resource regions (such as agricultural fields or coal mines). The demand for these intermediate goods and commodities is central to the business of some of the freight modes (e.g., the barge industry).

Likewise, the consumption of final goods directly determines the demand for freight transportation. Be it from production sites in the United States or from ports that receive imported goods, the number of finished goods that must move to consumption markets is the major determinant of the demand for freight transportation, especially trucking.

Although researchers usually focus on the growth in the nation's GDP as an indicator of the expected growth in the demand for freight, it is more useful to isolate growth in the number of goods that are manufactured in the United States for domestic and export markets and growth in the number of goods that are imported into the United States from other countries. This metric is more indicative of the number of goods that must move from production and import facilities to consumption and export facilities. As depicted in Table 5-1, this metric has been growing at a faster clip than GDP and other indicators commonly used to characterize economic activity from the perspective of freight transportation (e.g., U.S. manufacturing). The 4.26 percent annual growth in manufacturing plus imports shown in Table 5-1 is close to the overall growth in the demand for freight transportation over this period.

Table 5-1: Historic Growth Rates by Mode (Ton-Miles)

	1987 to 2000 Growth Rate
GDP*	3.19%
GDP Mfg.*	1.68%
GDP Mfg. + Imports*	4.26% ← This is the number that matters most.
Federal Reserve Board Mfg.**	3.60%
BEA Mfg.**	3.25%

* Value based

** Based on a combination of value and quantity

Note that the President's budget estimates 3.5 percent annual growth in GDP for the period from 2004 to 2009.

International Trade

Between 1970 and 1999 the portion of our nation's GDP that is attributable to international trade grew from 10.7 percent to 26.9 percent. According to Global Insight[52], U.S. trade will represent 27.1 percent of GDP in 2004 and 36.7 percent by 2025. As depicted in Figure 5-2, trade between the United States and Asia will grow to over 700 million tons by 2020, almost double that of today. Likewise, trade between the United States and South America is expected to reach almost 600 million tons by 2020.

According to FHWA, international trade-related transportation in the United States accounted for roughly 10 percent of the total tonnage moved on our domestic transportation system by the close of the 1990s.[53] As the portion of our nation's GDP that is attributable to trade grows, the effects on the transportation system can be expected to be significant.

First, the relative increase in trade, together with potential relative decreases in manufacturing's share of GDP, means that more finished goods will move directly from our ports to distribution and consumption centers across the country. This puts added pressure on carrier service flexibility and reliability, and influences the need for a leaner supply chain. It also means that the efficiency and reliability of connections between ports, railways, highways, and intermodal facilities will become even more important to the performance of the overall freight transportation system.

Figure 5-2: Growth in Trade

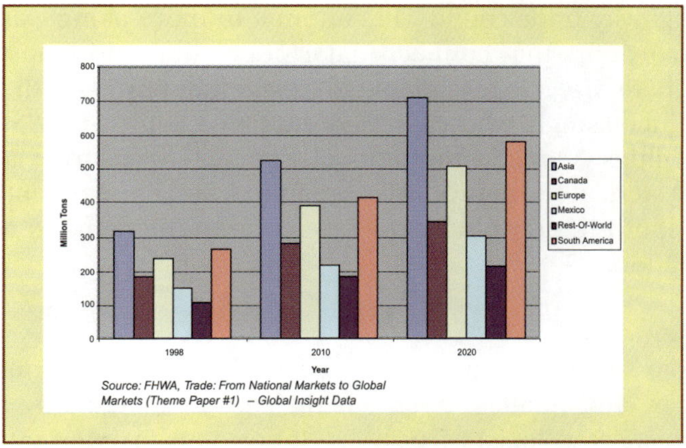

Source: FHWA, Trade: From National Markets to Global Markets (Theme Paper #1)—Glabal Insight Data

Second, depending on how trade patterns evolve, new trade-transportation corridors may need to be developed, or existing ones expanded to accommodate trade flows. Increased trade with Asia (especially China) will continue to put pressure on our Pacific-coast ports and on east-west inland transportation corridors. China's economy is not expected to take a major downturn, and as industries in China continue to develop significant economies of scale, productivity can be expected to increase. Productivity gains and relatively inexpensive labor costs likely will ensure that China's role in the global economy increases in importance as Chinese-made products offer increased value to consumers across the world (especially in the United States). An increased reliance on China and other Asian economies for our consumer goods will push the need for high performance of our Pacific-port gateways and the inland transportation systems that connect to them. This requirement could change the patterns of goods movement in the United States and the structure of the demand for freight transportation.

Third, the effect of China's comparative advantage in some industries is already being felt by Mexico. However, trade with both Mexico and Canada is expected to continue to increase, putting further pressure on the performance of our border crossings and north-south trade corridors. Based on work conducted by ICF for the Federal Motor Carrier Safety Administration, U.S. trade-truck vehicle miles traveled (VMT) is expected to nearly double between 2002 (the baseline year) and 2015 (from 3.8 billion to 7 billion VMT). It is expected that most of the future NAFTA highway trade traffic will continue to move along existing U.S. highway corridors that connect major population and manufacturing centers. Therefore, it is reasonable to expect that north-south trade will compete increasingly with passenger traffic on some of our most congested facilities.[54] Again, a multimodal approach to ensuring acceptable levels of system performance will be required, and these potential trends in north-south trade will alter the structure of the demand for freight transportation.

Technology

In today's highly competitive business world, many manufacturers, distributors, and retailers maintain their profit margins by means of ultra-sophisticated logistics systems. Innovation in information technology facilitates development of new products in robotics, just-in-time inventory control programs, networked dispatching, real-time schedule management, and other manifestations of intelligent production and transportation logistics.

Specifically, using advanced technology and algorithms to calculate optimal quantities in the supply chain, in warehouses, and in stores, logistics systems strike a fine balance between holding down inventories and keeping enough goods in the forward end of the chain to meet customer demand. Part of the design of these systems is the size and spacing of warehouses and distribution centers. Fewer distribution centers can mean lower inventory costs, but fewer distribution centers mean longer distances between supply sources and distribution centers and from distribution centers to stores. It takes speed and a high level of reliability in freight deliveries to make the system work with longer distances.

In this way, faced with some combination of lower truck rates, increased speed, and increased reliability, shippers will reconsider the amount of freight transportation they buy. In particular, this will take the form of reviewing basic logistics arrangements—the number and spacing of distribution centers, for example.[55] If fewer, more widely spaced warehouses can serve the same set of retail outlets or customers, a firm will be able to reduce inventory costs and increase its sales. The reduced real cost of freight transport lets a shipper buy more freight transport and reduce its inventory costs, thus reducing total logistics costs even though spending more on transportation.

As developed under FHWA's Freight Benefit-Cost Analysis (BCA) Study (conducted by ICF Consulting and HLB Decision-Economics), and as presented in Figure 5-3, a shipper's demand curve for freight

Figure 5-3: Logistics Reorganization and the Demand for Freight Transportation

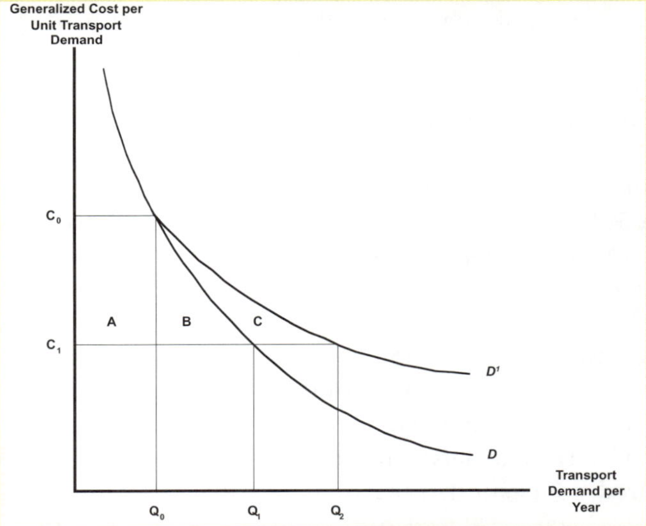

A shipper's demand curve reflects the benefits the shipper gets from buying freight transportation. The cost the shipper is willingto incur to obtain freight transportation is what managers believe the freight movement is worth to the firm. They will not incur a cost higher than what they think it is worth (although they will willingly take it at a lower cost if that is possible). Thus, the change in the demand curve reflects the greater benefits the shipper can get from the freight-carriage improvement, once the firm has reorganized its logistics set-up.

transportation (in this case trucking) takes two forms, D and D^1. D shows a shipper's demand for freight transportation before an improvement to the freight system (in particular a highway improvement). The new curve, D^1, shows the change in demand that follows the improvement. The shipper's reaction to the cost reduction can be thought of as occurring in three phases. In the very short run, the shipper makes no response and continues to buy the same number of vehicle miles of freight transportation, Q_0. (The benefit to the shipper is the area A, the cost reduction with the existing volume of freight.) In the next phase of response, the shipper takes advantage of the lower cost and buys more freight movement, Q_1. (This adds the area B to the benefit.) But this still reflects the shipper's original demand curve, D. The shipper has not made any changes in the firm's basic logistics. After managers have had time to consider the cost reduction, they may, as already noted, make changes in their logistics. This is when the shipper's demand for transportation would change, and there would be a new freight transportation demand curve, D^1. (The additional benefit from the reorganization is area C, the area between the old and new demand curves.) The freight improvement's full benefit is reflected in the sum of areas A, B, and C.

Table 5-2 provides a summary of findings of Phase II of FHWA's Freight BCA Study regarding the effect of changes in highway performance on the demand for trucking, using panel data and three different statistical approaches. Although these results should be interpreted with some caution given the difficulties and data limitations encountered in the course of that project, the estimated impact ranges from a 0.07 to 1.00 percent increase in the demand for trucking (measured by average daily truck traffic) for every 10 percent decrease in measured congestion (measured by delay and/or the volume to capacity, V/C, ratio). Based on that work, a highway improvement leading to a 10 percent decrease in measured congestion–from a V/C ratio of 0.60 to a V/C ratio of 0.54, for example–would increase truck movements along the improved highway segment by about 1.0 percent.

In this manner, technological innovation affects the logistics practices and decisions of shippers. As evidenced by the work under FHWA's Freight BCA Study, advanced logistics practices, enabled by technology, lead to increases in the demand for freight transportation as shippers use more transportation and thus hold less inventory and consolidate distribution centers.

Table 5-2: Estimated Impact of Changes in Highway Performance on Freight Demand

Model / Reference	Implied Relationship Between the Demand for Trucking and the Measure of Highway Performance	Interpretation
Pooled Regression Trucking Demand as a function of Delay per Mile and a number of other control variables.	-0.0072	Other things being equal, a 10% decrease in delay per mile increases the demand for trucking by 0.07%.
Fixed Effects Regression Trucking Demand as a function of Delay per Mile and a number of other control variables.	-0.0102	Other things being equal, a 10% decrease in delay per mile increases the demand for trucking by 0.1% (or a tenth of a percent).
Fixed Effects Regression Trucking Demand as a function of the V/C Ratio and a number of other control variables.	-0.0849	Other things being equal, a 10% decrease in the V/C ratio increases the demand for trucking by almost 1%.

Carrier Productivity

The ability to balance demand and supply is also influenced by increases (or decreases) in carrier productivity. For example, intermodal freight transport has directly affected the effective capacity of our freight system and has helped to optimize the number of necessary freight movements to meet freight transport demand. Today, large volumes of imported consumer goods move speedily and reliably from west-coast ports to the Midwest at low rates. Freight service of this quality and price allows major distributors and retailers to keep a tight rein on their logistics costs, to the benefit of their customers and the overall economy.

Intermodal transportation services exemplify the types of changes that have led to improvements in the reliability and quality of this nation's freight system. As shippers have changed their logistics practices to take advantage of a more flexible and demand-responsive freight system, carriers have also improved their operations. In this manner, improvements in carrier productivity are important to ensure that efficiency gains in the freight system are sustainable and that the overall number of freight movements necessary to meet demand is optimized (at the system level).

As depicted in Figure 5-4, both trucking and rail productivity have improved significantly since the mid-1980s (largely because of deregulation). However, the recent decline in trucking productivity suggests that the trucking industry may have difficulty in meeting short-term transportation demands from the manufacturing, service, and trade sectors over the next several years. Furthermore, due to intense competition the railroads have passed most of the productivity gains on to their customers in lower rates. Consequently, revenue losses due to competition may affect their ability to sustain demonstrated increases in productivity.

Figure 5-4: Productivity Trends in the Trucking and Railroad Industries

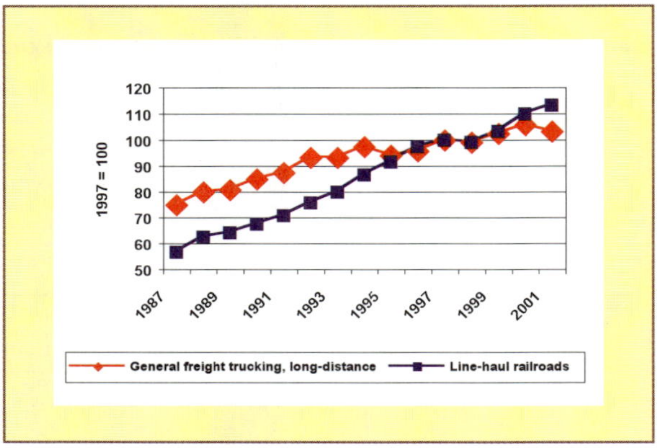

Overall, productivity losses in the transportation sector can lead to higher costs to the manufacturing, service, and trade sectors in the form of increased operating costs. This, in turn, can exert downward pressure on economic productivity, as transportation and warehousing costs rise relative to output. Coupled with the significant strains that currently exist in the capacity of our freight system, decreasing carrier productivity will result in an overall weakening of the U.S. economy as fewer products and services can be generated with the same amount of resources.

As discussed in Chapter 4, in the trucking industry, for example, truck size and weight limits, the hours of service (HOS) rules, and cabotage restrictions relevant to NAFTA are examples of regulations that directly affect cargo payloads and trucking operation cycles–and in turn carrier productivity.

Demand Forecasts

A central goal of this study is to characterize the future demand for freight transportation by mode. Demand projections enable a qualitative analysis of the severity of the capacity issues that are affecting the efficiency and reliability of our freight system, and consequently of the types of public policies that can be pursued.

Numerous recent studies have developed projections of freight transportation demand by mode. The information provided earlier in this chapter is used to construct a plausible demand scenario based on forecasts prepared by others.

A number of recent forecasts were gathered to determine a plausible demand scenario for the future, by mode. Specifically, the following three sources of freight demand projections were reviewed:

1. Bureau of Transportation Statistics (BTS) forecasts as reported in *The Changing Face of Transportation*
2. AASHTO's *Freight-Rail Bottom Line Report*
3. American Trucking Association's *U.S. Freight Transportation Forecast to 2014*

BTS's Changing Face of Transportation

Published in 2000, the BTS report entitled *The Changing Face of Transportation* covers transportation developments through the last quarter of the 20th century and forecasts the demand for freight transportation by intercity truck, rail, and air in 2025. The report investigates topics such as demand growth, deregulation, intermodalism, safety, globalization, technology, and national security, and presents forecasts based on empirical data and various econometric methods.[56]

Table 5-3 presents the BTS forecasts as reported in its publication. It is important to note that the forecasts do not account for the effects of the recent economic downturn that began in 2001 or the effects of 9/11. Nonetheless, the forecasts prepared by BTS are significantly lower than the historic growth rates discussed earlier in this chapter and provided in Figure 5-1. What is most striking about the BTS projections is the low annual growth rate that is estimated for rail (0.18 percent). As a benchmark, both the American Trucking Associations (ATA) and the Federal Railroad Administration (FRA) forecast a 2.0 percent annual growth rate for rail ton-miles over this period.

Table 5-3: BTS's U.S. Domestic Freight Ton-Mileage Growth Forecasts by Mode (2000 to 2025)

Mode	Ton-Miles in Billions (2000)	Ton-Miles in Billions (2025)	Percent Change (2000 to 2025)	Compound Annual Growth Rate (CAGR)
Intercity Truck	1,130.1	2,121.8	87.7%	2.55%
Rail	1,416.4	1,484.8	4.8%	0.18%
Air	15.9	33.9	113.2%	3.08%

AASHTO's Freight-Rail Bottom Line Report

The primary goal of AASHTO's *Freight-Rail Bottom Line Report* is to examine the performance and productivity of the nation's freight-rail system. Based upon anticipated levels of investment in that system, the study makes the case that the rail system requires significant investment to ensure that unsustainable volumes of traffic do not spill over onto the highway system as a result of insufficient capacity and service levels in the rail industry.

The report includes forecasts for the four major modes of freight transport (truck, rail, water and air).

The demand forecasts that are reported in AASHTO's Report are based on:

1. TRANSEARCH data for the baseline year (2000),[57] and
2. Growth rates developed under FHWA's Freight Analysis Framework (FAF).

Table 5-4 presents AASHTO's baseline forecasts by mode (truck, rail, water, air) in terms of ton-miles for the period 2000 to 2020.

Table 5-4: AASHTO's U.S. Domestic Freight Ton-Mileage Growth Forecasts by Mode (2000 – 2020)

Mode	Ton-Miles in Billions (2000)	Ton-Miles in Billions (2020)	Percent Change (2000 to 2020)	CAGR
Truck Total	2,639	4,174	58%	2.32%
Truck < 500 Miles	1,241	2,046	65%	2.53%
Truck > 500 Miles	1,398	2,128	52%	2.12%
Rail	1,239	1,821	47%	1.94%
Water	539	617	14%	0.68%
Air	9	27	200%	5.65%
Total	4,427	6,638	50%	2.05%

Note that AASHTO's baseline data shows a large volume of trucking ton-miles, compared to other data sources. For example, the BTS baseline data reported in Table 5-3 shows that in 2000 about 1.1 billion ton-miles of freight were moved by truck, less than half the estimate that is in AASHTO's Report. Conversations with staff from Reebie Associates revealed that the higher base used in the AASHTO Report was the result of: 1) incorporating local (non-intercity) truck movements, as well as intercity movements, 2) counting agricultural shipments not usually captured in other datasets on freight movements, and 3) using various data sources to derive ton-miles instead of relying on the carrier reported data that BTS uses.[58] AASHTO's baseline data for trucking ton-miles attributable to moves beyond 500 miles is more consistent with the BTS baseline estimate that only looks at intercity trucking (1.4 billion ton-miles versus 1.1 billion, respectively).

Nonetheless, AASHTO's annual growth rates by mode are lower than the historic averages presented in Figure 5-1. Moreover, the estimated 2.05 percent overall freight demand growth rate for the period between 2000 and 2020 is significantly lower than the historic growth rate in relevant economic activity (i.e., the 4.26 percent annual growth rate in manufacturing and imports that is presented in Table 5-1). The progression toward a service economy and our increased reliance on finished goods imports may account for some of the difference, since the 4.26 percent is a value-of-shipments based number. Yet, when compared with economic indicators that serve as a proxy for the demand for freight transportation, AASHTO's freight demand growth estimate appears to be conservative.

American Trucking Association's U.S. Freight Transportation Forecast to 2014

The American Trucking Assocation's (ATA's) *U.S. Freight Transportation Forecast to 2014* provides demand forecasts for trucking, rail, water, and air from 2002 to 2014. Global Insight and Martin Labbe Associates developed the forecasts for ATA using proprietary models, databases, and other available sources. While the actual model algorithms and supporting data are not documented, the study accounts for the U.S. economic outlook, energy prices, consumer spending, foreign trade, business investment, industrial output, regional economic growth, and the world economy; and applies models of freight flows.

Note that ATA's study provides ton-mile and tonnage forecasts by class of truck (Class 8, 6-7, 3-5). For other modes, however, forecasts are provided only in tons.[59] Additionally, for modes other than trucking, ATA's study only includes "primary shipments" (i.e., the first movement of freight from an origin to a destination). For trucking, ATA addresses both primary shipments and "secondary shipments" (i.e., additional truck hauls of the commodity that was primarily shipped).[60] Furthermore, forecasts for rail are broken down by total rail traffic and rail intermodal.

Table 5-5 presents ATA's freight volume forecasts in tons for trucking, rail, rail intermodal, water, and air. ATA's growth rates indicate that air freight will experience the highest level of growth, followed closely by rail intermodal, which is forecast to exceed even the air freight growth rate during the first half of the forecast period (2003 to 2008).[61] The primary driving force behind the high growth rate for rail intermodal is increased U.S. dependence on international trade, which is projected in ATA's study to grow by 5.0 to 6.5 percent per year. Alternatively, freight water volumes are predicted to grow at 1.6 percent per year from 2002 to 2014, while total rail tonnage is predicted to grow at an annual rate of 1.8 percent.

Table 5-5: ATA's U.S. Domestic Freight Forecast by Mode, 2002 - 2014

	Volume – Millions of Tons			Compound Annual Growth Rates		
Mode	2002	2008	2014	2003-2008	2009-2014	2003-2014
Truck	8,882.3	10,108.6	11,470.2	2.3%	2.2%	2.3%
Rail	1,751.2	1,983.8	2,142.5	2.2%	1.3%	1.8%
Rail Intermodal	155.8	201.2	252.1	4.9%	4.2%	4.6%
Air	17.4	22.3	29.1	4.7%	5.1%	4.9%
Water	1,006.7	1,129.7	1,213.6	2.0%	1.2%	1.6%
Total	11,813.4	13,445.6	15,107.5	2.2%	2.0%	2.1%

Table 5-6 presents ATA's trucking forecasts, by truck class, in ton-miles. Shipments by Class 8 trucks (primarily highway tractors pulling trailers) account for almost all of intercity trucking. Note, however, traffic from medium and light duty trucks (Classes 3-7) is expected to grow at a faster rate during the forecast period. Much of this is due to trends toward more frequent but smaller shipments that characterize modern supply-chain management (e.g. just-in-time shipments). Overall, ATA's study notes that the driving force behind the growth in trucking is general freight and small package shipments, which are expected to grow at a faster rate than bulk traffic.

Table 5-6: ATA's Trucking Ton-Mile Forecast by Class, 2002 - 2014

	Volume – Billions of Ton-Miles			CAGR		Percent Change
Truck Class	2002	2008	2014	2003-2008	2009-2014	2003-2014
Class 8	1,202	1,393	1,653	2.5%	2.9%	38.0%
Classes 6/7	115	138	169	2.7%	3.5%	44.0%
Classes 3-5	17	22	27	4.7%	4.0%	66.7%
Total	1,334	1,553	1,849	2.6%	2.9%	38.6%

Summary of Forecasts and Interpretation of Trends

Table 5-7 compares the recent history of growth rates and our plausible demand forecast by mode based on the studies discussed above and the factors that affect demand. The modes are listed in descending order of their historic and forecast growth rates. The exact amount of each future rate is certainly open to debate and adjustment, but there can be no doubt about the relative order of these rates, and that order is unlikely to change in the foreseeable future.

Table 5-7: Ton-Mile Percentage Annual Growth Rates (Recent History and Plausible Demand Forecast)

Mode	History 1990-2000	Forecast 2000-2020
Air	5.2	4.0
Truck	3.9	2.5
Rail	3.5	2.0
Water	-2.5	0.7

Interpretation of the Plausible Forecast Scenario

The forecasts presented in Exhibit 28 reflect both the price and service characteristics of the major freight modes and the evolving character of American industry and the economy. As discussed earlier, for some years now, there has been an increasing drive to reduce inventories throughout manufacturing and distribution supply chains. This has led to a substitution of transportation spending for inventory holding and, thus, to increased demand for fast and reliable goods transport. For longer moves, air transport is the fastest choice and by far the most expensive. That is why it accounts for a mere sliver of ton-miles (around one-half of a percent) but a significantly higher fraction of intercity freight revenue (more than two percent).

Truckload (TL) trucking with team drivers can also provide a relatively high-speed service, up to 1,000 miles in 24 hours. Even though the premium for team service over solo driving—in the range of $0.10 to $0.20 per mile—is not nearly as great as for air over truck, a comparatively small share of total truck-miles are in team operation.[62] This tells us that the great preponderance of shippers are not willing to pay extra to get speeds greater than those of solo trucking, roughly 500 miles a day in most of the country, around 400 miles per day in the I-95 corridor. Most shippers are willing, however, to pay the extra price of truck compared to rail to obtain the relative speed of highway service and the generally greater reliability and flexibility of trucking.

It is the higher-valued, time-sensitive traffic for which shippers are under pressure to reduce inventory costs and are, therefore, willing to pay for reliability and speed, especially the former. This traffic is also associated with newer, faster-growing sectors of manufacturing or fast-growing imports. This is the traffic where, for the most part, shippers will choose truck or air, and these modes will continue to grow faster than rail or water. Air will show the highest growth rate because it is starting from a small base, and pressures for a lean supply chain will continue to drive traffic to air cargo.

Traffic in bulk commodities—coal, grain, petroleum products, ores—does not grow as fast as the total economy. These commodities comprise almost all the inland waterway and other domestic water-borne traffic, and they are the major part of rail tonnage. This will keep the waterways at the bottom of the growth table. Railroads do have opportunities for growth aside from their bulk markets and will be able to grow much faster than water traffic but still not as fast as trucks.

Railroad markets can basically be divided into four categories: bulk, intermodal, carload, and automotive. Automotive traffic, both vehicles and parts, is technically carload traffic, but is a separate market segment with high-value traffic and a high standard for reliability. This business will grow as fast as the automotive industry does, but in tonnage terms it is a small percentage of the rail total. Bulk, the majority of tonnage, will continue to grow slowly.

Carload traffic comes from shippers who can never load enough cars at one time to make a whole train. This traffic must be collected by local service, put in mixed trains in a terminal, and then be moved through a succession of terminals in different trains before it is delivered by local service. Scheduled operation offers some hope of improvement in rail reliability, but growth of this traffic is constrained because a shipper cannot use it without a facility on a rail siding. The great majority of manufacturing and distributing facilities are no longer on rail sidings. Most shippers can use intermodal rail, and for that reason it is the one rail market-segment with a potential for strong growth. Rail intermodal is likely to grow faster than total trucking. Overall, however, rail growth will be slower than trucking growth.

Our plausible forecast shows future growth for air, truck, and rail at rates somewhat diminished from those of the 1990s. For air, this reflects a judgment that the recent high percentage growth rate (5.2 percent) will not be sustained as the base grows. For trucks, the drop from 3.9 percent in the past to 2.5 percent in the future may be based on a perception that the substitution of transportation for inventory holding has gone almost as far as it can go. Rail growth in the 1990s was driven more by increasing length of haul than by increasing tonnage, the longer hauls coming from the growth of intermodal traffic from west-coast ports and coal traffic from the Powder River basin. Future growth of 2 percent in ton-miles is an extension of the tonnage growth of the 1990s. The fall in water traffic in the 1990s was a result, in part, of falling grain exports and new offerings of low-priced rail service to the Pacific Northwest. The forecast for slow, positive growth is based on a belief that these negative factors have had their full effect.

Implications for System Performance

Based on an evaluation of multiple studies and on analyses of the primary factors that determine the demand for freight transport, a plausible demand growth scenario for each mode was developed for this analysis. Under our scenario, the annual growth rates in ton-miles for the period between 2000 and 2020 are as follows.

- Trucking = 2.5% per year
- Rail = 2.0% per year
- Barge = 0.70% per year
- Air freight = 4.0% per year

Given historic growth rates, expected growth in economic activity, expected increases in our dependence on imports to satisfy demand for finished goods, and the likelihood of continued technological innovation, one could argue that the growth rates provided above are conservative. As depicted in Figure 5-5, however, these growth rates mean that by the year 2020 our freight system will have experienced a 64 percent increase in trucking ton-miles, a 49 percent increase in rail ton-miles, and a 15 percent increase in barge traffic—all while the demand for air freight will have more than doubled.

In addition to the underlying drivers of the volume of freight transportation, a number of specific events could affect the structure of future demand (both modally and spatially), further straining specific parts of the system.

Shifts from Rail to Other Modes (Especially Trucking)

First, as estimated by AASHTO's *Freight-Rail Bottom Line Report*, significant investments are needed to ensure that the nation's railroads can accommodate future demand. AASHTO presents four investment scenarios.

Figure 5-5: What do these forecasts mean? (Billions of Ton-Miles)

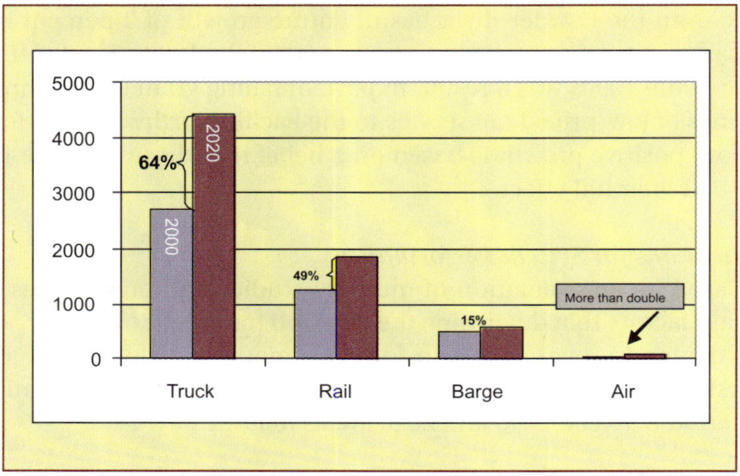

1. *No Growth*: This scenario assumes minimum investments in our rail industry, only sufficient to maintain current traffic volumes. Rail loses market share *vis a vis* the other modes.
2. *Constrained Investment*: Under this scenario, selected investments are made that to accommodate growth in traffic. However, the investments are not sufficient to accommodate the baseline forecast in 2020 (see Exhibit 26). In other words, rail traffic spills over to other modes.
3. *Base Case*: This scenario assumes that enough investments are made to retain the rail industry's current share of freight traffic.
4. *Aggressive Investment*: Under this scenario, the railroads make the investments and service improvements needed to more than accommodate the baseline forecast for 2020. Rail-freight increases its market share *vis-à-vis* other modes.

Table 5-8 summarizes the effects of the "no-growth," "constrained investment," and "aggressive investment" scenarios on the demand for trucking (in vehicle miles traveled). The AASHTO analysis shows that if significant investments are not made in our rail system, truck traffic will be much higher than predicted. Under the "no growth" scenario, the equivalent of 31 billion VMT would spill over onto our roadways. To put this in context, that amount of VMT represents about 22 percent of the total combination truck VMT reported by FHWA's Highway Statistics for

2002, and is roughly three times the VMT that is expected in 2015 for trade movements between Mexico and the United States.[63]

Hence, it will be critical that a holistic perspective be taken by decision-makers at all levels of government when it comes to investments in our freight transportation system. Lack of sufficient investment in one mode will affect the ability of other modes to deliver reliable and efficient performance, thus affecting the performance of the overall system.

Table 5-8: Effects of Trucking of Insufficient Investment in our Rail System

Shift Relative to Base Case Scenario, 2000 - 2020 Totals

	Equivalent Truck VMT
No Growth Scenario	+31 billion
Constrained Investment Scenario	+15 billion
Base Case Scenario	--
Aggressive Rail Investment Scenario	-25 billion

Source: AASHTO Freight-Rail Bottom Line Report

Widening of the Panama Canal and the Advent of Post-Panamax Vessels

A second consideration that likely will affect our nation's freight system both modally and spatially is the widening of the Panama Canal. The Panama Canal Authority has embarked on a $1-billion modernization and improvement program designed to meet growing transit demands with greater operating capacity and more flexible traffic scheduling. Once completed, two Panamax-sized vessels will be able to transit simultaneously without compromising navigational safety. In the future, the Panama Canal will offer nearly unrestricted two-way transit services to the world's merchant fleet 24 hours a day, and will be able to accommodate larger post-Panamax vessels that require deeper channels and harbors.[64]

Note that by the end of 2001, the Panama Canal Authority had finished the drilling and blasting portion of the Gaillard Cut segment, significantly ahead of original schedules. Once the Canal can accommodate fully post-Panamax vessels, the effects on the freight system in the United States could be significant:

First, changes in world trade patterns could effect the distribution of movements within our domestic freight system. East-to-west freight corridors that serve as land bridges today may not be as critical in the future as shippers take advantage of a more efficient and reliable Canal.

Second, the competitiveness of some of our ports will be affected as liners call on ports that can more readily accommodate post-Panamax vessels. Determining which ports should receive dredging resources will become even more important.

Third, some of our economic sectors may be adversely affected, especially agriculture as less costly transportation routes increase the competitiveness of producers in South America, for example. Should the agricultural sector be adversely affected, our inland waterways and major bulk port facilities would suffer as well.

Overall, the widening of the Panama Canal will necessitate additional investments in many of our busiest ports to ensure that larger vessels can be accommodated. Given current port capacity challenges, this development will further strain our maritime port system and increase the importance of well-crafted investment programs that account for changing trade patterns and new port facility requirements.

Increased Trade with China

Since the initiation of economic reforms in 1979, China has become one of the world's fastest growing economies. From 1979-1999, China's GDP grew at an average annual rate of 9.7 percent. Even with the effects of a global economic downturn, 9/11, SARS, and the Iraq war, China's economy still managed to grow at a rate of 8 percent in 2003. Some economists predict that China may be the world's largest economy by the middle of the 21st century.

The effects of China's continued growth on our domestic freight system could be very significant:

➢ First, the distribution of freight movements that are generated by international trade is shifting from ports-of-entry on the U.S.-Mexico border to our west-coast ports. Mexico's major export-oriented businesses (i.e., *maquiladoras*) are having difficulty competing with Chinese companies that pay significantly lower wage rates (roughly $2 per day compared with the $8 per day paid by Mexico's *maquiladoras*).[65] By December of 2002, trade with China accounted for 45 percent of the containerized imports in Los Angeles-Long Beach, compared with 39 percent in 2000.

During that same period, 529 factories in Mexico were closed.[66] If this trend continues, as is expected, the reliability and efficiency of our west-coast freight system (from ports to connecting rail and highway systems) will become even more important.

- Second, the relocation of production from Latin America, North America, and Europe to China is taking place rapidly. As trade patterns shift and the United States becomes even more reliant on imports to satisfy demand for finished goods, shipper logistics patterns will change, possibly leading to more movements over longer distances. In that case, carrier flexibility and reliability will become even more important.

Overall, federal, state, and local transportation agencies, in their decision-making, should account for increases in trade with China.[67] Specifically, changing trade patterns likely will affect the distribution of movements on our freight system. Special focus should be given to system reliability and efficiency needs in the west coast, as that part of the system becomes relatively more strained.

Technological Innovation (the "Second Wave" of the IT Revolution)

It is likely that future technological innovation will continue to affect our freight system. For instance, driven by the needs of "high-cycle" commerce, a "second wave" of improvements in information technology may enable the development of freight villages or city logistics. In turn, regional networks could develop, changing the spatial and institutional/organizational make-up of freight transport. Regional networks could further improve the productivity of carriers and directly affect the number of freight movements needed to satisfy customer demands. For example, city logistics is taking hold in some European cities and has decreased the number of truck trips into city centers. The European Union describes city logistics as follows.

> City logistics involves setting up new partnerships and styles of cooperation between all those involved in the logistics chain and in delivering/receiving goods in city centres. These partnerships offer significant reductions in vehicle kilometres and truck numbers and are currently in existence in Germany and Switzerland. City logistics is a very clear illustration of the importance of developing high-quality "software" to match high-quality "hardware." The hardware in a transport operation

is well understood and well managed, e.g. vehicles and depots. The 'software' relates to organisational linkages, cooperation, thinking about marketing and packaging strategies, and thinking about different ways of doing things. City logistics has taken transport operations into an area of development that builds links and emphasises cooperation across all players and interest groups.

In Germany partnerships between logistics contractors are reducing lorry numbers and improving the urban environment. These partnerships (known as City Logistik companies in Germany) are in operation in Berlin, Bremen, Ulm, Kassel and Freiburg. The Freiburg example has several pointers to the future shape of freight transport in urban areas. There are currently 12 partners in the scheme. Three of the partners leave city centre deliveries at the premises of a fourth. The latter then delivers all the goods involved in the city centre area. A second group of five partners delivers all its goods to one depot located near the city centre. An independent contractor (City Logistik) delivers them to city centre customers. A third group, this time with only two service providers, specialises in refrigerated fresh products. These partners form an unbroken relay chain, one partner collecting the goods from the other for delivery to the city centre.

The Freiburg scheme has reduced total journey times from 566 hours to 168 hours (per month), the monthly number of truck operations from 440 to 295 (a 33% reduction), and the time spent by lorries in the city from 612 hours to 317 hours (per month). The number of customers supplied or shipments made has remained the same. The Kassel scheme showed a reduction of vehicle kilometres travelled by 70 % and the number of delivering trucks by 11 %. This has reduced the costs of all the companies involved and increased the amount of work that can be done by each vehicle/driver combination.

It is interesting to note that the concepts of freight villages, city logistics, and regional networks are receiving the attention of carriers in the United States. During a presentation by JB Hunt at the TRB Annual Meeting in 2004, JB Hunt's representative discussed the evolution to regional networks. Part of the push is originating from driver shortage and retention issues, as well as the continued progression toward "high-cycle" commerce. Yet, without improvements in technology that enable advanced logistics systems, this progression would not be possible.

The ramifications on our freight system's inability to accommodate anticipated demand growth, partly driven by the events described above, could be severe, especially if there is little or no change in government policies and programs designed to enhance the system's effective capacity.

Chapter 6

Freight Transportation Policy

The findings of Chapters 4 and 5 indicate that given little or no change in government programs and policies there are likely to be significant strains on the capacity of the national freight system over the next 10 to 20 years. "Little or no change" means a continuation of past trends in funding levels and patterns of practice in programs and policies affecting freight-system performance. It does *not* mean a world in which there is no further investment in freight-transportation infrastructure and facilities. It means a world in which federal-aid highway funds continue to flow, states and local governments continue to spend on roads, railroad firms continue to invest in track and equipment, and so forth. But the current level of effort, allowing for some uptrend in funding in light of historical trends, is insufficient to maintain the current performance of the freight system, let alone enhance it.

There is no doubt, therefore, that the expected future strains on the freight system merit a policy response from the federal government. "Policy response" means some significant change; it could be a change in funding levels, changes in the structure of existing programs, creation of new programs, changes in regulatory practice, or some combination of these types of changes. The clear message thus far is that some significant response is definitely needed. The cost to the economy of a poorly performing freight system is too great to ignore.

It is important to recognize that the need to ensure an efficient, reliable, and safe freight transportation system is getting the attention of decision-makers at all levels of government. The Federal Highway Administration, for example, has for years focused on the needs of the freight system and has formalized its initiatives under the auspices of organizations such as the Office of Freight Management and Operations.

Similarly, many regions across the country have conducted detailed assessments of their freight system. As a result, progress is being made.

However, the capacity issues and demand trends that are discussed in this report highlight the urgency of the situation and the need to accelerate the pace of problem solving. As decision-makers consider how to move forward, three overarching needs should be accounted for in their deliberations:

- First, we need a national vision for our freight system as the basis for federal policy. The performance of our freight transportation system affects our national competitiveness. As a result, ensuring efficiency and reliability in the nation's system should be a national priority.
- Second, we need regional/local freight transport decisions that are consistent with national goals, objectives, and strategies. The transportation decision-making process is largely executed at the state and local levels. It is imperative that decisions at these levels do not result in suboptimal outcomes when it comes to the performance of the freight system as a whole.
- Third, we need strong, well-coordinated leadership to forge effective policy at all levels. Although it is true that freight shipments "don't vote," the people that own businesses do. Elected officials and other high-level decision-makers must recognize the importance of ensuring a high-performing freight transportation system as they formulate policies, design plans, and implement projects. Leadership is also critical in the forging of successful partnerships with business interests that have a direct stake on the performance of the system.

This section recommends specific actions that government can implement (relatively quickly) to get us on the path of ensuring a high-performing freight transportation system over the long term. To provide a more robust context for the specific recommendations put forth as part of this research effort, Appendix B reviews existing laws, regulations, and financing mechanisms, policy ideas that have been formulated by other researchers, and how ongoing legislative processes (in particular the highway bill) are dealing with freight needs.

Some Fundamental Guiding Principles

Appendix B provides summary information on the freight transport policies and programs that are in place today and on the kinds of policy levers that are available to forge change. Before offering recommendations on how to ensure that we make more progress toward the vision that is articulated in Table 6-1, however, we need to look broadly at the types of government actions that would be relevant, put forth some examples of those actions, and set out some of the criteria for choosing components of a package of measures designed to improve the efficiency, reliability, and safety of our freight transportation system. In doing so, it may be useful to step back and take a brief look at the fundamental nature of government intervention in the marketplace.

Table 6-1: Where do we want to be 10 or 20 years from now?

- An efficient, reliable, and integrated freight system, enabled by technology, that:
  - Optimizes generalized logistics costs
  - Helps to maximize manufacturing productivity
  - Helps to minimize the prices of imports
  - Enhances efforts to make our homeland more secure
  - Enhances our ability to deal with congestion in urban areas
  - Is energy and environmentally efficient
  - Limits effects on community livability and cohesiveness
  - Minimizes the probability of accidents and associated fatalities and injuries

Government acts to bring about results that would not occur if firms and individuals made all their decisions on the basis of the signals they get from the marketplace. At the most basic level, the government may act in three ways. It can spend, it can tax, and it can regulate:

- *Government spending* brings about a set of investments the private market would not have made. Spending in the form of operating subsidies can also sustain services (e.g., mass transit) that would not otherwise be provided. But note that government has other tools to change the market's choice of investments. Loan guarantees, special bonding authority, tax exemptions for interest on state and local-government bonds, and a host of other devices can steer investment towards projects or purposes favored by the government without any direct government outlay. But the economic effect is the same; the government has caused investments to be made that the market would not have made.

- *Taxes,* in the form of excise taxes, user fees, and the like are not just devices for raising money. They also change the prices of affected goods and services and, thus, change the decisions that firms and individuals make.
- With *regulation,* government affects behavior directly by prohibiting certain actions or requiring government approval for certain actions or types of activity. For example, you cannot offer commercial air service without government certification that your operations and safety practices meet certain standards. But the government may also modify behavior in other ways. It can attach conditions to financial assistance. The grants that flow to states and MPOs through the highway program, for example, come with strings attached–for instance, states and MPOs must follow certain planning practices.

These are the basics: the government can direct funds to certain purposes; it can use the taxing power to change prices; and it can regulate behavior directly with rules or with conditions on financial assistance. But if we consider the kinds of actions the government could take to improve the performance of the freight system, a number of nuances are introduced.

Consider, for example, the funds for highway, transit, and other purposes that flow through the federal-aid highway program. The issue is not simply one of whether, or by how much, to increase the amount of those funds. At least as important as the total funding level are issues of program structure. Important results could be obtained by changes that bring more focus on freight-related projects without any change in total program dollars. These could be changes regarding the eligibility of certain types of projects (e.g., rail freight). They could also be institutional changes of one kind or another that raise the profile of freight in planning and policy development. A list of possible variations would be almost endless.

A Spectrum of Choices

As can be discerned from the material in Appendix B, a wide spectrum of actions are available to policy-makers for addressing freight transportation needs and system inefficiencies. A set of responses that could be relevant and useful in ensuring a high level of performance in our freight-movement system are provided in this sub-section. One common element in these choices is a direct focus on freight movement. Simply increasing dollar levels for existing programs would not ensure that freight-system issues are addressed effectively.

Focus on Freight in Planning and Policy Development

- **At the U.S. DOT**–Either by creating a new office in the Office of the Secretary of Transportation (OST) or by changing the mandate of existing staff offices, the U.S. DOT should focus more of the policy-analysis and development effort on freight issues. A goal would be to ensure that freight issues receive priority attention in the staff's analytical efforts and in the development of budgets, legislative proposals, the Secretary's policy pronouncements, and so forth.
- **At State and Local Levels**–Encourage and exhort state DOTs and MPOs to develop and strengthen their freight policy and planning capabilities. This is an effort that could be led by FHWA or by OST staff newly focused on freight issues. Encourage, and perhaps require by legislation, MPOs to develop their freight capabilities and to identify and address freight issues in their planning activities.

Sharper Focus on Freight in Government Grants and Investments

- **Existing Highway Program**–Restructure the program to provide a categorical freight grant program for highway, intermodal, or rail projects of special significance. This could either be a discretionary program run by FHWA or a part of the funds apportioned to states, including MPO sub-allocations.
- **Strategic Freight Investment Program**–Set up a discretionary grant program to be operated by a group within the U.S. DOT. It would need its own program funds, completely free of any modal restraints regarding project eligibility. Its function would be to identify freight projects of national significance and provide financial assistance for projects that meet strict guidelines in terms of national significance and economic efficiency. A critical intermodal project such as the Alameda Corridor is a good example of the kind of investment this program would support.
- **National Port Planning**–Port-improvement projects, such as channel deepening or construction of major container handling

facilities, are frequently made in a decision process that focuses on one port at a time. There is, thus, a potential tendency to over-investment, as each port authority and its associated cities seek to maximize market share for their own port. A national planning body could analyze and recommend improvement projects in the framework of national freight movements and of ports' landside needs and capabilities as well as harbor capacities. Such a planning body could be somehow linked to the strategic freight investment program referred to above.

Pricing and Regulation

- **Demand Management on Inland Waterways**–Use demand-management techniques, including peak-period pricing, to reduce congestion levels at locks where delays are a major problem. The seasonal cycles in grain shipments and traffic surges at times of high export demand for grain make this a reasonable approach to solving congestion problems before resorting to new infrastructure investment. Peak pricing could be incorporated in user fees set to recover operation and maintenance costs for the river systems as well as the capital costs of replacing and expanding locks.
- Demand management could be the responsibility of new regional authorities for the overall management of the river transport system. Such authorities could have responsibility for identifying and recommending new investment where needed.
- **Enhance the Economics of Waterborne Movements Between U.S. Ports**–In the opinion of many analysts, the Jones Act has all but eliminated waterborne freight movement between U.S. ports. As discussed earlier in this report, the Jones Act restricts this trade to U.S.-flagged ships. It is argued that requirements that U.S.-flagged ships be crewed by U.S. citizens, and other rules, as well as the strength of the seafaring unions, push costs of U.S. ships up to the point where they cannot offer rail-competitive rates for domestic port-to-port moves. Opening this trade to foreign-flagged vessels could restore low-cost movement of bulk commodities along the coasts; some observers believe there is also a potential for short-haul container moves by water.
- **Open Skies for Air Freight**–Economic regulation of U.S. airlines has all but disappeared. Its remnant is restrictions on rights of foreign-flag airlines to carry goods between U.S. cities (i.e., to engage

in domestic freight movement). Barriers to entry in markets reduce competition and usually lead to higher prices than would otherwise be the case. Allowing foreign carriers to operate in these markets should reduce costs to American shippers and enhance the efficiency of the national freight system.

- **Truck Size and Weight Rules**–Many observers believe the current limits on truck size and weight, and on longer combination vehicles, need to be revisited. Limits now in effect were set by statute in 1983. Highway-freight costs per ton-mile would be reduced if a single tractor and driver could haul heavier loads. Finding a way to relax size and weight restrictions, without sacrificing public safety, could lead to significant efficiency gains.

Criteria for Choosing a Policy Response

For any potential policy response, careful analysis will reveal both advantages and disadvantages. The principal criteria that should be applied in judging the strengths and weaknesses of various actions are as follows:

- *Clear Focus on Freight*–Programs, especially those that involve financial aid, must be structured so that funds go to projects which clearly and significantly enhance the performance of the freight system. Without a requirement for direct and significant effects on freight, any program is in danger of being merely one more general-purpose transportation program.
- *Economic Efficiency*–Of all criteria, this is the most important. It should be demonstrable that any policy action, whether investment, regulation, pricing, subsidy, or some variant, returns economic benefits greater than its costs. And this should be determined through application of techniques such as benefit-cost analysis.
- *Benefit to the Public*–This criterion would apply in the case of investments in the facilities of a private firm, most likely a railroad. There would have to be clear and demonstrable benefits to the public from such an action, and it should be shown that the firm in question would not otherwise have made the investment.
- *Avoidance of Subsidy*–Any program of on-going subsidy for operations, whether for public or private entities, should have to pass an exceptionally rigorous benefit-cost test and require a demonstration that there is no other way to achieve the purpose in question.

Once subsidy programs are in place, it can be extremely difficult to terminate them, regardless of their actual effects in economic terms.

Recommendations

Selection of effective public-policy responses should be made in a careful process in which the above criteria are applied. But the choice of responses should also be based on a clear national vision for our freight system. The programs and projects that are implemented by states and localities in turn must support that vision, as well as the goals, objectives, and strategies that flow from it.

Table 6-1 articulates a vision for our freight transportation system, one that is predicated on economic efficiency and societal goals. Recognizing the numerous medium-term and long-term system performance challenges that are described in this report, achieving this vision will require the following:

- ➢ First, to address major capacity bottlenecks and to accelerate the development of projects that enhance the performance of the nation's freight system, consideration should be given to the development and implementation of a **National Strategic Freight Transportation Investment Program**. This grant program could be designed to select and help fund freight projects of national significance. It could be based on detailed and strict guidelines for project selection, monitoring, and evaluation, including an Annual Report to the President.
- ➢ Second, to address the need for meaningful freight planning at the state and local levels, consideration should be given to the development and implementation of an **Innovations Program for State and Local Freight Transportation Decision-Making**. This program could select and fund innovative multimodal freight planning and programming at the state and local levels, and help push the envelope on issues related to collaborative institutional arrangements, public/private partnerships, freight-passenger interferences, regional freight networks (e.g., freight villages, city logistics), land use needs, freight analysis data and tools, and operations-oriented strategies.
- ➢ Third, to address the current lack of national and/or regional focus for port planning, as well as needs related to changing trade patterns and to post-Panamax vessels, consideration should be

given to the development and implementation of a **National Harbor Improvement Program**. The program could help fund channel dredging projects according to the national interest and include an efficient user fee that adheres to trade treaties.

Certainly, as discussed above, a number of other choices are available to policy-makers, and consideration should be given to the full range of options for improving the performance of our freight transportation system. These three recommendations, however, can be implemented within the construct of current decision-making processes. In this way, they are actionable and if implemented should generate long-lasting benefits to the nation's economy.

Part III

Transportation Technology

by
Richard J. Weiland and
A. Merriman Boylan

Chapter 7

Twenty-First Century Vehicle Technology

This section of the book describes the technical transformation that the automobile has undergone in the past few years and provides a vision for its continuing transformation in the medium-term future. The most notable and dramatic part of this future will be the automobile's transformation from an essentially isolated island in the transportation system to a fully connected element of an integrated transportation system encompassing vehicles and their operators, and the infrastructure and its operators.

Vehicle operators have always been able to take note of their immediate driving environment and to expand this view slightly with the aid of car radios and roadside signs and signals. Infrastructure operators have always done surveillance on their road networks to try to operate the system as knowledgeably as possible. However, the new prospect is for vehicle *systems* to be able to interact with public and private infrastructure *systems* to provide better information to drivers and infrastructure managers and to allow the systems to facilitate accurate, broad-based, high-speed cooperation among all parties in the newly integrated environment.

Forces Driving Vehicle Transformation

The National ITS Program Plan,[68] recognizing both the difficulty and the promise of an integrated transportation system, draws an analogy to the Interstate Highway System. The Interstate Highway System was the bold vision of the second half of the twentieth century, building the physical surface transportation network. The integrated transportation system is the bold new vision for the next 50 years, building the logical, information-based and organization-based surface transportation network.

This integration has the potential to dramatically improve driving safety while, at the same time, making automobile travel accessible to a wider population and making the trip more comfortable, more efficient, and more productive. Successful integration will also encompass public transportation, improving its attractiveness and accessibility and providing new avenues for its financial support.

Many of the same technologies that will appear in the twenty-first century vehicle will also appear in twenty-first century buses and other transit vehicles. Indeed, transit vehicles are often the platform on which vehicle technology first appears, a result of the strong safety focus of transit agencies and the ability for higher-priced vehicles to better absorb the cost of new technology. A successful public transportation system not only contributes to mobility and safety, but also helps to mitigate congestion by providing alternatives to automobile travel.[69]

This paper defines "infrastructure" in this context broadly to include:

- The publicly managed physical roadway network and the intelligent transportation systems that help its managers to operate this network
- Transportation-related information and service systems operated by both the public and private sectors

Over the next 20 years, the automobile will go through a greater transformation – in how it works and in how it is used – than in any time in its history. This transformation could not come at a more opportune time. Even as the demand for the automobile to provide safe, flexible mobility continues to grow, the system through which this mobility is provided is increasingly under stress.

Road-Related Fatalities and Injuries

The total annual number of deaths related to road crashes, already a national tragedy and a national disgrace, is on the rise. Indeed, after a brief lull in the late 1990s, the death toll is once again rising steeply. Even the *rate* of fatalities – the number of deaths per 100 million vehicle miles traveled (VMT) – has begun to level out, an indication that the traditional approaches to controlling the carnage have basically made as much contribution as they can, and that new approaches are needed (see Figure 7-1). We could once take some small comfort in knowing that, even if the absolute number of deaths was increasing, road travel was, on average, still getting safer. This appears no longer to be the case.

Figure 7-1: Annual Fatalities Related to Road Crashes and Rate of Fatalities, 1994-2002

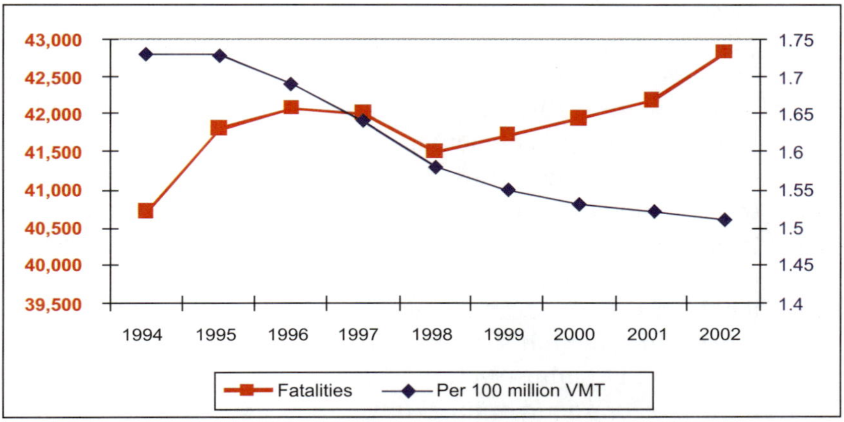

Source: U.S. DOT Fatal Accident Reporting Systems http://www-fars.nhtsa.dot.gov

The highway death toll is coming to be recognized as a serious public health issue – an epidemic that cannot be ignored and which needs to be controlled. The U.S. Department of Transportation's Strategic Plan for 2003-2008[70] includes a goal to reduce the fatality rate to one death per 100 million VMT by 2008. This is a significant decrease from the 1.5+ deaths per 100 million VMT in 2002 and more than twice the decline that was achieved between 1994 and 2002. This goal is, however, a modest one compared to the analogous goal set by the European Union, which aims to halve the number of highway fatalities by 2010 and eliminate them by 2020. This difference in goal setting is significant enough to warrant separate discussion below as one of the policy issues raised by this chapter.

Compounding the tragedy, roadway crashes represent a major drain on the nation's resources, a total cost to the American economy of $230 *billion* per year, according to the National Highway Traffic Safety Administration[71].

The evolving twenty-first century vehicle is the cornerstone for improving safety on the road.

Congestion Costs

In discussing its 2003 Urban Mobility Study of the 75 largest urban areas in the United States, the Texas Transportation Institute reported, "The cost of congestion continues to climb. 5.7 billion gallons of wasted fuel and 3.5 billion hours of lost productivity resulting from traffic congestion in 2001 cost the nation $69.5 billion, $4.5 billion more than the previous year.[72]"

Specifically addressing congestion is one of the major issues for the twenty-first vehicle and its driver, and for the managers of the twenty-first century infrastructure. This will necessarily be a multi-pronged effort. Better pre-trip information on actual and potential congestion can help travelers plan discretionary trips better, and the shift of these discretionary trips, in time or to other modes, will help moderate congestion. Safety systems on board vehicles that prevent crashes will help alleviate the major cause of nonrecurring congestion. Dynamic navigation systems will help drivers select and adapt to the best available route in the circumstances. Information systems that track and forecast congestion and demand will help infrastructure managers level the load over available resources, recommend optimal travel speed, and provide guidance on alternate routes, modes, and travel times. In-vehicle automatic crash notification (ACN) systems will instantly report the location and characteristics of crashes. This will help speed the right emergency responders to the scene to help victims and alert road authorities so that crashes can be cleared and traffic returned to normal as rapidly as possible.

Growing, Aging, and Less English-Speaking Population

The next 20 years will be characterized not only by continuing steady population growth in the United States, but by a major shift in the age distribution as the baby-boomers move through and past middle age. This very large population group grew up regarding the automobile as their fundamental means of transportation, but are finding that their reflexes and eyesight have started to show signs of age.

In addition, a major contributor to population growth will continue to be the immigration to the United States of people whose first language is not English, but who want and need to drive in an environment which remains very oriented to English speakers.

All of these factors contribute to a population which is at greater safety risk and for which providing mobility is a greater challenge[73]. The evolving twenty-first century vehicle can help mitigate the risk and enhance mobility.

Growing Demand for Mobility

For most of the second half of the twentieth century, the standard response to increased demand for automobile-related mobility was to build more roads. The development of the Interstate Highway System was the keystone of this effort, and it transformed the way people work and play and the places in which they work and live.

However, by the late twentieth century, it was apparent that achievable benefits from this approach had largely been realized. Some construction will obviously continue, especially in less developed areas, but the cost of new road construction has skyrocketed. This is particularly the case in densely populated areas where congestion is the worst, due to high land and relocation costs, as well as the increased cost of road building per se. More fundamentally in these areas, there is little room left where new roads can be built or existing roads expanded. A substantial fraction of the funding these days is needed simply to keep the roads we already have in adequate working condition.

The clear alternative is to do more and do better with the roadway infrastructure we have, and the emphasis among road agencies is moving away from construction and toward improved operations. A smarter infrastructure is being conceived whose promise is enormous, but which can be fully met only by interacting with smarter vehicles.[74]

Need for Information that only Vehicles Can Provide

One important way in which the twenty-first century vehicle will interact with the twenty-first century infrastructure is by serving as a source of information about the driving environment – the speed at which traffic is moving, weather at a microscopic level, current and evolving road and pavement conditions, the occurrence of incidents, etc. – all vital information streams for the safe and efficient operation of twenty-first century vehicles and the twenty-first century infrastructure.

Roadway-based sensors will never be able to economically cover more than a fraction of the roadway system. Automobiles (and other road vehicles) can gather and relay data wherever they travel. In addition, automobile-based sensors can do a far better job of providing continuous, micro-area data than sensors fixed at intervals in the infrastructure.

This ability for automobiles to serve as data probes is a major enabler of an intelligent twenty-first century transportation system. Its opportunities and challenges, all of which are significant, are discussed in detail later in this section of the book.

Need for Creative New Ways to Finance Roadway Infrastructure

A major challenge of fulfilling the promise of the twenty-first century vehicle is the continuing development and maintenance of the twenty-first century infrastructure, both the physical roadway infrastructure and the information infrastructure that will move information between vehicles and the land. Most of the physical infrastructure and much of the intelligent transportation systems infrastructure has traditionally been funded by gasoline taxes through the Federal Highway Trust Fund. However, the Highway Trust Fund is increasingly proving inadequate for ongoing development and maintenance, and there is great political resistance to increasing the gasoline tax which funds the Trust Fund.

Considerable discussion is taking place about alternative mechanisms for paying for the infrastructure,[75] many of which are based on having vehicles pay for their use of the infrastructure in more sophisticated ways than simply in proportion to fuel consumption. For example, road usage could be charged by mileage, time and day of usage, actual speed, local congestion levels, pollution levels or demand levels, based on the number of passengers on board, the type of vehicle, use of particular lanes (e.g., higher charges for express lanes), and a variety of other parameters. These same mechanisms can help to more flexibly fund the public transportation system as well.

So far as the twenty-first century vehicle is concerned, there are no technological barriers to this kind of usage charging, other than the creation of the communications infrastructure for transmitting information to and from vehicles.[76] Vehicles will be able to record and report their use of the infrastructure in any detail required. For this kind of revenue generation to be accomplished, a wide range of political issues will have to be successfully addressed for which policy approaches are clearly needed. The other principal obstacle relates to timing.

It would obviously be helpful if the gasoline tax could be replaced, at a stroke, by another collection mechanism that was revenue neutral and no less fair than the current arrangement. However, advanced mechanisms for revenue collection require vehicles to be equipped with many of the advanced technologies described below. The appearance of these technologies in automobiles is fairly inevitable, but they will not appear all at once in all automobiles. A significant challenge to shifting the revenue mechanism is providing for the transition period in which some vehicles will be equipped for alternative infrastructure charging and some won't. Unequipped vehicles will presumably have to continue paying traditional gasoline taxes (or use some other method which is not technology dependent), while equipped vehicles wouldn't. Managing this transition over the necessary extended timeframe will require carefully crafted public policy to ensure equity for all motorists and reliable collections.

Need to Stay Connected, Informed, Entertained

Twenty-first century Americans expect to have access to information and services wherever they are. This expectation began to take hold in the late twentieth century with the widespread adoption of cellular telephones, email, pocket radios and music players, and wireless digital assistants. News, sports, business information, and entertainment have been available in automobiles for many years, but with relatively little choice and very little personalization beyond setting the buttons on the car radio.

The twenty-first century vehicle will help to create a seamless lifestyle, with personalized information and services available to users no matter where they are. Far wider choices of audio information and entertainment will be available for all vehicle occupants. Video entertainment, including movies and games, will be readily available for passengers in the back seat. While "infotainment" lacks the drama of life-saving technology, its widespread appeal may very well provide the financial base to make the life-saving technology and services economically viable.

Connectivity, however, is not just for fun or for business as usual. Connectivity is a lifeline in an emergency, whether the emergency is a one-car crash or a major natural or human-caused disaster. Vehicle connectivity allows vehicles to provide and to make use of collectively gathered, detailed, microscopic information on the state of traffic, the roads, and the weather. Connectivity is the pipeline through which calls for help will be delivered and responses received. In a major emergency, connectivity provides the best hope of helping responders effectively get to the scene and of helping people at risk get evacuated.

The benefits that the twenty-first century vehicle can provide in terms of safety, productivity, and comfort will clearly not be realized in a vacuum. The capabilities of the twenty-first century vehicle will be refined and enhanced by being part of an integrated system. In many cases, full capabilities *depend* on being part of such an integrated system. This integration will connect vehicles and vehicle systems to one another and to the infrastructure and to infrastructure-based and other land-based systems. The industry is talking seriously and enthusiastically about integrating vehicles and the infrastructure through wireless communications. This integration must also make enthusiastically cooperating partners of the people who operate vehicles and the people who operate and manage the infrastructure and the public transportation system. It must also recognize that the landside systems to which vehicles will connect will be operated by private industry as well as by public authorities.

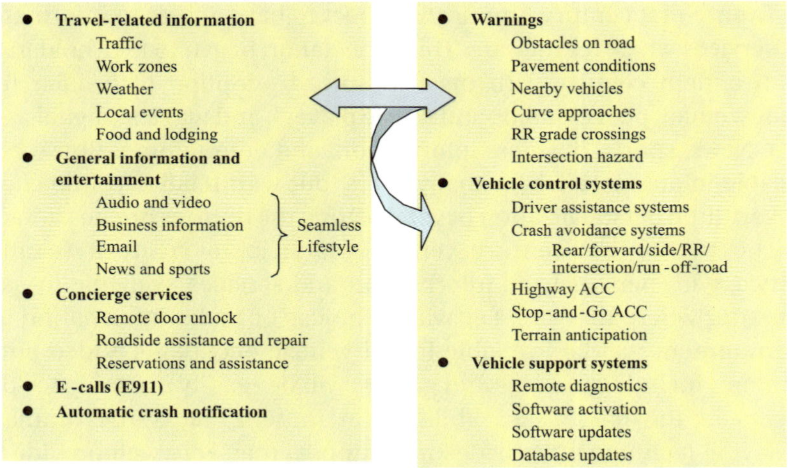

Multiple Dimensions of Emerging and Evolving Vehicle Technology

New Vehicle Technologies

There are two primary technical advances enabling the transformation of the twenty-first century vehicle:

- The availability of cheap, powerful information technologies – processors, sensors, databases, data storage devices, and communications devices – for incorporation into the vehicle
- The ability, through wireless communications technology, to link vehicles to other vehicles, to the immediate environment in which they are traveling, and to the surrounding overall environment, forming a single integrated system

There will be very little technology in the vehicle of 2010 that is not already well understood and available in the marketplace in 2004. This is largely due to the long development cycles for automobiles and the particular care that is required in developing and deploying systems that affect safety. On the other hand, technology which is developed between now and 2010 can be expected to appear in vehicles over the succeeding five to ten years.

New technology will undoubtedly follow the familiar pattern of becoming available first in high-end vehicles where cost is less of a consideration. Technology which proves its worth and is well accepted by the marketplace will then start to diffuse into less expensive and more mainstream vehicle models. Technology now available at the high end (e.g., adaptive cruise control) will be well on its way into the mass market.

This technology is emerging and evolving on many fronts to provide safer, more productive, and more comfortable travel. In-vehicle applications will continue to evolve as new technologies and capabilities become available and affordable. The evolution will follow two basic paths: the incorporation of new and more sophisticated functionality that follows a progression from information to warnings to control; and the incorporation of new and better ways to accomplish the functionality.

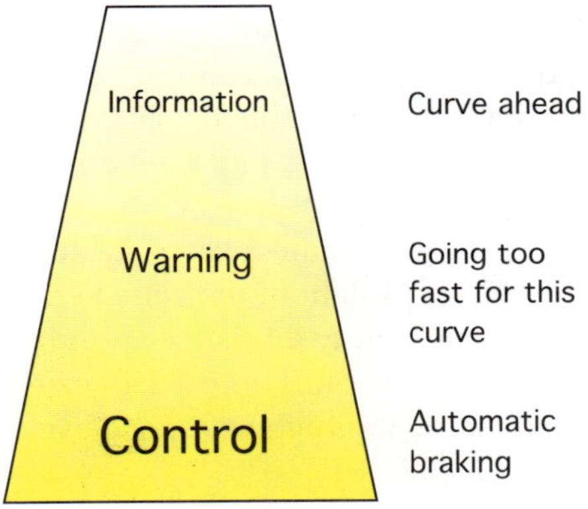

For example, consider the potential evolution of a product oriented to safe driving around curves. In its first stage, the function is simply informative, advising that a curve is ahead, based either on data in an onboard map database, on video recognition, or on the detection of a roadside beacon that advises the vehicle that it is approaching a curve. In the second stage, the function is to provide a warning to the driver if the vehicle is approaching the curve too fast for conditions based, for example, on the radius of curvature of the road ahead as recorded in the onboard map database. This information could be combined with information on vehicle speed, road conditions, and weather that provides insight on traction. In the third stage, the function is for onboard technology to temporarily take control of the brakes, automatically slowing the vehicle if a curve-related crash is imminent and the driver is not responding adequately.

The evolution of more sophisticated ways of handling the same basic task can be illustrated by cruise control, whose objective is to permit safe, steady highway driving with minimum need for intervention by the driver.

- In traditional cruise control, the driver simply sets a speed which the vehicle maintains until the driver intervenes by applying the brakes or adjusting the cruise control settings.
- Adaptive cruise control (ACC), now widespread in high-end vehicles in Europe and Asia and beginning to enter the high-end market in the United States, adds a ranging sensor (e.g., radar) that allows the driver to set a safe forward interval as well as a desired speed. Upon approaching a slower moving vehicle ahead or if another vehicle enters the same lane in front of the equipped car, ACC slows the car to maintain the interval, resuming the preset speed when the interval is restored.
- This process can be made far more reliable and much less computationally intensive by introducing an onboard digital map. By knowing the configuration of the road ahead, ACC can much more accurately determine, for example, whether the car ahead has changed lanes or simply entered a curve first; or whether a lead car which seems to have gone away may actually have just gone over a hill ahead, out of sight of the vehicle radar.
- With the addition of a route guidance system, the ACC can know, for example, when the car has entered an exit ramp and be smart enough not to resume full highway speed even if there is no vehicle immediately ahead.
- In a fully connected environment, vehicles can advise their intentions in advance (e.g., to change lanes), allowing the ACC to operate smoothly and reliably to keep cars safely separated.

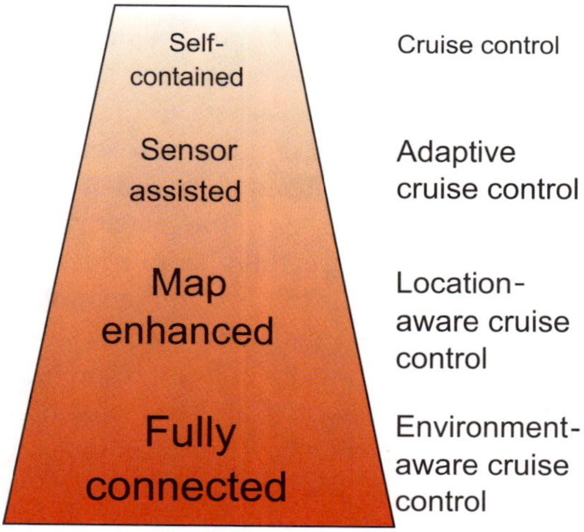

The descriptions that follow cover a wide range of technology which is likely to appear in vehicles over the next 10-20 years. In many cases, early versions of this technology are already being offered, at least selectively. A survey of existing vehicle technology appears as appendix C.

Crash Prevention

The greatest positive result of technology in the twenty-first century vehicle will clearly be in reducing deaths and injuries. The overwhelming majority of crashes are the result of driver failure – lack of skill, lack of attention, lack of judgment, lack of sobriety. The real prospect exists for in-vehicle technology to compensate for driver deficiencies and to help correct driver errors.

The ways in which the technology can and will be applied is a matter which impinges on social issues as well as technical ones. It is clearly not the purpose of intelligent vehicle systems to enable motorists to drive drunk. However, one reasonable objective is to use technology to *prevent* drug or alcohol impaired people from operating motor vehicles. The question remains whether vehicle manufacturers and purchasers are prepared to countenance or to pay for this kind of technology. Other technologies will be able to evaluate situations in which a crash is imminent, possibly at a point in which conditions are beyond the driver's ability to avoid a crash, and to intervene by taking temporary control of the brakes, throttle, and steering to prevent the crash from occurring.

Avoiding crashes successfully will require a combination of technologies: sensors (to tell the vehicle exactly where it is and to create an awareness of the immediate driving environment) and very carefully crafted algorithms to identify and respond to impending crash situations. Major vehicle manufacturers around the world are devoting significant attention and resources to the development of this technology.

Crash warning and avoidance systems are arising through an evolution of technology that helps the vehicle and the driver perform better. Antilock brake systems (ABS), which help a vehicle stop in a straight line on slippery road surfaces, are already all but universal in new automobiles. In the United States, they are mandatory equipment on heavy trucks. Traction control systems and stability control systems, now in most high-end automobiles, are already starting to work their way into the mass market. To a very large extent these systems work behind the scenes, their operation mostly invisible to the driver.

Other products provide active assistance to drivers. Radar-assisted adaptive cruise control (ACC) helps to maintain a safe interval to the vehicle in front. Maintaining the interval takes precedence over maintaining a steady, preset speed. As ACC becomes more sophisticated, incorporating the use of digital maps and environmental data, its technologies begin to evolve into forward collision avoidance systems. Similarly, future generations of ABS may evolve from simply enabling straight-line stops to enabling stops that automatically follow the curvature of a winding road, using video and positional sensors and map databases.

Navigation products are currently regarded mostly as driver convenience systems, enhancing productivity and reducing stress by helping the driver plan and follow efficient routes and avoid getting lost. However, a good digital copilot can also help the driver avoid sudden turns and sudden multi-lane changes by providing advance notice of upcoming driving maneuvers. The next generation of navigation products will be able to incorporate real-time traffic data into the calculation to permit mid-trip route adjustments that help drivers avoid congestion, work zones, incidents, etc. where crashes are more likely to occur.

All crash warning and avoidance systems are complex. Part of this complexity is reliably recognizing and responding to dangerous situations, and part is the need to avoid excessive false alarms. The least complex are those which involve the state and actions of a single vehicle. These include advanced navigation systems that help keep vehicles out of congested and potentially dangerous areas, and curve warning and lane/road departure crash avoidance systems. These systems primarily need to know the vehicle's operating characteristics (most notably how fast it is going and in what direction) and its relationship to the road (where the vehicle is, shape of the curves ahead, tendency to drift out of lane or off the road), and in the case of the navigation product, where the driver wants to go.

More complex safety systems are those aimed at preventing crashes between two or more vehicles. The additional complexity comes, of course, from having to plan very rapid crash avoidance actions that appropriately coordinate with another moving object which may (or may not) also be taking evasive action. Coordinating these actions, so that both don't zig when one should zag, is potentially very complicated. Two approaches can help. One is to have consistent crash avoidance protocols in all equipped vehicles, so that each vehicle understands what the other vehicle is likely to do in the situation. The other is to establish a wireless link among vehicles in an area so that they can more actively cooperate in ensuring safety. This linkage could be an ad hoc network strictly among the vehicles, or it could be a star network mediated by a land-based system through which all of the vehicles in an area are in communication.

Ultimately, land-based systems will provide support and assistance in preventing crashes. One important way in which they will do this is to collect and fuse sensor data from multiple vehicles to determine and transmit a broader understanding of the driving environment than can be gotten by an individual vehicle using its own sensors only. This function is called Probe Processing and it is discussed in the next chapter.

A variety of other opportunities exist for vehicle-based and land-based systems to cooperate to the benefit of all. This vehicle-infrastructure cooperation is also discussed in greater detail below.

Intelligent Vehicle Initiative

The mission of the U.S. DOT's recently concluded Intelligent Vehicle Initiative (IVI program)[77] was to reduce the number and severity of crashes through driver assistance systems, both vehicle-based systems and vehicle-infrastructure cooperative systems. The program, which assembled both public and private partners for technical exploration, identified a number of areas for the application of in-vehicle safety technology.

After several years of successful explorations, U.S. DOT recently announced that the IVI program was being concluded, and that the department would focus its resources on the most challenging areas of traffic safety and management:

- Intersection collision avoidance
- Vehicle safety system integration
- Vehicle-infrastructure cooperation

Intersection collision avoidance products on vehicles are challenging because, to work at all, they need to be cooperative with the infrastructure. Vehicles on intersecting paths will often be out of the line of sight of each other's sensors. Until all vehicles can communicate and coordinate with one another (a prospect with a probable 30-40 year horizon), intersection collision avoidance will depend on infrastructure-based sensors that detect potential collisions and warn vehicles, either via in-vehicle warnings or via warning signs and signals at the intersection.

Vehicle safety system integration is the challenge of getting multiple safety functions – collision avoidance, traction control, ACC, road departure prevention, etc. – to work in concert with one another and with the driver. In the absence of this integration, multiple safety products could all be calling for control of the brakes and steering at once in an emergency situation and end up canceling each other out.

Vehicle-infrastructure cooperation is discussed in its own section below.

Automatic Crash Notification (ACN)

An automatic crash notification is an emergency message automatically transmitted by a vehicle when onboard sensors determine that a crash is occurring, usually the same sensors that deploy the airbags. ACN is already being offered as a service in the United States by OnStar® and ATX Technologies through a number of car lines.

The automatic emergency message, including vehicle location, is transmitted to a service center, which contacts the appropriate public safety answering point to summon help. The service center will usually try to contact the occupants of the crashed car, to seek further information and advise that help is on the way. Currently this is done by a cellular telephone call to the car. In the future, Voice over IP (VoIP), a mechanism for transmitting voice in data packets over the internet, will also be available. (See "Data Communications" below for further discussion.) Emergency services will be dispatched regardless of whether the call gets through to the vehicle, unless the driver specifically advises that no help is wanted. ACN helps to get the right assistance to a crash site as rapidly as possible.

ACN has particular lifesaving potential for rural, single-car crashes, most often road departure crashes. Road departure crashes account for as many as one-third of highway fatalities in the United States, and two-thirds of rural fatalities[78], which are the least likely to be witnessed by outside parties. Urban crashes, especially during the day, will invariably be called in by multiple bystanders on their cellular phones. This is far less likely for rural road departure crashes, which, if the driver is incapacitated, may go unnoticed for hours. Further aggravating this scenario is that, in rural areas, emergency responders will generally have to travel farther to reach a crash site. Anything which can increase the likelihood of promptly detecting a crash and speeding the dispatch of assistance can make a significant difference in crash survivability.

In the future, additional information characterizing the crash and the state of the vehicle and its occupants will be included in the ACN message or in follow-on messages.

ACN presents some interesting business and institutional issues that need to be resolved:

- Vehicle manufacturers are coming to the conclusion that ACN, once made available, cannot acceptably be turned off, for example for nonpayment of a service subscription. A fatality that is partly attributable to just-switched-off ACN service could produce a level of liability exposure and bad press that is probably not tolerable. This basically means that lifetime service would have to be provided, potentially by including its cost in the purchase price of the vehicle.
- Current ACN systems use cellular as their primary communications technology. Unfortunately, cellular is not well suited for sending large volumes of data messages. In addition, cellular is slow to make a reliable connection if the phone is not already registered with a local carrier, and coverage is not universal, particularly in the rural areas where ACN would be most valuable. Cellular data messaging (like the GPRS service of GSM) may be serviceable while volumes are small, particularly if an arrangement can be made to put through ACN messages without carrier registration (similar to the way wireless 911 calls are required to be handled). In the long term, however, other communications approaches may well supersede cellular, although legacy systems would still have to be supported.
- The probability that an ACN message will get through can be improved, particularly in marginal areas, by allowing the vehicle's communications device to use the cellular network with the strongest signal, regardless of the business arrangements between wireless carriers and the user. Further, if the cellular signal is weak or absent, the vehicle could be enabled to send a very high-power ACN data message on multiple frequencies to try to get the message through. Such a variable power approach is currently being considered by the European Telecommunications Standards Institute (ETSI) and explored by the FCC.

Telematics

Under the American definition, telematics[79] is the wireless provision of information and services to vehicles. In its broadest sense, telematics includes two general classes of services:

- **Vehicle-centric services:** primarily safety- and security-oriented services like ACN and stolen vehicle tracking, and the identification to onboard systems of safety hazards ahead (e.g., location of work zones and slippery spots on the road).

- **User-centric services:** generally information and services unrelated to safety: music and video download, news and sports, traffic alerts, remote door unlock, concierge services, office in the car services, etc.

The typical telematics services currently offered include:

- Automatic crash notification when the airbag deploys
- Emergency assistance on request in situations that do not necessarily trigger ACN
- Roadside assistance
- Tracking of stolen vehicles
- Driving directions
- Remote door unlock for equipped vehicles
- Information services
- Personal calling via an included cellular phone
- Concierge services (e.g., restaurant recommendations and reservations)

Some telematics services also offer remote diagnostics and internet connectivity. Some telematics services offer to keep track of medical information about the vehicle owner's family to relay to emergency services in case of a crash or medical emergency in the automobile.

Telematics services have been offered around the world by vehicle manufacturers, telephone companies (mainly wireless carriers), and independent technology firms. Nearly all of these ventures have failed to develop a significant subscriber base or to make money. Among the failed telematics ventures: ComROAD AG (Germany), Comworxx (U.S.), Monet (Toyota in Japan), Signant (Ford, PSA, and Renault-Nissan in Europe), Tegaron (Deutsche Telecom), Tiger Telematics (U.S.), Vodafone Passo (Europe), and Wingcast (Ford and Qualcomm).

A few companies in Europe, notably Trafficmaster and ITIS (UK) and MediaMobile (France) have had limited success selling rudimentary real-time traffic information, but have little prospect of branching out into other telematics services. Even OnStar, whose two million plus subscribers represent the majority of the total worldwide customers for telematics, is estimated to have a renewal rate of under 50% (in some estimates far under 50%). Unless this is improved significantly, there may be insufficient continuing business to cover costs, especially considering the high startup hardware and marketing costs for new customers.[80]

Although there is a widespread expectation that telematics will eventually be a successful and profitable enterprise, entrants have so far been unsuccessful in establishing a business model which is attractive to its participants and self-sustaining financially.

One of the clear problems with current telematics offerings is that most of the offered services can be gotten just as easily by telephone, notably including the automobile occupants' personal cell phone, without any need for specialized onboard equipment or a separate subscription fee. There is clearly some convenience in being able to access these services by pressing a dashboard button rather than an autodial key on a cell phone. However, subscribers do not appear to be willing to pay much for this convenience.

Another feature of current in-vehicle telematics products is that they can send a data message containing the vehicle's location along with the voice request, providing a destination for emergency responders and roadside assistance, and a location for location-based services (e.g., requesting the location of a nearby florist). However, as part of the wireless E-911 initiative, it will soon be the case that *every* cellular telephone call will have the ability to include caller location, diminishing the value of this telematics feature. One near-future model now gaining some interest has all user-centric services provided via mobile telephone, with the automobile simply serving to provide peripheral support: better sound, data entry capabilities, and graphics than the phone can provide by itself. Under this model, services would be provided consistently via the mobile telephone, regardless of whether the user was at home, at work, walking, or in a vehicle.

Two services that have clearly appealed to consumers are ACN and remote door unlock (and as a result, these services are the focus of most telematics provider advertising). However, a small amount of economic analysis shows that the cost of providing these clearly useful services, in volume, is only a few dollars per equipped vehicle per year.[81] This helps to explain why the current cost for telematics services, typically $15 to $60 per month, produces a low renewal rate and does not obviously make for a viable telematics business.

Connected Safety Systems

The current lackluster state of the telematics industry is potentially a serious issue for connected vehicle safety systems. These systems depend (among other things) on widespread, readily affordable communications to carry ACN and probe data messages. If such a communications network cannot be provided by a successful telematics industry, the only other alternative for providing it may be a massive public investment.

In general, successful telematics depends on meeting five challenges related to functionality and cost:

- Cheap, universally available, high-speed wireless packet data communications. Data communication issues are discussed as part of "Technology Around the Vehicle" below.
- Interface protocols that work both in a moving vehicle and in a handheld device (smart cell phone or wireless-enabled PDA). Such protocols would allow service providers already in the handheld market to enter the vehicle market with relatively low startup costs. The leading candidates are the protocols already being used to deliver information and services to 3G cellular phones, along with XML to define messages.
- User applications, from information and service providers, that a critical mass of users is willing to pay for.
- Lower in-vehicle hardware costs, possibly by integrating telematics capabilities into multimedia electronics or navigation systems.
- Flexible billing capabilities that allow users to pay only for the services that they use, without requiring users to make periodic payments if they don't use any services.

As with ACN, it would be very helpful if basic telematics connectivity could be available for the vehicle's service life through a reasonable upfront payment built into the purchase price of the vehicle. Excluding hardware, some industry experts believe that this upfront cost could be as little as $250 in the 2007-2010 timeframe, even less as volumes grow over the next 20 years. This would allow vehicle manufacturers always to be connected to their vehicles for customer relations, wireless diagnostics, wireless software updates, etc. and would provide a customer base ready to do business with information and service providers as attractive applications are developed and offered. Some vehicle manufacturers are beginning to explore such a model, which could be in the market by 2007 or so.

One of the challenges of providing connectivity for the life of the vehicle for a single upfront payment is that the lives of vehicles are getting longer and longer – up to 20 years or more. Among other things, this means having data communications devices in the vehicle that are serviceable throughout this long lifespan. The main issue is not physical durability (although this is clearly a challenge in the demanding in-vehicle environment), but the changes that are likely to occur in wireless technology, spectrum, protocols, etc. over an extended time period. One promising avenue is the current preliminary exploration of "smart" or "cognitive" radios that can adapt their behavior to new frequencies and protocols. The FCC recently issued a notice of proposed rulemaking (NPRM) and order[82] that seeks comment on the uses and applications of cognitive radio systems.

A future approach to telematics that may improve the viability of the business model is to make a much clearer separation between voice-oriented services that can be accessed from any telephone (landline or wireless) and purely data transactions like ACN, remote diagnostics, remote door unlock, delivery of externally selected destinations to the vehicle navigation system, in-vehicle software configuration management and maintenance, etc. Telematics would concentrate on the data transactions, taking itself out of the voice services supply chain to which it makes no obvious contribution.

Chapter 8

Technologies Inside and Outside the Vehicle

The three major technology application areas discussed in the previous chapter – crash prevention, ACN, and telematics – all depend on a variety of underlying in-vehicle technologies which are briefly discussed below. In many cases, these technologies represent enhanced versions of computer technologies that have already begun to appear in the vehicle.

Positioning

The twenty-first century vehicle will know very precisely where it is.

Current vehicles with navigation products already know their position to within about 16 meters, the approximate unassisted resolution provided by the Global Positioning Satellite (GPS) system. Many navigation products can refine the resolution to within 10 meters through the use of *+map matching*, a process onboard the vehicle that tracks the vehicle's progress and maneuvers against the onboard map, paying attention particularly to how the shape of the vehicle's travel path fits the shape of the road. This resolution is sufficient for route guidance and for early versions of some driver assistance systems like curve warning.

More advanced driver assistance systems and future collision avoidance systems need far more accurate positioning as well as far more accurate digital road maps than are currently available in the marketplace. Simply knowing the latitude and longitude of the vehicle to more decimal places is not helpful by itself. The important knowledge is where the vehicle is with respect to the road system, to features and obstacles on and near the road system, and to other vehicles. This requires collaboration between positioning and ranging technology and the digital map. The goal is sub-meter accuracy, which is needed for applications that depend on knowing which lane the vehicle is in and its relationship to other vehicles. Some safety applications may require resolutions of 10 cm or better.

Positioning accuracy can be improved by:

- *Differential GPS (DGPS)* – DGPS is a land-based service which transmits corrections of the standard GPS signal. A base station is set up in a fixed place whose location is known very accurately. The base station receives the GPS signal and notes the difference between its true location and the GPS-derived location. It then transmits this difference to users in the area, including vehicles, which can combine it with their own GPS-derived location to get a much more accurate position. This kind of service is available selectively throughout the United States. DGPS is not yet being used in automobiles, partly because of cost, but mainly because current in-vehicle applications do not require this level of accuracy. However, future in-vehicle applications will be inhibited if DGPS is not fully available throughout the United States
- *Improved Satellite Systems* – Satellite positioning systems are being planned by the EU and by China. The EU claims that its Galileo system[83], now in development, will be able to deliver real-time positioning accuracy of one meter. The U.S. Dept. of Defense was reported[84] to have selectively enhanced the accuracy of the GPS system to three meters to support air and ground forces during the Iraq war.
- *Trilateration (Triangulation)* – Trilateration is a process which helps a vehicle fix its position by noting its instantaneous distance from two[85] or more external objects whose locations are precisely known. The distance and bearing can be measured by radar or lidar, and the objects and their locations can be recorded in the map database. This is a future approach. At present, commercial map databases do not include these kinds of objects, and trilateration capabilities are not currently present in automobiles.

Projects conducted by the European Commission (NextMAP and ActMAP) and by U.S. DOT (EDMap) have focused on determining requirements for digital road maps to support safety systems. Requirements include identifying the features to be included, the needed accuracy of representation of these features, and the ability for the map database in the vehicle to be updated in real time with new and corrected feature information. This updating is a far greater challenge than simply getting updated characteristics to the automobile. It is a particular challenge when new geometry needs to added, not just changes to the characteristics of existing roads. At present, map databases get updated by replacement, either via a whole new CD/DVD or a rewritten hard disk file. Although incremental updating is being actively explored, technology does not presently exist to allow a map database to have just changes installed rather than a whole new copy of the database.

Getting the necessary level of geometric road network accuracy for future map databases will probably require equipping a large number of vehicles with positioning technology, recording their driving paths, and post-analyzing this data to arrive at a statistically accurate determination of the location, configuration, and shape of roads and lanes. A relevant issue is determining how much public sector support is appropriate and desirable for building better map databases and what the impact of this support would be on ownership and distribution of the results.

Sensors

The twenty-first century vehicle already has a large number of sensors that provide data about the vehicle and its immediate environment. The reasonably advanced vehicle of today already knows how fast it is going and in what direction, the level of outside light, the outside temperature, whether it is raining, how slippery and how rough the pavement is, and a variety of facts about the internal operation and state of the vehicle. All reasonably new vehicles can sense a crash, which is how airbags are deployed. Some vehicles having ranging sensors – radar or lidar – to detect obstacles and leading vehicles, and some have infrared sensors to provide improved night vision. Some vehicles can sense the characteristics (size, weight) of passengers to more safely control airbag deployment.

Sensors in the evolving twenty-first century vehicle are more likely to add refinement and precision to existing capabilities than to provide totally new data. No major breakthroughs are obviously needed; however, sensors, like other information technology, will become cheaper and more capable. The most notable expansion will probably be video imaging capabilities to capture large amounts of data about the vehicle's immediate environment. For the most part, video capabilities will work with other sensors to refine and improve data capture and analysis. For example, video image analysis can help to characterize obstacles, help to determine the lane in which the vehicle (or another vehicle) is traveling, and help to locate and categorize roadside features for more accurate positioning.

In addition to supporting a variety of in-vehicle functions, sensors on board the vehicle are the raw material for probe processing, a key external technology surrounding the twenty-first century vehicle, discussed further below.

Microprocessors and Software

Microprocessors were already showing up in quantity in late twentieth century vehicles. By the beginning of the twenty-first century, some high-end vehicles included as many as 60 processors for controlling a variety of functionality in the automobile, including separate processors for engine control, emissions, cruise control, ABS, transmission control, etc. In general, processors tended to focus on particular functions. The number and power of these processors is sure to increase as electronic functionality grows and as the price of processors continues to decline. The popular press recently reported the availability of specialized computer chips that can be installed in vehicles to provide new vehicle functionality or adjust existing functionality.

Processor functionality depends on software. Traditionally, many in-vehicle processors used read-only memory (ROM) or programmable read-only memory (PROM) to help keep programs from being corrupted. This approach is applicable when processors are focused enough and programs are short enough for the entire program to remain in memory all the time. As memory continues to get cheaper, this approach may continue to work as programs grow larger, at least for a while. Although this approach is very stable, the software cannot be upgraded or updated except through a physical visit to a service facility to replace a module. This is not an issue for basic functionality like engine control, which does not generally change during the life of the automobile. However, it may be a problem in areas of more rapid technological change, for example the software controlling onboard communications devices, which may need to adapt to new protocols and frequencies over the life of the vehicle.

Fortunately, a connected automobile in wireless communication with its manufacturer or a service facility offers the prospect of updating in-vehicle software wirelessly. There are a variety of concerns that have to be addressed to make this feasible and foolproof. These include very well-controlled software configuration management and mechanisms to authenticate and verify the transmission of software updates. A hacker who introduces malicious code in a PC is a serious nuisance, but malicious code in the drive train of a vehicle could be deadly. As the software content of the vehicle grows, this kind of software updating will become increasingly appealing, but meeting the challenges of doing the updating utterly reliably probably means that it is at least ten years into the future.

Data Storage

The twenty-first century vehicle will need a significant quantity of updatable data storage – a hard disk or large-size solid-state memory. A primary reason for this storage is to maintain up-to-date map databases, both for navigation/route guidance and to support probe processing. Some navigation map databases are already being kept on in-vehicle hard disks.

Once the problem of incremental updating has been solved, the reasonable expectation is that automobiles will periodically receive wireless updates to navigation map databases that reflect changes to the road network, including new road construction, new maneuver restrictions, and new points of interest.

Data storage is also needed to support economical probe processing in the automobile. The database allows probe messages (which describe the sensed driving environment) to be sent by exception; that is, only when onboard sensors detect a situation that is different than the one recorded in the in-vehicle database. When the database is updated with a new situation, probe messages will be suppressed until the situation once again changes. This area is discussed further below.

In-Vehicle Networking

The twenty-first century vehicle is characterized by a large number of electronic components, many of which need to communicate with one another and with vehicle occupants. One of the dramatic advances of the fairly recent past has been to replace the bundles of individual wires and cables with databuses – smart cables to which a variety of components can be connected, forming networks through which information traffic can be directed among onboard devices.[86]

As a matter of both safety and practicality, vehicle manufacturers have been creating multiple, largely independent networks in their vehicles based on functionality[87]. Vehicles may have several internal networks for controlling different classes of devices. One network/databus could handle basic vehicle functionality: engine control, transmission, traction and stability control, etc. Another might control devices in the vehicle's interior: power seats, door locks, power mirrors, air conditioning, etc. A third network could handle vehicle diagnostics. A fourth could focus on multimedia products: radio, CD-player, etc. These networks are largely isolated from one another to minimize the possibility that a non-critical function (CD player control) might interfere with a critical function (engine control). Non-multimedia networks are sometimes characterized as controller-area networks (CANs). CAN buses are typically copper-based and relatively slow speed, but highly reliable for operation in the demanding in-vehicle environment. Multimedia buses are newer on the scene. They are much higher speed, to handle audio and video information, and are typically optical fiber based. The one adopted by the Automotive Multimedia Interface Collaboration is the MOST bus, whose name comes from the name of its German manufacturer[88]. Another multimedia bus being considered is IDB-1394[89] based on a high-speed standard developed by the Institute of Electrical and Electronics Engineers (IEEE).

One of the challenges to be addressed in the evolving twenty-first century vehicle is that many emerging applications, particularly safety applications, cut across various kinds of multimedia devices and vehicle control devices. In particular, information from the outside world on road conditions and the driving environment will begin to play a larger role in the management of traction and stability control and emergency maneuvers for collision avoidance. Making sure that information flows appropriately between the networks without compromising safety and security will be a significant issue.

Drive-by-Wire

Over the next 20 years, the operation of the twenty-first century vehicle will increasingly be characterized as "drive-by-wire." Drive-by-wire means that control devices in the hands (and beneath the feet) of the driver will communicate electronically to throttle, steering, and braking devices through an in-vehicle network rather than through mechanical and hydraulic linkages. Aircraft are already flying by wire. Some new commercial vehicles have introduced electronic braking (in which airbrakes are engaged by an electronic command) which is far more responsive than traditional braking and allows better braking coordination between tractor and trailer. Some automobile manufacturers, mainly European and Japanese, have developed drive-by-wire concept cars.[90, 91]

Rudimentary drive-by-wire capabilities already exist in the twenty-first century vehicle. For example, many automobiles have electronic door locks that can be activated by a switch, by a remote control device, or by a signal from a telematics provider bounced to the automobile off a satellite. In each case, the "door unlock" command is delivered to the lock over a databus. The only difference is where the command originated.

The advantages of drive-by-wire are: the number of moving parts is greatly reduced, sensor-based controls can be made that are far more accurate than mechanical controls, and there is far greater freedom in the form and placement of the controls. For example, some drive-by-wire prototypes replace the steering wheel, accelerator, and brake pedal with a single joystick (sometimes two joysticks). Being able to remove the steering column eliminates one of the objects most dangerous to the driver in a crash.

Possibly more important for the twenty-first century vehicle, drive-by-wire provides the basis for coordinated vehicle control in an emergency situation, when collision avoidance, stability control, and traction control systems, along with the driver, are all putting urgent simultaneous demands on steering and braking devices. Creating the in-vehicle intelligence to do this coordination is a primary technical and design challenge for the developers of the twenty-first century vehicle and a major new focus of the U.S. Department of Transportation's ITS Joint Program Office. An equal challenge is to make sure that drive-by-wire is at least as reliable as mechanical and hydraulic systems and that these electronic systems will not stop working if the vehicle's engine stops or its electrical system has a simple failure. In current cars, regular braking and steering are still available if power steering or power brake assists fail. Similar failsafe provisions are needed in drive-by-wire vehicles. A further challenge will be to develop trust for drive-by-wire in a car buying public that knows how often its PCs need to be rebooted.

Voice Recognition and Speech Recognition and Synthesis

The first thing to be clear about is that voice recognition and speech recognition are two different technologies.

Voice recognition is a biometric – a process for determining a person's identity by analyzing the characteristics of his or her voice. Voice recognition can be helpful for applications such as determining which family member is currently driving, so that various preset preferences (radio stations, suspension setting, climate control) can be invoked. Voice recognition could also be a component of validating the user of electronic payment mechanisms, although this is certainly not restricted to in-vehicle use. Good voice recognition could be particularly helpful for ensuring that the right person is actually behind the wheel, for example of a truck carrying hazardous materials or operating in a sensitive area. Voices cannot be mislaid or stolen like identify cards, and very simple mechanisms can be used to prevent prerecorded misuse of someone's voice (e.g., by asking the subject to repeat randomly selected words or phrases).

Speech recognition is technology to correctly interpret a sequence of one or more spoken words. Vehicle manufacturers are already experimenting with speech recognition and synthesis as a hands-free way for vehicle occupants to interact with onboard systems. Speech recognition is a particularly valuable approach for in-vehicle user interfaces as an alternative to selecting choices from a screen or doing some other more conventional type of data entry. For navigation, for example, it would be very helpful if the traveler could say: "I want to go to 127 Maple Lane in Springfield, Missouri" and have this correctly interpreted by the navigation system. It would even be helpful if the traveler could participate in a more stylized dialog to the same end:

Traveler: "New destination!"
Nav System: "Destination State?"
Traveler: "Missouri"
Nav System: "Destination City?"
Traveler: "Springfield"

or for frequent destinations, being able to respond "Office" to the first prompt.

Considerable progress has been made in speech recognition over the past few years as evidenced by its use by airlines to deliver arrival and departure information over the telephone, its use to do toll-free directory assistance, deliver stock quotes over the telephone, etc. Limiting the universe of allowable responses obviously improves accuracy (e.g., to the names of publicly traded companies, or to the names of streets in a particular town). Pre-training the speech recognition system by individual users also helps to compensate for individual idiosyncrasies and accents.

The other side of the coin is speech synthesis: computer generated speech. Done well, synthesized speech can provide information to the driver of the twenty-first century vehicle in a manner that does not require moving eyes off the road. However, the distraction potential of synthesized speech is currently an open issue.

The ability for computers to *understand* the meaning and context of free-form text is still many years away, regardless of whether the text is spoken or typed.

Interconnection Technologies

One of the most important characteristics of the twenty-first century vehicle is that it will be connected – to the land and to other vehicles – for a variety of safety and productivity enhancing purposes. This section describes some of the more important ways in which the twenty-first century vehicle will be connected and why.

Probe Processing

Probe processing is the centralized fusion and analysis of sensor data obtained from many vehicles, combined with data from multiple other public and private sources. These sources can include infrastructure-based sensors, weather reports, police and fire reports, event listings, road construction and repair plans, etc.

Probe processing is a principal enabler of several crucial activities in and around the twenty-first century vehicle, and it is a key component of the cooperation between vehicle-based and land-based technology that will characterize twenty-first century surface transportation:

- First, probe processing is the basis for enhancing the performance of onboard preventive safety products and advanced driver assistance systems. Probe processing extends the reach and the precision of the sensors on board any particular vehicle by aggregating and refining information from multiple vehicles and other sources to build an accurate, enlarged, real-time picture of the driving environment.
- Second, probe processing can build an accurate real-time and predictive picture of traffic, to enable vehicles to select and modify driving routes to optimize trips based on current and forecast traffic conditions. For good traffic modeling, one important ingredient is a good historical database of traffic patterns and behavior that takes note of the baseline differences in traffic patterns by time of day, day of the week, season, weather, whether school is in or out, the occurrence and timing of major sports/entertainment/political events, the typical impact of

various kinds of crashes and other nonrecurring traffic incidents, etc.

- Third, probe processing is the information basis for enhancing the operation of the roadway infrastructure. Probe processing can provide information on the state and performance of a far wider range of roads than it is practical to instrument directly. Through probe processing, road authorities can know about the state of arterials as well as major highways, to help redirect traffic to viable alternative routes.
- Fourth, probe processing appears to be the only economic way to gather the large volume of road geometry data needed to build map databases with the accuracy required to support preventive safety applications in the vehicle.
- Finally, probe processing provides vital information in times of emergency to help assess the impact on surface transportation and to help devise good mechanisms for getting emergency responders to the scene and at-risk populations evacuated as smoothly and efficiently as possible.

Probe data starts mainly as vehicle sensor data, relayed to a central point for processing. In general, as shown in Table 8-1, sensors are not introduced into the vehicle primarily to serve as sources of probe data. Rather, probe processing makes use of sensors that already are (or will be) in the car for other purposes. At the probe processing center, vehicle sensor data is combined with similar data from other vehicles and from a wide variety of other fixed and mobile, public and private data sources that help to characterize the driving environment.

The other primary in-vehicle hardware ingredient for probe processing is a wireless data communications capability. Again, it is unlikely that this capability will be incorporated in the vehicle primarily to serve the probe application. Rather probe data transmission will use the communications capability that already is (or will be) in the vehicle for other purposes, most notably automatic crash notification (ACN), telematics (i.e., the wireless provision of information and services to the vehicle), and vehicle-manufacturer-centric services (e.g., wireless diagnostics, customer relationship management, wireless updating of in-vehicle software, etc.). The communications issue is discussed in more detail in the next chapter.

Probe data transmitted from the vehicle has some characteristics which distinguish it from other kinds of vehicle-based data transmission.

Table 8-1:

Sensor Data	Source	Use in the Vehicle	Use as Probe Data
Vehicle location	Enhanced differential GPS, dead reckoning, map matching, trilateration against known road features	Route guidance, lane keeping, adaptive cruise control, mayday and other calls for assistance, enabling location-based services	Foundation for all location-related analysis including vehicle tracking and map refinement
Vehicle speed	Speedometer feed	Driver feedback, cruise control	Traffic reporting and prediction
Air temperature	Temperature sensor	Driver information, air conditioning fine tuning, engine performance fine tuning	Weather reporting and forecasting
Precipitation (start/stop/intensity)	Rain detector	Automatic wipers, traction control	Weather reporting and forecasting, safety alerts to other vehicles
Wind direction and speed	Steering sensors, stability control system	Stability control, lane keeping	Weather reporting and forecasting, safety alerts to other vehicles
Pavement traction	Traction sensor	Traction control system	Safety alerts to other vehicles and to road authorities
Pavement condition	Suspension sensors	Stability control, suspension control	Alerts to other vehicles, maintenance alert to road authorities
Roadway geometry or feature variance	Route guidance system, map matching subsystem	Alert driver to variances	Feedback to map vendors, alerts to other vehicles, maintenance alert to road authorities
Presence/location of obstacles and other vehicles	Radar/lidar/vision systems in conjunction with map data	Adaptive cruise control, lane change warning, collision warning and avoidance, knowledge of vehicles and obstacles that are outside the field of view (e.g., over a hill)	Alerting authorities to clear obstacles, coordinating collision avoidance among multiple vehicles

Adapted from Gomi & Weiland, "The Future of Probe Data to Support ITS," Proceedings of the 2002 FISITA Conference, with the authors' permission

Most important, probe data will be totally anonymous. It does not contain any information which directly or indirectly identifies the vehicle from which it was sent or any of its occupants. The probe message contains only the relayed sensor reading and a time/location stamp to indicate when and where the reading was taken. This assurance of anonymity is generally agreed to be critical for getting vehicle owners and users to participate in contributing probe data. Since probe processing is the aggregation of sensor readings from multiple vehicles, vehicle and occupant identity is irrelevant in practically all cases anyway.

There are a few cases in which knowing vehicle identify might be helpful. For example, if the probe processing center determines that some vehicle is transmitting bad data (i.e., data which is inconsistent with all other reports from the same area); it would be helpful to be able to notify the vehicle to recalibrate or switch off data transmission. However, the examination of such cases by the ISO committee developing probe data standards (ISO TC204/WG16.3) has found that all of them could be dealt with without compromising anonymity. For example, in the case given above, the probe center can send a message to all vehicles in the area identifying the bad value and the correct value, asking any vehicle generating the bad value to take corrective action.

Another important characteristic of probe data is that vehicles will typically send a probe message only when its sensors detect a situation different than the most recent one known (e.g., traffic is moving significantly slower or faster than the most recent report). Reporting by exception makes a major difference in the volume and cost of communication traffic, especially when the number of probe-equipped vehicles becomes large. Once the probe processing center sends out an update, the new information becomes the most recent report, and the vehicle will stop sending probe messages until the situation once again changes. Probe architectures under development do include a provision for the probe processing center to request vehicles in a particular area to begin reporting unconditionally for a time, rather than by exception, for intensive data gathering in special circumstances.

Other requirements for successful and productive probe processing include[92]:

- A low-cost wireless data communications capability in the vehicle in an environment that allows it to send messages, particularly safety-related messages, from wherever it is.
- An effective, low-cost mechanism for wide-area communications *to* the vehicle. Note that the mechanism for sending probe results *to* vehicles typically targets areas, not particular vehicles; it is not point-to-point. In the medium term, this communications technology will probably not be the same as the one used for inbound probe data message transmission.
- An in-vehicle data network that interconnects sensors, processors, communication systems, and in-vehicle applications, discussed above.
- Fairly large-scale, updatable, in-vehicle data storage. Also discussed above.
- A high-quality telematics platform in the vehicle, eventually integrated with the navigation system and other multimedia electronics. The existence of such a platform provides most of hardware

needed to support vehicle-side probe processing and makes the incremental cost of adding probe capabilities fairly insignificant.

- High-quality landside operations to support telematics, landside data communications, and probe processing. The first two of these are clearly prerequisite to the third, from both an economic and logistics viewpoint.

Fairly extensive trials of probe data and probe processing have taken place or are ongoing in Japan and Europe.

Efforts in Japan have been sponsored by the Internet CAR and Internet ITS consortiums, public-private partnerships working with the Japan Automobile Research Institute (JARI). These trials have been ongoing since 1996. The most recent, in Nagoya, was a trial that included over 1,500 taxis reporting on traffic and weather via cellular, mobile packet switching, DSRC, and wireless LAN.

In Europe, traffic information based on probe data is being provided commercially on a limited scale (mostly major roads) by Trafficmaster and ITIS Holdings (UK) and by MediaMobile (France). A major UK field demonstration of probe data and vehicle communications is being conducted by a public-private partnership that includes vehicle and electronics manufacturers under the overall management of Britain's Transport Research Laboratory. The OPTIS project, a joint effort of the Swedish government and Swedish vehicle manufacturers, used probe data to provide better traveler information, optimize travel, and reduce fuel consumption and emissions. ERTICO (ITS Europe) is leading an investigation of Extended Floating Car Data (an alternative term for probe data) in conjunction with BMW. Several other European trials and demonstrations took place starting in the middle 1990s.

Activities in the United States are much sparser. A "Probe Vehicle Test Bed" project was added at FHWA's request to the iFlorida model deployment project, to serve as a testbed for private sector probe vehicle technologies. The iFlorida effort intends to demonstrate the operational functions that are enabled or enhanced with a surface transportation information system. However, according to the iFlorida website, the probe project is on hold pending further direction from FHWA.

Ford Research has announced a two-part initiative, in cooperation with the city of Dearborn Heights, Michigan, and with the Minnesota Department of Transportation, to equip public vehicles to gather and transmit probe data. This involves 15 police cars in Dearborn Heights and 50-100 state-owned cars and buses in Minnesota with sensing devices that will communicate traffic and weather information to a central processing point. The test was scheduled to begin in April 2004.[93]

Ownership of Probe Processing Center

An interesting issue for production-level probe processing that is far from being resolved or even adequately addressed is: Who should own and operate the probe processing center?

There is, first, a good argument for there being only a single probe processing center covering each particular region. Multiple parallel probe processing centers simply have the effect of multiplying development and operational costs while dividing up revenue and the number of vehicles providing data. Particularly for less-traveled roads, this could produce a situation in which none of multiple probe processing centers gets the critical mass of data needed to create an effective picture of the driving environment that could be created if the data were collected by a single center. In addition, multiple probe processing centers for a region could potentially result in multiple, systematically inconsistent pictures of the driving environment, which could easily produce confusion among vehicles that need to interact smoothly and consistently, particularly in a developing emergency situation.

Unfortunately, public ownership of the probe processing center has many associated problems. Not the least of these is that, in the early years, the center would be operated primarily for the benefit of the owners and operators of late-model, high-end vehicles, an unattractive political prospect for a very expensive public works project. Another problem is that there is widespread public unease about having government agencies collect information about the behavior of vehicles and drivers, regardless of the assurances that the data is collected anonymously. There is less discomfort with having a private venture do the collection.

One possibility is for the probe center to be operated as a utility that is jointly owned by the vehicle manufacturers. This would help to ensure that probe processing and its resulting safety benefits would function as a level playing field and it would help to ensure that all vehicles operate with a consistent model of the driving environment.

While the ultimate objective of probe processing is to enhance vehicle safety, a useful additional outcome could be the availability of real-time and (more important) predictive traffic information on all roads except the smallest and least traveled.

One model suggests that focusing initial probe processing on producing good traffic data can help finance probe processing to produce good safety data. Traffic data can be used more widely and in a much shorter timeframe than safety data. It requires much the same infrastructure for data collection and processing as safety data, and it is potentially revenue producing. By focusing first on probe processing for traffic data, the groundwork can be laid for making safety-oriented probe data available when in-vehicle systems are ready to make use of it, and potentially to move this date forward by several years.

Data Communications

Probe data is not, of course, the only kind of information that will be moving between the twenty-first century vehicle and the land. Data communications will be needed to support the two general classes of services discussed above under Telematics – vehicle-centric and user-centric services – plus a third category, vehicle-manufacturer-centric services, which make use of the ability to connect the vehicle with its manufacturer's information technology systems. These services can include wireless diagnostics, in-vehicle software configuration control, and, eventually, wireless software updates for some components in the vehicle. Vehicle-manufacturer-centric services can help the vehicle manufacturer maintain good customer relationships and lower the cost of keeping the vehicle well maintained.

In addition, in future years, the capability will exist for data communications among vehicles, either directly as area broadcasts within an ad hoc local network or by relay through a central point. The primary purpose of vehicle-vehicle communication is safety: for one vehicle to advise other nearby vehicles of detected safety hazards (e.g., slippery spots or obstacles on the road) at the same time that it notifies road authorities and to help coordinate crash avoidance among potentially involved vehicles. Coordinating crash avoidance includes advising connected vehicles about the status of all vehicle in the vicinity, especially those which are determined not to be connected. DSRC and CALM, discussed below, include provisions for vehicle-vehicle communication as well as vehicle-infrastructure communication.

Separating Voice from Data. Although voice conversations are a significant part of current telematics services, there is a good argument for separating voice communications from data communications. Under this separation, voice communications are the exclusive purview of users' personal communication devices (i.e., cell phones and wireless-enabled PDAs), while interactions with the in-vehicle communications device are exclusively via data messages. This provides for a much simpler onboard system architecture and eliminates an arguably unnecessary link in the voice communication chain.

As discussed above, approaches to the handling of automatic crash notification (ACN) messages generally include attempting to contact vehicle occupants after a crash to seek further information about the crash that may be useful to emergency responders or to determine if no help is actually wanted[94]. In the twenty-first century vehicle, this call can be made to the cell phone embedded in the car, if one exists, or to any cell phone belonging to an occupant that is registered with the ACN service (through an advance call or over the web), or in real time via device registration in the vehicle using Bluetooth (or an analogous approach). In addition, a voice conversation can be attempted over the data connection using Voice over IP (VoIP), which has a much higher probability than a regular cell phone call of getting through in areas of marginal cellular coverage.

The current technologies for vehicle-land communication are cellular telephony and dedicated short-range communications (DSRC) at 5.9 GHz, both of which are capable of handling data traffic including internet activities like VoIP. A generalization of vehicle-land communications called CALM, which incorporates both cellular and DSRC, is being explored in the ITS Technical Committee of the International Standards Organization (ISO TC204).

Cellular. Cellular is the only mobile communication technology which has any current claim for widespread, high volume deployment across the United States. Current commercial telematics services in the United States mainly use analog cellular (AMPS), for all transmissions, including ACN data messages. In August 2002, the FCC ruled that cellular carriers would not be required to support AMPS after 2007, providing a five-year period for the transition to digital cellular.

The major cellular carriers are gravitating toward two different types of digital cellular, CDMA and GSM. Industry projections are that by the 2010 timeframe, coverage for both technologies will be widespread in the United States, each represented by about half of the major wireless carriers.

CDMA (Code Division Multiple Access) is a more compact encoding than GSM (that is, more capacity on the same bandwidth), but is technically somewhat more complex. GSM (Global System for Mobile Communications) is the standard used in Europe and in much of the Asia-Pacific region, although not Japan. GSM has the advantage of incorporating mechanisms for sending data messages (the Short Message

Service, SMS, suitable for messages of up to 160 bytes, and its successor, the General Packet Radio Service, GPRS, which is designed for general data dialogs including interaction with the internet).

Nonetheless, in the long term, cellular is not well suited for high-volume, low-cost data messaging, and even its data message services do not connect instantaneously, requiring a high level of armor to ensure that a message will get out when a crash occurs.

DSRC/WAVE. Dedicated short-range communication (DSRC) for vehicles[95] was designed originally for electronic toll collection and for electronically checking commercial vehicle credentials at borders and weigh stations. Early versions of DSRC used the unlicensed 915 MHz band, which has many attractive propagation characteristics. However, this band is shared by a large number of other applications, and the resulting potential for interference makes it unsuitable for safety services. The FCC recently allocated 75 MHz of bandwidth (a very substantial chunk) in the 5.9 GHz band, specifically for intelligent transportation system (ITS) use, with particular emphasis on safety services. In this band, ITS has co-primary status which eliminates interference from other applications. The other co-primary user is a narrow class of satellite services which are highly unlikely to interfere with vehicle-land communications.

With the decision to use the IEEE 802.11 wireless LAN standards as a basis for DSRC communications at 5.9 GHz, a new name has been adopted: Wireless Access for Vehicular Environments (WAVE). Standards for this service are being developed cooperatively in IEEE (in IEEE 1609 and IEEE 802.11) and in ISO TC204 (as ISO 21210). At the same time, a request has been made (by Canada) to the International Telecommunications Union (ITU) to reserve the 75 MHz of spectrum between 5.850 GHz and 5.925 GHz as a band for ITS safety services worldwide. This band exactly corresponds to the spectrum allocated in the United States for ITS applications of DSRC. At this writing, Japan has objected to this allocation to protect its existing investment in electronic user fee collection technology in other bands, and as a result, European interests are beginning to consider other applications for this band.

CALM. ISO TC204 is working on a set of standards for more general vehicle-land communications called Continuous Air interface for Long and Medium distance (CALM), which incorporates digital cellular (2.5G and 3G), DSRC/WAVE, and other communications media including infrared and millimeter wave (~63 GHz). CALM takes the viewpoint that different communication media will be appropriate in different places based on terrain and population density. CALM provides for communication sessions to be handed off, not only from place to place like cellular, but also across communication media depending on what is available at various places that the vehicle travels.

The primary advantage of cellular is that its infrastructure is already in place. The absence of an existing infrastructure is the primary challenge of the other, otherwise more suitable communications technologies. Planning and financing this communications infrastructure will require a partnership of communications companies, vehicle manufacturers, state and local transportation agencies, and U.S. DOT.

Vehicle-Infrastructure Cooperation

In many discussions of vehicle-infrastructure cooperation to promote road safety and productivity, "infrastructure" means the road network and its related operators and systems. The road network and other aspects of the publicly operated surface transportation infrastructure will clearly have a large and crucial role to play in this cooperation. However, it is also clear that important aspects of the land-based part of this cooperation can and should be developed and operated by the private sector, probably including:

- Wireless communications
- Telematics
- Probe processing

The notion of vehicle-infrastructure cooperation is certainly not new. The requirement to demonstrate an automated highway system (AHS) was included in the language of the Intermodal Surface Transportation Efficiency Act of 1991 (ISTEA), the first ITS-aware transportation bill. However, fully automated highways with relatively little vehicle-based intelligence turned out not to be a fruitful pursuit. Vehicle-landside cooperation in the form of initial forays into telematics were (and are being) pursued. However, except for isolated pockets of research activity, very little headway in cooperation between vehicles and the roadway network was made between the mandated 1997 demonstration of AHS and the January 2002 publication, by the Intelligent Transportation Society of America (ITS America), of the *National ITS Program Plan: A Ten-Year Vision.*

One of the leading themes of this plan was a call for the development of an Integrated Network of Transportation Information that would link vehicles of all kinds, the road and rail networks, public agencies (notably, but not exclusively transportation agencies) at all levels, private sector organizations, and the general traveling public. The road vehicle / road network portion of this theme was explored in an August 2002 workshop sponsored by the Transportation Research Board (National Research Council) to explore the Roadway INFOstructure.[96] The INFOstructure term had been suggested by the U.S. DOT's ITS Joint Program Office in January 2002, to express its interest in a transportation-oriented information network that would link vehicles with the roads.

The initial U.S. DOT vision of the INFOstructure was primarily infrastructure based, with sensors and communications devices installed in traffic signals. However, the TRB workshop greatly broadened this perspective, recognizing the fundamental role of vehicles in the cooperative environment. This was further expanded in a February 2003 workshop, sponsored by ITS America, on the Integrated Network of Transportation Information (INTI).[97] This workshop was well attended by public sector representatives from federal, state, and local government and by private sector representatives including vehicle manufacturers, communications carriers, trucking companies, railroads, electronics manufacturers, and transportation consultants.

A significant outcome of this activity is the current collaboration getting under way between state DOTs under the auspices of the American Association of State Highway and Transportation Officials (AASHTO), vehicle manufacturers under the auspices of the Alliance of Automobile Manufacturers (AAM), and the U.S. DOT ITS Joint Program Office. This Vehicle-Infrastructure Integration (VII) collaboration is still in its early days of formation, but it appears that all participants agree that an integrated system of vehicles and the infrastructure has significant benefits for all of them and for other stakeholders who will later join the collaboration.

Chapter 9

Challenges of Developing the Twenty-First Century Vehicle

While the potential of the twenty-first century vehicle to improve safety, mobility, productivity, and comfort is enormous, so are the challenges.

Technical challenges include:

- Creating and refining onboard safety products and making them effective, reliable, and affordable
- Developing the in-vehicle networks to gather and distribute information throughout the vehicle and to and from in-vehicle communications devices
- Establishing the communications infrastructure that will connect vehicles no matter where they are
- Effectively managing, filtering, and productively digesting the vast quantities of information that vehicles can deliver
- Modeling the overall driving environment in real time
- Effectively combining this model with onboard technology to make vehicles more crash-proof
- Developing a profound understanding of driver behavior in both routine and emergency situations

Institutional challenges include:

- Fostering cooperation between and among:
  - ➢ Public sector organizations with public safety and infrastructure management responsibilities
  - ➢ Manufacturers of vehicles and vehicle technology
- Encouraging technology transfer from the military, leveraging its use of ITS in conducting the Iraq war and in counterterrorist activities

- Addressing liability and antitrust issues that can limit and delay the deployment of life-saving technologies
- Addressing privacy concerns of the drivers and vehicle owners who will be supplying most of the needed information
- Providing reliable funding for high-risk, high-payoff technology research and development and appropriately safeguarding the intellectual property that results from this R&D
- Getting this whole process going expeditiously

Many of these challenges are properly left to the marketplace to sort out. However, there is a clear public interest in accelerating and facilitating the reduction of traffic fatalities and in encouraging developments that benefit American industry and the American public. The following section identifies and discusses some of the more important policy issues that can help realize the potential benefits of the twenty-first century vehicle.

Setting the Right Goal

Reducing traffic deaths and injuries is high on the list of goals for governments around the world. Europe's goal is to halve its traffic fatalities by 2010, targeting "zero traffic fatalities" as a goal for 2020. In September 2003, the European Commission (EC) produced a communication to the Council and European Parliament entitled "Information and Communications Technologies for Safe and Intelligent Vehicles."[98] It describes how the EC will accelerate the development, large-scale deployment, and use of intelligent vehicle safety systems throughout Europe.

The EC identifies three categories for action:

1. Promoting intelligent vehicle safety systems
2. Adapting regulatory and standardization provisions
3. Removing societal and business obstacles

Table 9-1 shows the EC's proposed timetable for deployment of in-vehicle safety technology in Europe.

In contrast, the goal in the United States is to lower the *rate* of traffic deaths by about one-third between now and 2008, from about 1.5 deaths per hundred million vehicle miles traveled (VMT) to 1 death per hundred million VMT. With the continuing increase in VMT, the actual death toll will fall by a smaller percentage than this rate.

Table 9-1:

Year	Item	Description
2004	Antilock Braking Systems (ABS)	All new motor vehicles will be equipped with ABS starting in July 2004.
2005	Electronic Stability Program (ESP)	ESP available on all cars in 2005.
2006	E-call	E-call provides a location-enhanced automatic or manual emergency call to a Public Safety Answering Point. The goal of E-call is to cut down on emergency response times. Some business and infrastructure investment issues need to be resolved before E-call can be deployed; however, the EC considers 2006 a realistic target year for E-call.
2007	Crash Warning and Mitigation systems	The EC considers 2007 a possible target year for these systems. A current major issue is that the underlying technical implementations of these systems are not compatible from one vehicle manufacturer to another. There are also liability and regulatory issues, including spectrum allocation for short-range radar.
2008	Safe Speed	The EC is promoting research on a Safe Speed concept: onboard systems that always maintain a safe speed in relation to the road and environment. These systems still need further development and infrastructure investment and are therefore targeted for 2008.
2010 & Beyond	Zero Fatalities	Europe's target is to cut the number of road fatalities in half by 2010 and to move towards "zero fatalities" by 2020.

Is the U.S. goal more realistic than the European goal, or is the United States simply aiming too low? There are many factors in the relative speed at which safety technology can be introduced in the United States and Europe. To begin with, Europe is simply further ahead in developing and deploying vehicle safety technology than the United States and continues to take a much more proactive approach than in the United States. The reasons for this, and several other factors affecting the safety gap, are part of the policy discussion below. However, an overall public policy that resolutely sets and relentlessly pursues more aggressive goals for reducing traffic fatalities in the United States will profoundly affect all other public policy in this arena.

Liability

Vehicle manufacturers operate in a peculiar paradox, particularly in litigious America. Their offering of in-vehicle products with demonstrable net safety benefits potentially exposes them to far greater product liability risk if the product fails than not offering the product at all. Public policy which tolerates (or even encourages) this situation has resulted in the introduction of safety products far later and far less aggressively in the United States than in Europe and Asia. As a result, lives have been lost and injuries sustained that could have been prevented by wider, faster safety product deployment. This situation is complicated by the patchwork of inconsistent product liability laws from state to state across the United States.

The current state of product liability includes the concept of "strict liability," which works against the introduction of new leading-edge safety equipment. Strict liability entitles a person injured by a defective or unexpectedly dangerous product to compensation from the maker or seller of the product without having to show that the manufacturer or seller was negligent. A recent trend in vehicle product liability cases has been increased awards of punitive damages to add to the potential cost of design defects.

Recently, there have been efforts in Congress and in some state legislatures to establish a principle that vehicle manufacturer compliance with government safety standards is a valid defense to a vehicle defect claim. However, courts are continuing to rule that, regardless of federal standards, vehicle manufacturers have a duty to build a car that is as safe as is reasonably possible under the present state of mechanical technology, vehicle design, and safety. This potentially creates a situation in which vehicle manufacturers are liable if they introduce new safety technology and liable as well if they don't.

Obviously, despite these obstacles, automakers continue to develop and deliver safer cars, but this development might be accelerated if the liability environment for vehicle manufacturers was less hostile to technology innovation and more consistent from state to state.

Privacy, Enforcement, Security

Privacy of data is critical to the acceptance of new vehicle technology. Public concern is already being raised about the ability that new vehicle systems possess to allow others to track the vehicle location, trip characteristics (time, origin/destination), and driver behavior (speed, for example). There is clearly a legitimate public safety interest in enforcing traffic laws. There is at least as clear a public safety interest in saving lives. The concern is that the monitoring of personal behavior, even the *possibility* that personal behavior will be monitored, whether for routine enforcement or general snooping, will discourage the adoption and use of systems whose net result would be the saving of lives and the reduction of injuries. The assurance of personal privacy is a central public policy issue that could have an enormous impact on the speed and breadth of safety system deployment.

The Intelligent Transportation Society of America (ITS America) developed a set of privacy principles[99] for intelligent vehicle systems. These principles include the recognition of the individual's interest in privacy and in how intelligent transportation systems use the personal information they are capable of gathering. The fifth of these privacy principles states that "absent consent, government authority, or appropriate legal process, information [from intelligent transportation systems] identifying individuals will not be disclosed to law enforcement."[100]

Another principle touches on **information security**, stating that ITS applications and communications systems should make conscientious use of information security technology and processes. For the most part, the development and standardizing of information security resources is the realm of the information technology and wired and wireless communications industries. However, recognizing the importance of requiring and adopting the use of these resources in a transportation context is a matter for public policy.

Information security also helps to ensure that the information that is collected and disseminated is authentic and accurate and that it can be accessed only by people and organizations with a legitimate right to do so. Besides ensuring privacy, intelligent transportation systems must not allow hackers, criminals, or terrorists to introduce spurious information about traffic, incidents, weather, or obstacles. Allowing them to do so could result in the misdirection of vehicle systems and of public safety resources, potentially causing deaths and injuries and massive snarls in the system. Again, the technology and processes for authentication and verification will largely arise from outside the transportation industry, but the adoption and use of these resources must be made an explicit part of the way the transportation industry does business, by both the public and private sectors.

Costs and Incentives

A major potential impediment to the prompt and widespread adoption of twenty-first century vehicle technology is its cost. It makes good sense to let the marketplace work its will in its own time in areas like information and entertainment. However, the clear public interest in safety could potentially translate into incentives (tax subsidies, for example) to reduce the cost of developing and acquiring vehicle technology that will help reduce the annual loss of 43,000 lives and the estimated $230 billion annual cost to the American economy of vehicle crashes.

Data Ownership and Use

Beyond privacy and security, there is a serious question as to who owns the data produced by a vehicle (not all of which can be anonymous) and who may have access to it for what purposes. For example, developing the real-time picture of the driving environment to enable and enhance safety systems requires data from a critical mass of vehicles. Can vehicles be required to participate in delivering this data? Should they be permitted to opt out? Should they have to opt in? What data developed by the vehicle can be subpoenaed? Is real-time data different than data accumulated on an event data recorder?

Our society has put very strict limits on access to medical records, concluding that the benefits of these strict limits outweigh their disadvantages. Might this notion extend to data, created in a private automobile, that could have a positive impact on public health and safety? Resolving the data ownership and access issue is a key prerequisite to the successful widespread development and deployment of twenty-first century vehicle technology.

Industrial Policy and Antitrust

A byproduct of the liability paradox is that the development and refinement of leading-edge vehicle technology, notably but not exclusively safety-enhancing technology, has been largely spearheaded by European and Asian manufacturers. This situation is further exacerbated, to America's disadvantage, by differences in industrial policy. European and Asian industry has been far better supported by European and Asian governments in the research and development of advanced vehicle technology. Much of the advanced technology for the twenty-first century vehicle is being designed and manufactured outside the United States. Profits from the eventual sale of these products tend to go abroad, and the jobs with high intellectual and managerial content continue to move offshore. In addition, developers of these products regard the needs and interests of the U.S. market as secondary to the requirements of their home markets, further delaying and constraining their introduction in the United States.

Technology in vehicles, particularly safety technology that interacts with vehicle occupants, needs to operate consistently from automobile to automobile to avoid confusion in emergency situations where appropriate responses and fast reaction time are crucial. In addition, safety-related systems are costly to develop. These two factors combine to suggest that a relatively high level of cooperation among technology developers and vehicle manufacturers is needed for safety technology to be developed as quickly, economically, and consistently as possible. While there are already some avenues for doing this, for example through industry alliances and standards development organizations, it is good public policy to make sure that antitrust rules do not unreasonably constrain cooperative development where safety is at stake.

Allocation of Spectrum

Wireless communications is the basic fabric for connecting vehicles with landside services and the infrastructure. Some applications will use cellular technology, for which spectrum is secured through mechanisms unrelated to transportation per se. Some applications will use Dedicated Short Range Communications (DSRC) in the 5.9 GHz band fairly recently allocated by the FCC for use by ITS, mainly for public safety. However, over the next 20 years, applications and situations will inevitably arise for which neither cellular nor DSRC is a good fit. Public policy which favors the allocation of spectrum to enhance vehicle safety can be an important ingredient for success and for prompt deployment.

Differential GPS and Improved Map Databases

As discussed above, Differential GPS (DGPS) is a service that helps improve the positional accuracy derived from the GPS system. Within the next 20 years, there is near certainty that the primary customers for DGPS will be automobiles and their onboard safety systems, which will need very precise positioning capabilities. The mechanics of providing DGPS are well known, but DGPS coverage is currently spotty. Although a plan has been articulated for creating national DGPS coverage, little progress is being made.

It is not a foregone conclusion that public authorities must build, own, and operate the DGPS system – this could be a private sector opportunity, although probably regulated. However, it is an important matter of public policy to ensure that DGPS is universally available in the United States by the time vehicle safety systems need it. The timing of this assurance is equally important, so that vehicle makers can appropriately plan the introduction of onboard systems to make use of DGPS.

As also discussed above, improved vehicle positioning technology is meaningful for safety systems only if correspondingly improved digital maps of the road network are also available. Joint government-industry efforts in the United States and Europe have been exploring the requirements for map databases that are accurate and detailed enough to support and enhance preventive safety products in the twenty-first century vehicle. These efforts are also exploring the mapmaking technology needed to produce digital map databases that will meet these requirements. There is a clear public interest in having these maps available in the same timeframe as the in-vehicle safety products that need them. Indeed, the schedule for developing safety products will depend significantly on when developers believe the right map databases will be available. Public policy is needed to define the public sector role in the development of these map databases. Issues include ownership of intellectual property, appropriate areas for public funding, and the basis on which map databases are made available if their development is partially funded by the public sector.

Human Factors and Driver Behavior

The introduction of additional technology into the vehicle raises a wide range of human factor issues, even when the technology does not interact directly with vehicle occupants. For example, there is a concern that introducing safety technology could produce driver complacence and dependence, diminishing safety benefits. Where technology *does* interact with occupants, the issue is how to elicit quick, appropriate responses and how to avoid distracting the driver from the primary task of driving safely.

Underlying all of these concerns is the fact that a deep, fundamental, comprehensive understanding of driver behavior does not exist, although portions of this understanding are being pursued on many fronts. Such a comprehensive understanding could be of enormous value in designing technology for the maximum positive effect on safety. Public policy could help to encourage and help to fund the prompt and well-managed development of this understanding.

Part IV

Transportation Management

by
Richard Mudge

Chapter 10

Managing Twenty-First Century Transportation Systems

This chapter examines the role that technology might play in helping transportation agencies to better manage the nation's highway and transit network. The focus is on improvements to management, but the implications go well beyond what one conceives as day-to-day operations. The quality and quantity of information that technology can provide also offer opportunities for transport agencies to improve how they support overall economic growth and open the door to financial techniques that may also encourage economic productivity.

The ability to collect information from the vehicle also means it will be possible to provide drivers with the information they need to make more effective use of existing capacity (which mode to take, when to stay at home a bit longer, when you *must* leave for the airport, and so forth) and how to improve safety (avoid vehicles that may create a dangerous situation, or adjust for risky road conditions). This chapter does not focus on what technologies transport agencies will need within the agency in order to take full advantage of these data.

Three significant opportunities derive from the ability to know where everything is and the condition of everything, whether vehicle or infrastructure:

1. **Apply more business-like management techniques**. These data will provide DOTs and transit agencies with the real-time information they need in order to manage their system using direct measures of the quality of service their customers receive. Most private businesses already operate with this advantage. This change has implications for operations, planning, design, and even how agencies interact with some of their customers (for example, see item three below).

2. **Implement performance-based pricing**. Real-time information on the quality of service on all significant roads and transit lines could open the door to large-scale use of performance based pricing. That is, travelers can be told the travel times they can expect – and how much they will pay to receive this level of service. This approach will encourage more effective use of our limited transportation capacity. It differs in concept from most congestion pricing schemes and differs in scale from HOT lanes (although very similar in concept).
3. **Improve link with economy.** Today's economy depends on reliability and predictability – also true of course for much of our non-work travel. Real-time information on the quality of service on all roads can be a powerful economic tool for a world that behaves as if everything were part of a supply chain. Transportation agencies can now develop a different business model, one that involves an active partnership with private industry, rather than making physical improvements and then hoping that industry responds positively. By integrating travel information, predicted travel times, and a performance-based system of rewards, highway and transit services could be coordinated to match the demands of today's businesses, with business being encouraged to shift how they use the network as one way to improve its efficiency. The result would be a transportation system based on "*No Surprises.*"

Much work remains before such a comprehensive system of real-time information is available. A business case is needed, followed by dedicated funding – and at a higher level than typical of recent years. In some cases (such as expanded ITS) the public sector has a lead role, in some (such as use of traffic probes) the private sector has a clear lead, while others (such as VII or the proposed system of vehicle-infrastructure integration) require a combination of public and private activity.

Trends in Technology

The U.S. transportation network is the largest and most complex in the world. An efficient transportation system is essential for economic growth and to support an enjoyable and secure daily life. Nearly one in every eight dollars spent on goods and services in the United States economy is absorbed by transportation products and services. Yet the efficiency of our transportation system remains at risk since congestion decreases reliability. In addition, an aging infrastructure needs constant attention and re-investment.

Day-to-day management of our surface transportation system – and thus the search for solutions – is largely in the hands of the fifty state DOTs, local transport agencies, and public transit authorities. Traditional solutions, including the addition of new lanes of highway and new bus and rail facilities, will continue to add tangible value. New physical capacity alone is not enough. Indeed, many public agencies already emphasize operations approach. Technology can produce the information needed to take this new emphasis to a new level.

It is important to consider these opportunities within a broader framework.

Networks are key to economic and social progress. The average economic rate of return to private business from investment in the nation's highway network exceeds the average rate of return from private sector investments as a whole.[101] This has been true for at least the last 50 years. Of course, there is no inherent reason why similar returns should not apply to other modes including airports and mass transit.

Returns are highest during periods that experience significant new capacity addition (for example, 50-60 percent a year while we built the Interstate System) and are highest for higher level roads such as the National Highway System. Unfortunately, public spending on technology (as with ITS) has often been deliberate in its pace, thus placing the full range of potential gains at risk. Since completion of the Interstate Highway System, the nation's transportation leaders have struggled to find the next national-scale network.

Economic and location patterns have changed dramatically from when we built the Interstate Highway System – indeed they have changed from just ten to twenty years ago. We now live in an age of supply chain economics, just-in-time delivery, global competition across almost every industry, continual change in the nature and organization of industry, complex urban patterns that are rarely oriented toward a single central business district (CBD), and an economy dominated by services and high-tech manufacturing.

The peak-hour work trip may create much congestion, but it no longer dominates travel. Workforce participation has increased significantly, placing greater pressures on how we use our transportation system. Reliability is important around the clock. Examples flow more easily from the business side of life, but these effects occur in almost every aspect of our daily lives.

Technology should be viewed as an important management tool and a way to provide higher quality services for less money. There is more here than ITS and a clever way to collect user fees. Technology makes it possible to implement basic economic principles in areas where action is not typically shaped by market forces.

Relative to most other industries, transportation has been slow to adopt technology (see Figure 10-1, Phil Tarnoff's famous "Progress is Glacial" chart that shows ITS deployment growing at 2-3 percent a year). One positive aspect of this fact is that a wide array of opportunities exists to "leapfrog" this trend – the equivalent of "going vertical" on the "Progress is Glacial" chart. Examples include

- The ability to locate and track almost anything, whether by GPS or cellular tracking, with accuracy within meters
- Wireless communication that makes it possible to exchange data among vehicles and between vehicles and the highway
- An internet that allows low-cost, rapid communication worldwide

Figure 10-1: Progress Is Glacial

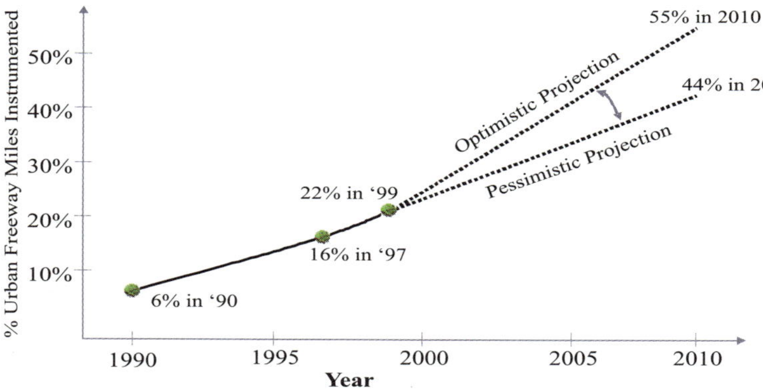

In recent years there has been a growing split in the pace of technology growth between the vehicle side (increasingly high tech) and the infrastructure side (business as usual). The number of sensors in each vehicle has grown rapidly, in part due to public demand for safety – and some believe that even more could be done as public agencies take a more active interest, perhaps including the purchase of data.[102]

A tangible sign of this change is interest in developing a VII network, or Vehicle-Infrastructure Integration (an extension of earlier concepts such as FHWA's proposed INFOstructure and ITS America's concept of the INTI). AASHTO, Automobile OEMs (original equipment manufacturers), and U.S. DOT have formed a working group to see how best to release the information available in many new cars so that the public sector might make full use of it – and of course so information could be recycled back to the driver. Many details remain to be established, including the exact technical nature of the VII, who will build it, who will operate it, and of course, who will pay for it. Not surprisingly, the exact timing for when this new network will appear is uncertain, but estimates in the five to ten-year range seem reasonable.

A key part of the VII will be its reliance on a broadband wireless network to communicate among vehicles and between vehicles and the infrastructure. This effort to integrate wireless communication with the surface transportation system represents a break from past practice – and one in keeping with the needs of a twenty-first Century transportation system. Certainly transportation and telecommunications form a logical economic partnership since both provide ways to overcome distance.

Management and Operations

Most transportation agencies now think of their business as one that relies on operations as much (maybe even more than) it does on construction. We need new measures of performance that match today's (and maybe even tomorrow's) economic structure. Ton-miles and VMT were 19th century measures of value. Cost measures have not been forgotten, but are less important in a world where reliability, predictability, and *completed trips* are what matter. This shift in value should have major implications for what we build and how we manage it. Technology can help make an effective measuring system possible, thus opening the door to a family of new management approaches. These changes, in turn, will require a new "corporate culture" within DOTs and other transport agencies.

Pure privatization has been an interesting sideshow but of limited value (except to some consultants). Our ability to apply **private-sector management principles** requires real-time, ubiquitous (beyond a few urban expressways) measures of performance that have a direct meaning for the traveling public. Speed and travel time information could fill this need, but only if they covered all roadways all the time.[103] If this were available, DOTs would have the opportunity to manage their systems with private-sector principles of accountability.

Defining the System

This chapter considers three primary frameworks: Intelligent Transportation Systems, the Vehicle Infrastructure Integration program, and traffic probes. These approaches are under development along parallel tracks. Figure 10-2 provides a very conceptual picture of the evolution for each category.

Intelligent Transportation Systems (ITS)

ITS is primarily a public-sector program. ITS aims to use advanced technologies to help accomplish the public sector's mission of improved safety, increased system capacity, reduced travel times, and improved productivity. These efforts began to mature in the late 1980s, and in 1991 Congress called for a "national system of travel support technology, smoothly coordinated among modes and jurisdictions to promote safe, expeditious, and economical movement of goods and people."[104] Adequate funding to meet this goal did not follow.

Figure 10-2

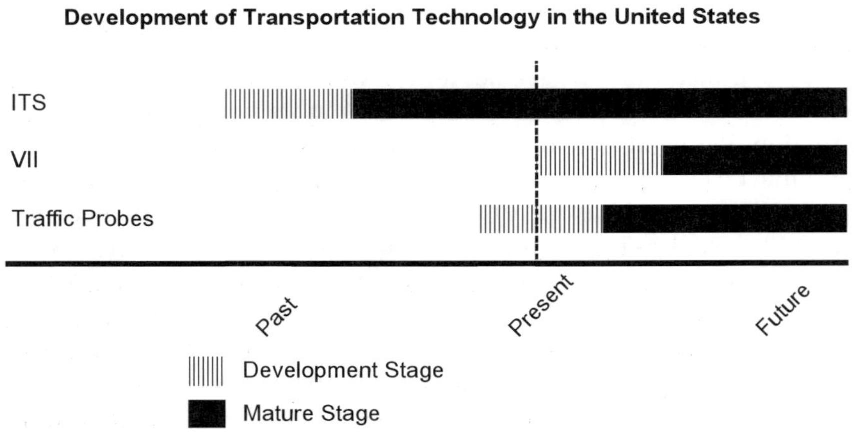

ITS technologies encompass a broad range of hardware and software. FHWA has put a significant amount of funds into research, testing, standards development, and deployment of these technologies. The private sector, however, typically provides the equipment under contract to DOTs and other public agencies. Table 10-1 shows examples of specific ITS technologies and their uses.

Although a large suite of ITS technologies exist, actual ITS deployment has been slower than expected. In 1996, Secretary of

Transportation, Federico Pena, stated, "I want 75 of our largest metropolitan areas with a complete ITS infrastructure in 10 years." By 2002, however, these 75 largest metropolitan areas had deployed only 26.8 percent of needed capital.[105] This leaves $33 billion to complete full deployment. This figure, however, assumes a very thorough system with redundancies and multiple technologies covering the same physical space.[106] As discussed below, the VII network and traffic probes could provide a more cost-effective option for parts of this system. Even so, remaining costs are likely in the $10 to $20 billion range. This is not a small sum, but one that the nation could fund over the next five to ten years if it chose to do so.

Table 10-1: Commonly Deployed ITS Technologies

Technology	Use
Loop detectors and other sensors	Monitor speeds and volumes on roadways
Variable message signs	Provide safety and traffic information to travelers
Traffic signal controllers	Adjust traffic signal timing to reflect traffic flow
Closed circuit television cameras	Traffic surveillance and incident detection
Radio frequency identification (RFID)	Collect user fees automatically

Traffic Probes

As noted in the previous chapter, traffic probe systems use vehicles or cell phones to collect data on speed and travel times on most roads and do this in near real-time.[107] These vehicle-oriented systems are sometimes referred to as Floating Car Data (FCD). Typical methods to obtain FCD include:

- Transponders such as those issued for Electronic Toll Collection – these collect travel time, but only between fixed points where readers have been installed.[108] While not "true" traffic probes since they rely on sensors, transponders differ in concept from traditional fixed sensors.
- GPS devices installed on commercial or public-sector vehicles – these then require some regular means of communication to download data.
- Cellular phones — most proposed systems apply sophisticated statistical models to analyze data already collected by wireless firms.

One important aspect of FCD is its relative low cost. The industry has proven many times that no market exists for poor-quality traffic data, but FCD systems are capable of delivering real-time traffic data that are valuable to public and private entities alike. For example, ITIS Holdings has developed a national FCD network in the United Kingdom. Their customers include automobile manufacturers (Toyota, Ford, BMW, Nissan), telecoms (Vodaphone, T-Mobile, Orange), the British Automobile Association, and the UK Ministry of Transportation.

Several firms, including ITIS, have regional tests underway in the United States, although no wide-scale deployments have yet come to fruition. AirSage has tested cell phones as traffic probes around Knoxville, TN, and Norfolk, VA. Another firm, Zipdash, uses GPS enabled phones to collect data in San Francisco. As firms such as these refine their services and establish working business models, traffic probes will become more commonplace in the United States. OnStar is rumored to have examined floating car data possibilities based on their fleet of some three million equipped vehicles.

Vehicle Infrastructure Integration (VII)

VII is a consortium that includes AASHTO, the Federal Highway Administration, and several automotive manufacturers. Its goal is to share real-time information between vehicle and infrastructure with a focus on safety implications. As of May 2004, however, few characteristics have been defined. These include timelines for the program's development and deployment, the appropriate broadband communications medium, overall business case, and a host of institutional issues and operating implications.

Nevertheless, the value of a nationwide Vehicle-Infrastructure system is understood on a conceptual basis. The applications and benefits from such a framework are far reaching. Table 10-2 illustrates a sample of the consumer-oriented applications that such a system could facilitate.

Table 10-2: Potential Applications of a Systemwide VII Type Solution

Infrastructure-to-Vehicle	Vehicle-to-Infrastructure	Vehicle-to-Vehicle
Intersection Collision	Post-Crash Warning	Vehicle-Based Road Condition Warning
In-Vehicle Signage	SOS Service	Post-Crash Warning
Road Condition Warning	Stop Sign Movement Assistance	Blind Merge Warning
Stop Sign Warning	Floating Vehicle Data	Adaptive Cruise Control
Adaptive Headlight	Intelligent On-Ramp Metering	Wrong-Way Driver Warning
Curve Speed Warning	Intelligent Traffic Lights	Blind Spot Warning
Dynamic Navigation	Electronic Toll Collection	Instant Messaging
Rail Collision	Emergency Vehicle Signal Preemption	Vehicle-Based Road Feature Notification
Low Bridge Warning	Remote Diagnostics/Repair Warning	Visibility Enhancer
Work Zone Warning	Air Quality Warning	Lane Change Assistant

The success of the VII program will hinge upon having strong support from both public and private sectors. This will require compromise and patience from both sectors since they have their own ways of working through issues and making decisions. Automobile OEMs have begun to equip vehicles with sensors that offer potential value for transportation operations and traffic management (Table 10-3). Additional guidance from the public sector (perhaps reinforced with some hard cash), would give OEMs a clearer picture of the types of sensors and technological modifications they might consider including in their vehicles.

Table 10-3: AMI-C's Sensor Penetration Forecast for 2005 Vehicles

Sensor	Penetration	Sensor	Penetration
Air Bag	100%	Rear Window Defrost	50%
Vehicle Speed	100%	Exterior Temperature	25%
Hazard Signal	75%	Sun Sensor	20%
Headlights	75%	Antilock Brake System State	20%
Brake Applied Status	50%	Rain Sensor	20%
Cruise Control Set Speed	50%	Traction Control State	20%
Fog Lamps	50%	Vehicle Location	10%
Wiper Speed	50%	Obstacle Distance	10%

A major requirement for the VII is to build and operate a broadband wireless network that covers a significant portion of the nation's highway system. The cost to build the broadband wireless infrastructure portion of such a system is relatively modest, perhaps in the range of $2 billion to $3 billion. Automobile OEMs would provide the appropriate in-vehicle equipment, and state and local transport agencies would fund the costs to analyze and use the new data. Presumably, OEMs would deploy the sensors that would best fit within their business model, although federal, state, and local agencies might appeal to OEMs to install certain additional sensors in some cases. In such a situation, government subsidies to the producer or consumer could help speed this process and ensure that services meet specific needs.

Chapter 11

Transportation Technologies and Transportation Management

You've got to think about big things while you're doing small things, so the small things go in the right direction

– Alvin Toffler

Transportation technology is typically delivered piece by piece, whether via a consumer who purchases an automobile with new equipment or a transportation agency that makes an ITS investment. Each individual consumer must assess whether the safety, convenience, security, or entertainment benefits they expect to receive will offset the price they pay for the vehicle. The transportation agency looks at each ITS investment relative to the value provided by other specific investment opportunities that it faces. These decisions can be relatively well defined.

When viewed as a system or a network, however, the potential benefits and costs change in nature and magnitude. This shift in point of view may have broad implications for how we manage and operate our transportation systems. A better understanding of these potential effects is important in helping to make decisions about potential large-scale systems such as the proposed VII. In particular, what is the overall value to public agencies, and which aspects are most useful?

This chapter reviews the possible implications that information from system-wide investments in technology might have for transportation agencies. This review covers six major DOT functions:

- Management and operations
- Planning
- Design
- Safety
- Economic linkages
- Finance

Management and Operations

Transportation systems today face two fundamental problems: one is chronic congestion, particularly in urban areas. A second is the *lack of meaningful interaction with their customers.* That is, unlike most other industries, a traveler who receives poor service (misses a meeting or has a shipment delayed, for example) has no immediate recourse with the state DOT, local transportation agency, or transit authority.

The menu of data that could come from full deployment of ITS, traffic probes (as an interim step), and the VII offer a chance to quantify and track performance in real time. The focus here is often on travel times, but the potential data cover much more, including weather conditions (exactly where and when is the roadway ready to freeze – or not freeze), accident characteristics (how severe was the accident and thus which type of emergency vehicle should respond), and early warning signals about congestion (as indicated by changes in headway between vehicles or a shift in braking patterns).

All of these open the door to performance-based management approaches, such as many private firms use as a matter of course. Movement towards this concept is consistent with the recent emphasis on operations by DOTs and transit agencies. An important difference, however, is the new ability to measure travel times and speeds across a full range of roadways and to do so in close to real-time. These measures are closer to performance measures of direct value to travelers. Publishing these data on a regular (maybe even real-time) basis may serve to help focus day-to-day management on measures of quality as perceived by the average citizen. Most private firms already have such information and use it as part of how they manage their businesses. There can be an important feedback with customers as well if they know that "the owner" is aware of the quality of the service they receive.

In-vehicle sensors also have the potential to collect data for asset management. It is possible to equip vehicles with sensors that measure pavement conditions, for example. These data could then be incorporated into pavement management systems. One obvious advantage is that these data would be collected continuously.

Asset management is "a systematic process of maintaining, upgrading, and operating physical assets cost effectively."[109] The ability of asset management to live up to its potential requires accurate and timely information on the condition and location of the assets. Technology can help in a number of ways. For example, roadway sign asset management has traditionally been conducted manually with visual observation by employees. Sensors and GPS technology, however, make it possible to monitor roadway sign inventories in close to real time. This method is more timely and more efficient.

Additionally, with better data, transportation agencies will be able to devise better performance measures and metrics of cost efficiency in relation to their assets. Ideally, asset management should form a multi-disciplinary approach incorporating engineering, economics, and business practices. Asset management then becomes an important component of the planning process.

Transportation Planning

Technologies such as adaptive cruise control and dynamic navigation enable drivers to use the road differently, leading to new traffic characteristics. This will affect capacity utilization, effective levels of service, trip choice, and other factors. As these realities change, transportation planning must also change in order to capture them.

For instance, many of the assumptions that form the basis of travel demand and planning models are likely to become obsolete as technology changes driver behavior. Consider the traditional four-step planning process of forecasting trip generation, trip distribution, mode split, and trip assignment. New technologies may change characteristics within each of these steps.

New technologies such as adaptive cruise control (ACC) and lane departure monitors may have big impacts on effective highway capacity. Recent research suggests that autonomous adaptive cruise control (AACC)[110] has the potential to significantly increase highway capacity. The findings of this research suggest that the way ACC technology is used is crucial to the impact of this technology.

Figure 11-1 shows vehicle throughput on the vertical axis and the percentage of vehicles equipped with ACC on the horizontal axis. The plotted lines represent overall capacity based upon the headways between vehicles (i.e., the time it would take for a following vehicle to reach the rear of the vehicle traveling in front of it). With no ACC present, vehicle throughput is around 2,100 vehicles per hour. When ACC is introduced and calibrated to maintain a one second headway (the top line plotted) potential vehicle throughput increases, even with only 20 percent of vehicles equipped with ACC. As the percentage of vehicles equipped with ACC increases, capacity increases further, reaching 2,700 vehicles per hour or about 30 percent more than the base. If the ACC is set for longer headways, however, the opposite happens. The bottom line illustrates the case with headways set at two seconds. In this scenario capacity decreases as more vehicles equipped with ACC are added to the road. This example shows that *how* a technology is used is at least as important as *that* a technology is used.

Figure 11-1

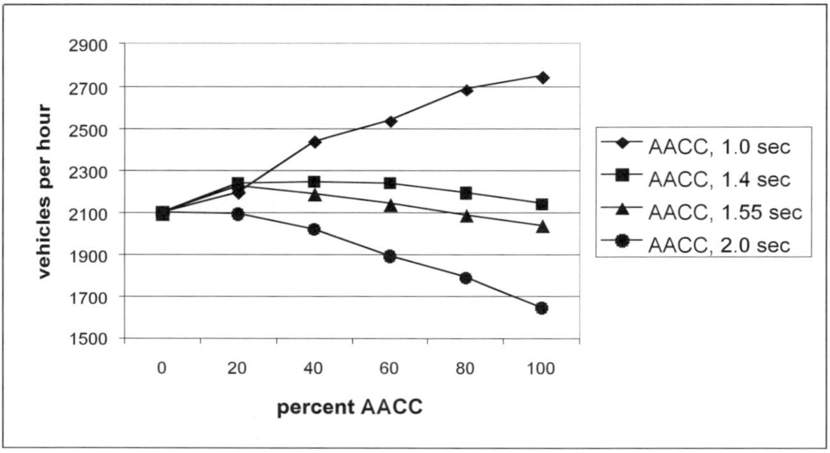

Source: Evaluation of the Effects of Adaptive Cruise Control Systems on Highway Traffic Flow Capacity and Implications for Deployment of Future Automated Systems; Kourjanskaia, Natalia; Miller, Mark A.; Shladover, Steven E.; VanderWerf, Joel; California PATH Program; 2003

Technologies such as ACC assist the driver in making decisions or may even make decisions for the driver. This has implications beyond capacity utilization. Models that incorporate assumptions about driver behavior may need to be recalibrated as these technologies begin to be deployed in large numbers.

Technologies can also provide new data to help improve planning. In particular, much of these data will be available in close to real-time, making it easier to track rapid changes in the location of business and individuals and shifts in travel patterns. Much of the necessary data will be provided as a by-product of other purposes, and thus should be available at modest cost.

Highway Design

New in-vehicle technologies also have implications for the design of roads, much in the same way as they do for planning. For example, if adaptive cruise control allows drivers to reduce headways and still operate safely, there will be significant implications for the effective capacity of highways and perhaps for their design. An important variable here is the pace with which such devices move into the marketplace and the fraction of vehicles that need to be equipped before a noticeable effect can be seen. But, since planning and design both look to future requirements, we need not wait to see the effect before reacting.[111]

One instance where this has been explored is the design of truck-only lanes. The design of truck-only lanes typically necessitates two lanes since an accident in a single lane could cause a significant and costly backup. Due to limited space, constructing truck-only lanes to these specifications on SR-60 in Los Angeles County was estimated to cost approximately $4.3 billion. Much of this high cost resulted from design constraints where SR-60 interferes with the truck lanes. The use of automated truck lanes would reduce the initial capital costs to $1.4 billion. These automated truck lanes would only require one lane since they automate all aspects of driving the vehicle while on the facility.[112]

Assumptions regarding driver behavior are of critical importance in highway design. Engineers strive to design a road that is both safe and offers the best mobility possible. These two interests are often in conflict, and roads designed for higher speeds require lower grades, wider shoulders, more gradual curves, and greater lines of sight in order to meet safety standards. Designers are also constrained by land characteristics and available funds. Highways designed for travel at higher speeds generally use more land and require acreage that allows the creation of long, straight paths. New transportation technologies, however, may make it possible to ease design constraints by allowing vehicles to navigate points safely that would be considered design exceptions. Table 11-1 illustrates some conventional tools and strategies for dealing with design exceptions and compares them to various technological solutions.

Vision enhancement devices, for example, allow users to see the road in different ways, identifying and illuminating signs and other objects and even allowing drivers to "see" through inclement weather and around curves. Although still being defined, these technologies could have major impacts on geometry and other aspects of the roadway.

Economic Links

Today's economy is dominated by services and light manufacturing. This means that the movement of people and goods has high value and that timely arrivals and departures are more important than a generation ago when we measured success in terms of ton-miles or vehicle miles. Part of this concept is captured in the phrase "supply chain logistics," but the implications go beyond the reliable movement of goods worldwide. The ability to attract a skilled and cost-effective labor force faces some of the same problems as a supply chain system.

Table 11-1: Technological and Conventional Tools for Mitigating the Potential Safety Risk from Design Exceptions[113]

Design Exception	Conventional Mitigation Tool	Technology Tool
Narrow Lanes or Shoulders	• Pavement edge lines • Raised reflective markers • Delineators • Shoulder rumble strips • Centerline rumble strips	Lane departure warning system
Steep Sideslopes, Roadside Obstacles	• Roadside object markers • Slope flattening • Rounded ditches • Obstacle removal • Breakaway safety hardware • Guardrail or crash cushions	• Driver vision enhancement • Lane Departure System • Dynamic Navigation System
Narrow Bridge	• Approach guardrail • Pavement edge lines • Warning signs and/or object markers	• Collision avoidance system • Vision Enhancement
Limited Sign Distance at Crest of Vertical Curve	• Advance warning signs • Obstacle removal • Shoulder widening • Driveway or intersection relocation	• Adaptive Cruise Control • Vision Enhancement
Sharp Horizontal Curve	• Advance warning signs • Shoulder widening and/or paving • Improved superelevation • Transverse rumble strips or pavement markings • Slope flattening • Pavement and anti-skid treatment • Guardrail or crash cushions	• Adaptive Cruise Control • Lane Departure System • In-Vehicle Navigation
Hazardous Intersection	• Upgrade intersection traffic control • Warning signs • Street lighting • Pavement anti-skid treatment • Sight distance improvements	• Collision avoidance system • Adaptive Cruise Control • Vision Enhancement

The ability to collect real-time performance information on all roadss — and the parallel ability to make short-term forecasts of travel times — opens the door to new ways for DOTs to work directly with business. An active sharing of information on system performance, including actions by the public sector that could affect that performance, may make it possible to work with major shippers on when they move goods or schedule shifts. Such active management would work best if there were reliable measures of travel times so that performance could be tracked.

Combining financial incentives with performance measures would help – at what point is it more cost-effective for a DOT to reduce registration fees (or simply write a check) for businesses that schedule movements to maximize the effective capacity of the system. Of course, this is easier said than done – witness the problems the Ports of LA and Long Beach have had in encouraging container traffic to shift to off-hours when plenty of highway capacity exists.

Highway Finance

The technology exists to implement variable roadway pricing, with charges based on where and when one travels. The policy implications of this concept are explored in detail in the final section of this book.

Highway Safety

Safety is often cited as the number one priority for federal, state, and local transportation agencies. Technology, in the form of ITS, is a tool that has been used for a number of years to make the nation's roads safer. In-vehicle technologies and infrastructure-vehicle communication have the potential for even greater safety benefits.

Already, there are a number of in-vehicle technologies available in the marketplace (or coming soon) that make driving safer. Many of these will be installed in vehicles based on consumer demand, as noted in chapters 7 and 8 of this book.

The public sector can work with these features and add additional safety values by installing compatible infrastructure. The type of infrastructure installed will likely vary from location to location, although most will depend on effective means of communication between vehicle and roadway. Road intersections are one logical choice and are a major focus of FHWA's vision for the VII. The public sector can install infrastructure that alerts drivers to the presence and location of other drivers, helping coordinate the safe flow of traffic.

The public sector could also significantly reduce accidents and injuries from accidents through in-vehicle technologies providing that there is the political will to do so. For instance, the government could mandate the OEMs build into cars devices that render a vehicle inoperable if the driver is intoxicated.

Next Steps in Transportation Management

The result of technological applications in transportation is not clearly defined. Although a national program exists, it often seems to be carried out in a disjointed fashion. It is unclear whether improvements in one corner of the nation have anything to do with what is going on elsewhere.

New technologies in combination with a new interest in a national perspective can help to speed deployment of transportation-related technologies and do so in a way that allows both public and private entities to take full advantage.

While many details will vary, three primary characteristics appear essential for a future system that can create a "virtuous cycle" of productivity growth similar to the successes of past generations:

1. *National Scale* – Although discrete technological deployments are usually beneficial, a systemwide deployment should generate much higher returns and benefits. This is analogous to the Interstate Highway System or the internet. A system also supports economic stimulus from economies of scale and the seamless use of standard technical components.
2. *Assured Finances* – A future system should have an assured financial mechanism. This need not be as grand as the Highway Trust Fund, of course, but a well-defined and reliable source of funds provides the assurance that private and public entities need in order to make ambitious changes. While almost anything planners may dream up is possible (as long as it conforms to the laws of physics), as a society we prefer options where scarce resources are spent in the most effective way. This aspect may be the difference between a nationwide Automated Highway System requiring huge amounts of capital and maintenance and a system that emphasizes a more commercial approach.
3. *Rapid Deployment* – Resources will be used more efficiently and cost effectively if they bring a system to deployment rapidly. There is a close linkage here with an assured source of funding.

Define Broadband Wireless Network

A key to the success of VII is an effective means of communication between the vehicle and the infrastructure and among vehicles. This should be:

- Near universal – 10 percent of highway miles account for 80-90 percent of vehicle miles traveled, so we need not cover everything
- Continuous – once on the road, gaps are undesirable
- Always on – no waiting for the network to be ready
- Low-cost – at least very low marginal cost once the network is in place
- Non-prescriptive – that is, easy for suppliers and other firms to adapt to the technology (the internet and the interstate offer good examples)

A group of wireless technologies are candidates to meet these needs, including: DSRC; 802.11 a, b, g, (WiFi, WiMAX, Mobile-Fi); Digital Cellular/PCS/2.5-3G; Ultra Wideband; and Infrared.

In all likelihood, these communications technologies would work together in some combination. As with any national infrastructure project, significant engineering details need to be solved. Depending on the technology selected, using highways as the backbone could support adjacent non-mobile business activity.

Define Roles for Public and Private Partners

Who does what in a new public-private partnership? What are the characteristics of such a partnership for a transportation communications system and what roles will the public and private partners play? Although important institutional roles remain undefined:

The public sector could provide:

- Access to rights of way across the country. Shared resource deals show that barter works better than cash, with DOTs receiving communication services and access to floating car data.
- Access to power. Urban areas and rural interchanges have light poles and traffic lights which offer power and places to locate communications equipment.
- Access to backhaul telecommunications – at least where fiber optics are in place
- Soft loans. TIFIA is an option and many states have their own State Infrastructure Banks. Their basic structure makes these tools attractive for businesses with unproven markets.
- A customer – DOTs need traffic information that only vehicle probes can provide

The private sector could:

- Provide technical knowledge
- Construct and operate the network
- Fill in places not covered by the backbone
- Market commercial services
- Provide part of the capital, including repayment of public loans

Public-private partnerships of this scale do not happen automatically. Usually, one partner takes a lead role. In the case of the Interstate Highway system, this was the federal government; for transcontinental railroads, it was the private sector. Given the technology involved, an integrated national wireless network probably requires leadership by the private sector. Speed argues for a small number of firms rather than a consortium. An active public sector role is required as well. Given the important role played by access to highway rights of way, AASHTO is a necessary partner.

Create a Corporate Culture

The changes discussed here imply a more business-like management style for many transportation agencies. Managers will now be held accountable for changes in travel times and related performance – response time to incidents, for example. The concept of showing the public data on how well the highway and transit system performs is new. Private firms do this, but not more often than quarterly.

The pace of technology change is faster than the normal pace at which we change transportation policies and investments. Success will require finding more than a few advocates for change within the DOT.

Resolve Policy Issues

Government policies greatly affect both the kinds of vehicles and transportation management systems that will be viable and available. A matter of critical importance is to answer the policy challenges noted in chapter 9 of this book.

Part V

The Future of Transportation

by
Jeffrey A. Parker and
Tom Warne

Chapter 12

Issues Driving the Future of Public Transportation

The Underlying Resource Question

For a financial consultant to the public transport industry, the answer to the question, "What is the greatest variable affecting the future of public transit?" is obvious: funding levels. No doubt, the same can be said for highway programs, the exploration of outer space, education, job training, and national defense.

However, the case for increased capital investment in public transportation and greater resources for operating support is bound in a conundrum of cause and effect. Passengers cannot ride systems that do not exist, are partially built, are overcrowded, or operate in a state of disrepair.

To the extent that greater investment is made in fixed guideway facilities and improved bus services, the attractiveness of public transportation as an option for mobility increases. Networks must achieve a critical mass of geographic coverage, service frequency, and quality to satisfy customer expectations. Therefore, there is a dynamic quality to public transportation investment – the more robust public transit networks become, the greater their utilization.

Heavy Rail

Every day, cities with established transit networks like New York, Chicago, Boston, Philadelphia, Pittsburgh, and Cleveland prove the ability of public transit to address high proportions of total travel demand within traditional urban cores. This example has been replicated in cities like Atlanta, San Francisco, and Washington D.C., where investments in high capacity transit systems have resulted in the attainment of significant market shares for transit along corridors served by fixed guideway networks. It is notable that gains for public transport have occurred even in regions with multi-nucleated urban cores.

However, these successes have yielded new needs – capacity constraints that limit future patronage growth. For example, capacity constraints in New York City alone have triggered over $20 billion of planned programming for the East Side Access, Second Avenue Subway, and Number 7 Extension projects, with additional investment totaling more than $10 billion for direct access to John F. Kennedy International Airport from Lower Manhattan, commuter rail upgrades to NJTransit under the Access to the Region's Core Project, and the package of station and intermodal improvements being made as part of the reconstruction of Lower Manhattan. Similar and costly-to-resolve capacity and intermodal constraints exist in the Bay Area, Chicago's regional commuter rail network, Washington DC, and other major cities. In Washington DC, capacity constraints and state of good repair shortfalls have triggered a $1.5-billion, "Mobility Matters" initiative that includes expansion of bus services, acquisition of 120 railcars, construction of supporting facilities, homeland security measures, and modernization of 30-year old infrastructure.

Light Rail

Cities like Portland, OR, Dallas, San Diego, Denver, Salt Lake City, Miami, St. Louis, Sacramento, Los Angeles, Memphis, Pasadena, and San Jose have demonstrated that fixed guideway investment can achieve similar results in the context of smaller, less dense central core areas and, in most cases, using smaller-scale rail systems. In almost all these examples, investments have been funded in large measure by voter-backed initiatives that may also require super-majorities for approval.

Transit investments are defining future density patterns in these "new" cities, and triggering economic spin-offs by minimizing land requirements for roadways and parking to accommodate growth. Such successes are underscored by the initiation of extensions in almost all the cases noted above, as well as additional fixed guideway initiatives in high-growth regions such as Houston, Minneapolis, Seattle, Phoenix, Charlotte, the Research Triangle, and Las Vegas. The latter projects are either currently in construction or have received endorsements to move forward in the President's FY 2005 budget. Again, voter-backed initiatives are underwriting the majority of construction and long term operating costs of these projects. The fixed guideway expansions also are accompanied by significant changes in zoning and land use planning to maximize their transportation and urban development benefits – a notable accomplishment in locales with heavy auto dependency.

Commuter Rail

The rapid expansion of commuter rail services in Washington, D.C. (Maryland and Virginia), New Jersey, Miami/South Florida, Seattle, Los Angeles, Dallas/Fort Worth, Boston, San Francisco, San Diego, San Jose, and Chicago demonstrate the potential of public transportation to serve broadly dispersed regions, particularly when regional and local transit systems are linked conveniently.

Bus Rapid Transit

Increasing attention to bus rapid transit (BRT) technologies is allowing higher service levels to be offered at relatively modest cost in areas as diverse as Phoenix, Los Angeles, Houston, Dallas, Charlotte, Kansas City, Minneapolis, New York, Orlando, Portland, OR, San Diego, San Jose, Seattle, and Washington, D.C. These investments are yielding higher ridership, faster travel times, and greater public transit productivity, while offering innovative opportunities to share investment costs with highway agencies. These services also incorporate rapidly developing technologies for signal prioritization, vehicle location, and customer information systems.

Rural and Alternative Transit Strategies

In rural areas, the expansion of demand response and route deviation services is facilitated by the application of new technologies in dispatching and vehicle location, making public transportation an increasingly relevant and affordable option even in non-traditional settings. Folding paratransit services and vanpool/carpool services under the public transit umbrella further expands the reach of public transportation in urban, suburban and rural areas, creating interesting models for "mobility management" experimentation. In jurisdictions like San Diego, Houston, Orange County, CA, and New York/New Jersey, toll agencies have partnered with public transportation and carpooling initiatives to offer multi-modal travel and financing options on high occupancy vehicle facilities that foreshadow future modal integration.

Investment Required

Thus, the conundrum remains: the promise of public transportation in the future is dependent upon investments made today for new systems, expanding the capacity of existing systems, providing for homeland security measures, and underwriting the costs of maintaining a state of good repair.

The background factors identified earlier in this book tend to suggest that there will be future growth in demand for public transportation and indicate the need for modal balance in national transportation investment:

- An aging domestic population
- Generally favorable economic outlook
- Trip requirements increasing at faster rates than available road capacity
- Increased population concentration in urban and suburban areas
- Continued high levels of immigration
- Likelihood of higher fuel prices over time and potential spot shortages
- Increased efficiency in the rail freight industry freeing rights of way for alternative use
- Growing use of open road user fee collection technologies for new highway capacity that also support transit and HOV use
- Central cities becoming special event venues that impose surge requirements best met by mass transit
- Greater recognition of transport infrastructure costs in land use decisions
- Increased attention to homeland security requirements that necessitate balanced investment policies in order to achieve transportation system redundancies, provide strategically located intermodal crossover points, and create the capability to evacuate large numbers of people from concentrated areas.

Will U.S. public transit systems have the resources to meet the challenges posed by these factors driving future service needs? The answer is uncertain.

Considerable progress has been made under ISTEA and TEA-21 in reducing the transit industry's backlog of deferred maintenance and achieving a state of good repair. These gains have resulted from higher levels of federal funding and the even greater levels of non-federal matching commitments they have leveraged. (See following section for trends in non-federal match.)

Ramping up outlays over the next six years to accelerate attainment of a state of good repair and expand the national transit network does not appear to be likely. At issue to a greater extent than the debate over "needs" are fundamental policy differences over how to fund spending increases during a period of resistance to new taxes and large federal budget deficits.

As discussed in the next section, federal grants are the foundation for capital funding for mass transit in the United States. Locally enacted dedicated tax measures, primarily sales taxes, now generate about as much revenue for public transportation as federal aid. The leveraging incentives offered by federal funding have accelerated the trend toward increased non-federal support by encouraging public backing for ballot measures.

The current national debate over how to fund transportation will affect the public transit industry across two broad dimensions. The first dimension is the most pressing because it bears directly on the near term – the next 10 to 15 years: *Will public transportation receive adequate resources to provide the level of service necessary to achieve a balanced, multi-modal transport network across the United States?*

The second dimension is longer-term, perhaps 15 to 20 years off, because it entails the development of new technologies, turnover of the vehicle inventory in the United States, and profound change in public opinion: *Will the mix of funding strategies used to support transport investment evolve toward market-based mechanisms that allow market pricing to help balance supply and demand for transportation services?*

If the near-term outcome of the resource debate is a growth scenario, the transit industry will be well-positioned by 2010 to incorporate new business models and organizational strategies: stronger federal funding commitments will attract even higher levels of non-federal matching revenues, accelerated investment levels will increase the market for new technologies, innovative ideas will be tested, incentives will be available to broaden applications of "best practices," and enough "new money" will be flowing through the system to permit the negotiation of gains-sharing arrangements needed to advance institutional changes. Increased opportunity for the private sector in public transportation also is facilitated in an expansion environment because existing jobs are not threatened and there is less resistance to change when new systems are involved.

A scarcity of resources over the next six years would reduce prospects for investment and incentives to grow non-federal funding commitments, shrink potential demand for new technologies, increase resistance to new business models, and eliminate the incentives required to promote new ideas and encourage "best practices." Interest groups that define the institutional structure of public transportation will be forced to retrench in order to protect jobs and preserve benefits in the face of static or declining (relative to inflation) resource levels.

Most importantly, the transit industry's ability to serve growing markets will be limited and its physical assets will deteriorate, reducing the quality of existing services and ultimately raising public safety concerns. Unable to keep up with demand or retain existing customers, the decline of public transportation caused by funding shortfalls in the coming years will exacerbate road congestion, lost productivity, freight movement inefficiencies, and erosion of highway safety.

How much money will be required to sustain a competitive public transportation industry and position it for a positive future?

The U.S. Department of Transportation's (USDOT) *2002 Conditions and Performance Report* indicated that an average of roughly $22 billion ($2004) per year in public transportation investment over a 20-year period would be needed in order to improve the condition of the existing asset base and initiate sufficient capital programming to alleviate crowding, accommodate limited ridership growth, and increase average vehicle speeds.[114] In addition, homeland security considerations have resulted in over $6 billion in additional funding requirements for public transportation, according to the American Public Transit Association, that are not included in these estimates.[115]

By comparison, current annual investment levels from federal and non-federal sources are in the range of $10 billion per year – roughly one-half the amount required to achieve modest gains according to the parameters established by USDOT.

The American Association of State Highway and Transportation Officials (AASHTO) also conducted an independent condition and performance assessment in 2002 that used an adjusted baseline condition and a level of patronage growth that is more in line with recent trends to anticipate investment needs under improved service levels.[116] The result was an annualized level of investment that doubled the Federal Transit Administration's (FTA) *2002 Conditions and Performance Report* assessment without accounting for Homeland Security funding requirements. The comparison between the USDOT and the AASHTO funding needs forecasts is shown in Table 12-1 and is projected for the next five years through 2009 in Table 12-2.

Based upon this range of outcomes, the American Public Transportation Association (APTA) adopted a comprehensive recommendation for reauthorization of federal transportation legislation that called for federal funding levels totaling $65.7 billion between Federal FY 2004 – 2009, as indicated in Table 12-2.[117]

Assuming that trends discussed in the next section regarding non-federal capital matching shares continue, the APTA proposal would yield a total investment program (federal funding plus non-federal match) slightly higher than the FTA *2002 Condition and Performance Report* level shown in Table 12-2.

Table 12-1: Average Annual Transit Investment Requirements 2001 – 2020 *(billions)*

Annual Average Costs					
		2000$	2004$	2000$	2004$
Conditions	Performance	USDOT		AASHTO	
Maintain	Maintain	$14.8	$16.0	$18.9	$20.5
Improve	Maintain	$16.0	$17.3		
Maintain	Improve	$19.5	$21.1		
Improve	Improve	$20.6	$22.3	$43.9	$47.5

Inflated at 2.0% per year

Table 12-2: Forecast Capital Outlays to Improve Assets and Provide for Expansion *(billions)*

	2004	2005	2006	2007	2008	2009	Total
USDOT 2002 C&P	$22.3	$22.7	$23.2	$23.7	$24.1	$24.6	**$140.7**
AASHTO Bottom Line	$47.5	$48.5	$49.4	$50.4	$51.4	$52.5	**$299.8**
APTA Reauthorization Proposal	*$8.1*	*$9.1*	*$10.2*	*$11.4*	*$12.7*	*$14.3*	**$65.7**

Inflated at 2.0% per year

Linking the level of investment in public transportation to the amount required to bring the current asset base to a state of good repair and provide sufficient expansion to meet the demand for public transportation in urban, suburban, and rural communities based upon ridership trends over the prior five to ten years represents a quantifiable, objective goal for assessing investment need.

This concept parallels a proposal made by the American Road and Transportation Builders Association (ARTBA)[118] that would create a performance goal for federal surface transportation programs at a level of investment that at least maintains current physical and structural conditions, maintains or improves safety, and maintains traffic congestion and mobility conditions.

Experience under TEA-21 has demonstrated that the level of federal funding is only part of the resource equation. Under TEA-21's unique "firewalls," public transportation and highway agencies were able to leverage multi-year funding commitments to finance large capital projects. The "firewall" concept is explained in the box below. This feature of the federal statute has allowed public transportation agencies and state departments of transportation to borrow against future federal funding to accelerate the delivery of needed infrastructure, as well as to address the inherently "lumpy" nature of state of good repair projects.

Transit agencies in San Francisco, New Jersey, Chicago, and Denver have borrowed against federal Full Funding Grant Agreements to accelerate construction of New Start fixed guideway projects, while New Jersey Transit and states such as Virginia, Colorado, Arkansas, Arizona, New Mexico, Massachusetts, Ohio, Michigan, and Mississippi have issued over $5 billion of bonds backed by future formula funding provided under the federal transit and highway programs in order to expedite needed capital investment.

The statutory funding guarantees also reinforce the concept that the federal fuel tax is in fact a user fee that is being dedicated to highway and mass transportation programs. Since "guaranteed" dollars are more valuable than dollars subject to annual appropriation, building the "firewalls" into the future of surface transportation funding will be important to preserving this stream of non-cash benefits.

What Are the TEA 21 Funding Guarantees?

Funds for the federal transit and highway programs are *authorized* by Congress for five or six year periods. Annual appropriations are then required to make the authorized funds available. Prior to TEA 21 it was not possible to anticipate how much of the authorized funding levels would actually be *appropriated* each year. The significance of TEA 21 is that it authorized $41 billion for transit programs between FY 1998 and FY 2003 *and* established a "funding guarantee mechanism" that assured a minimum of $36 billion would be appropriated.

The $36 billion was divided annually and allocated to individual transit programs. For formula grants such as Section 5307 Urbanized Area, Section 5311 Non-Urbanized Area, and Section 5309 Fixed Guideway Modernization, the annual guaranteed amounts allowed individual transit agencies to plan their future capital programs with an unprecedented amount of certainty.

How does the guarantee mechanism work in practice? Uniquely, Title VII of TEA 21 provides "offsets" in discretionary spending, which mean that the guaranteed annual levels are already "paid for" under congressional budgetary rules.

Each year since enactment of TEA 21, Congress has honored the funding guarantees. This study shows just how important funding guarantees have been in providing safe, reliable and high-quality public transportation services that help communities increase accessibility, improve highway performance, upgrade air quality and enhance urban and rural environments.

Source: TEA 21 – A Summary of Transit-Related Provisions, APTA

Chapter 13

Funding Strategies for Twenty-First Century Transit

Sources of Funding

Stable, reliable federal funding in recent years is attracting even higher levels of stable, reliable non-federal funding, largely in the form of dedicated sales taxes at the local level.[119] These trends are likely to prevail for the next six years. Beyond 2010, new strategies may need to be explored in order to supplement the current array of funding options due to flattening fuel tax yields. The details of existing and future funding sources are reviewed in chapters 1 and 2 of this book.

Public transportation in the United States is supported by four revenue sources (see figure 13-1)–federal funds (about 17 percent), state funds (about 18 percent), local funds (about 33 percent), and system-generated income such as fares, concessions, advertising, and real estate development (about 32 percent).[120]

Figure 13-1: All Sources of Transit System Revenue – 2000

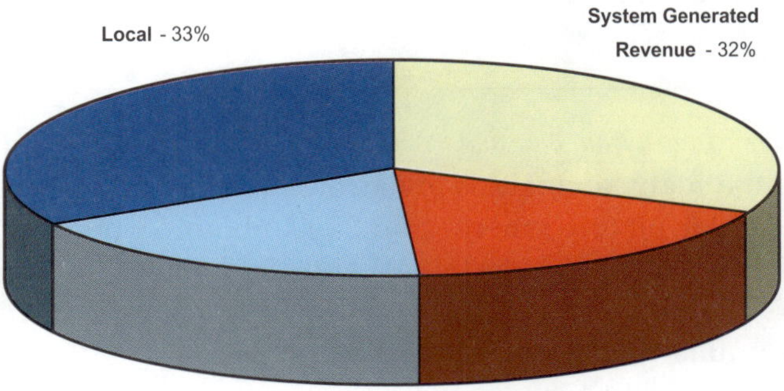

Source: National Transit Data Base

The current distribution of transit funding between federal, state, and local governments was not always the case. Federal funds comprised 43 percent of public grants to mass transit systems in the early 1980s when about $8.5 billion in external support was provided. By 2000, the level of subsidies to the nation's transit systems had grown to $21 billion, but the federal share had declined to 25 percent.

Figure 13-2 illustrates the historic trend in funding for public transportation from federal and non-federal sources. The data demonstrates that federal grants for public transit have been matched to an increasing extent by state and local revenues.

Figure 13-2: Federal and Non-Federal Funding for Public Transportation ***(millions of year-of-expenditure dollars)***

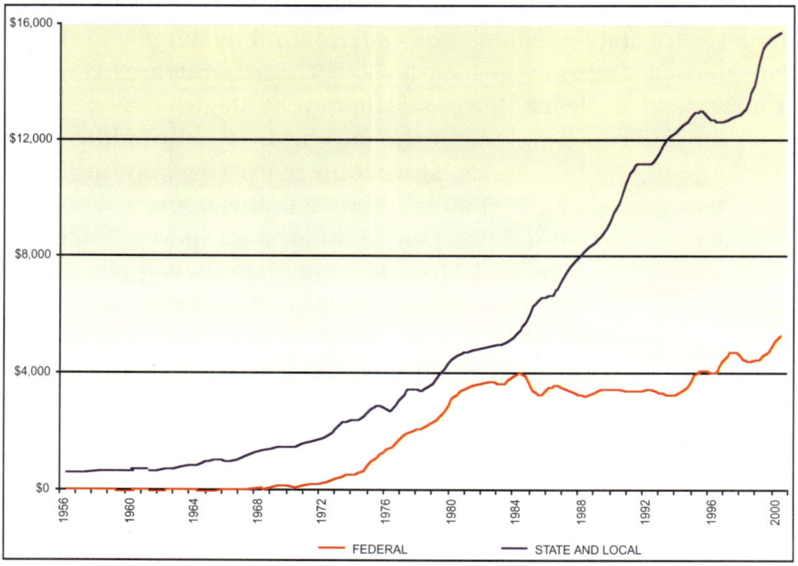

Source: National Transit Data Base and FY 2003 Federal Budget

When the focus of analysis is narrowed to capital investment programs, a similar picture emerges. In 2000, about 31 percent of transit outlays were for capital investment, and the balance were applied to operations. Federal grants represented over 58 percent of capital revenues for public transportation in 1990; however, by 2000 the federal share had declined to 47 percent.

Between 1990 and 2000, the FTA has estimated that federal capital funding for public transportation grew at an average annual rate of 5.0 percent.

Over the same time period state funding increased by an annual average of 4.2 percent, while local contributions climbed by 11.7 percent per year.

Figure 13-3 confirms that the rapid increase in federal support for capital investment in the transit industry has been more than matched by non-federal revenues – local revenues have increased their share of capital funding from about 28 percent in 1990, or about $1.25 billion, to 42 percent, or $3.8 billion in 2000.

Figure 13-3: Funding Shares for Transit Capital Investment

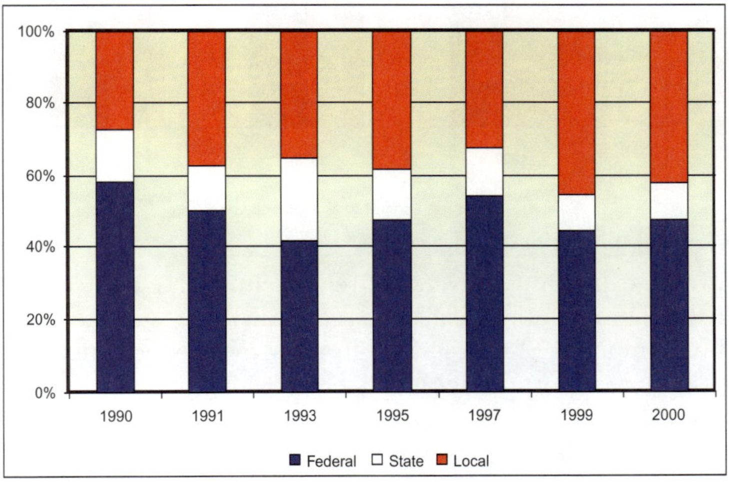

Source: National Transit Data Base

For data covering the TEA-21 authorization period between 1997 and 2000, local funding for public transit capital programs jumped from $2.5 billion to over $3.8 billion, while federal commitments increased about $137 million and state outlays were virtually unchanged. The net results of these shifts are shown in Figure 13-4.

Perhaps most importantly, these trends are unlikely to change because the bulk of local revenues are derived from dedicated sources. Sales taxes alone represented over 40 percent of local funding for public transit in 2000. Dedicated sales taxes for transit generated $4.8 billion in 2000, compared to total federal support of $5.3 billion.[121] Subsequent successful sales tax and bonding referenda in communities such as Miami, Dallas, Phoenix, and Houston have increased the number of regions with dedicated sales taxes for public transportation and raised the leveraging potential of these revenue streams to generate capital investment in the near-term.

Figure 13-4: Transit Capital Commitments since TEA 21
(millions of year-of-expenditure dollars)

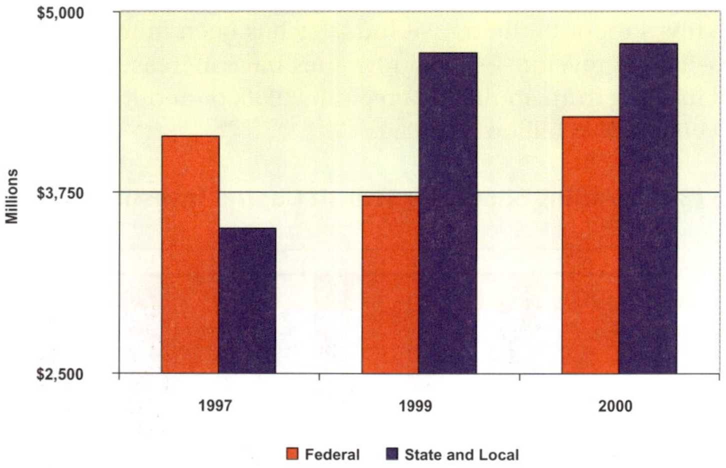

Source: National Transit Data Base

With the expanding universe of regions imposing dedicated transit sales taxes demonstrating year-over-year growth rates in excess of inflation, the dominance of non-federal funding over federal fuel tax-based appropriations/apportionments is likely to widen over time.

Even as federal appropriations for public transportation increased under ISTEA and TEA-21, the federal share of all public transportation outlays has *declined* from 43 to 25 percent over the past 20 years. While federal support grew almost 60 percent in year-of-expenditure dollars over the past two decades, state and local support for transit operations and capital investment has grown *240 percent*. Figure 13-5 summarizes this discussion by taking snapshots of total federal and non-federal transit funding levels at the start of each decade since 1960.

The ability of stable, reliable federal funding to leverage even larger increases in matching grants is one of the true success stories of TEA-21 and validates the notion that a growing federal transportation program is a critical incentive to overall investment in public transit.

How can federal support for public transportation be increased in the near-term? Relative to international experience, there is significant "head room" for growth in federal motor fuel taxes in the United States. Although alternative fuels and increased fleet efficiency are expected to erode yields from motor fuel taxes over time, the current levels of state and local levies are well below international benchmarks.[122]

Figure 13-5: Funding Levels for Public Transportation
(millions of year-of-expenditure dollars)

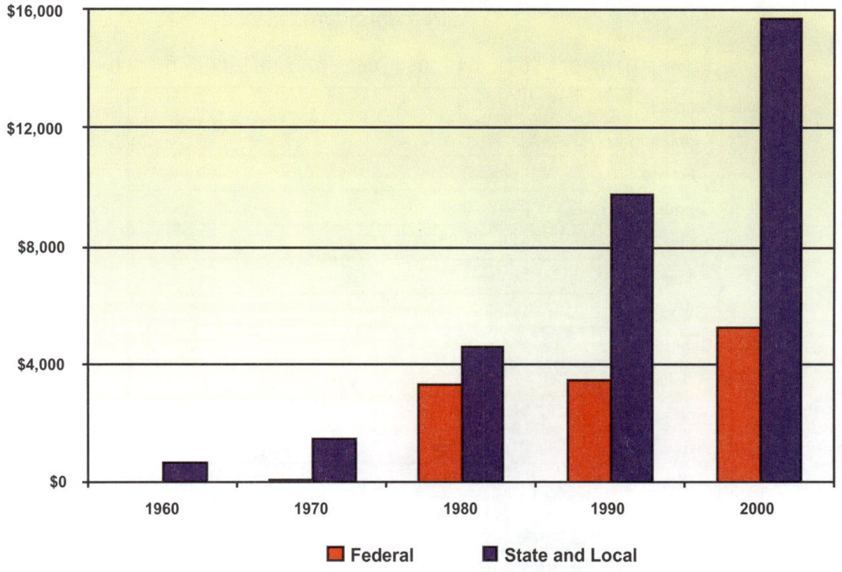

Source: National Transit Data Base

Table 13-1 shows that the proportion of retail motor fuel prices for unleaded gasoline comprised of taxes (about 25%) is lower in the United States than any of the countries listed, other than Mexico. The next lowest proportion of motor fuel taxes is found in Canada at 42%, with eight major nations taxing motor fuels at 70% or more of retail prices (Denmark, Sweden, Turkey, Netherlands, Germany, France, Finland, and United Kingdom). A similar condition prevails with regard to diesel fuels, which tend to be more prevalent for auto use in other countries.[123]

Table 13-2 demonstrates that not only is the proportion of retail prices attributable to taxes in the United States significantly below international benchmarks, the total price of unleaded gasoline is the lowest of all the countries studied as of the first quarter of 2004.[124] More extensive data collected by the German Federal Ministry for Economic Cooperation and Development[125] indicates that retail gasoline prices in the United States are 40% of the price in the Central African Republic and Djibouti, 47% of the retail price in Singapore, 50% of the price in Albania, 54% of the price in Bosnia, 58% of pump prices in Gabon, Bolivia, Lithuania, and the Congo, 73% of North Korea's fuel prices, and about 80% of Australia's.

Table 13-1: Motor Fuel Taxes as a Percentage of Retail Unleaded Gasoline Prices - 1Q2004

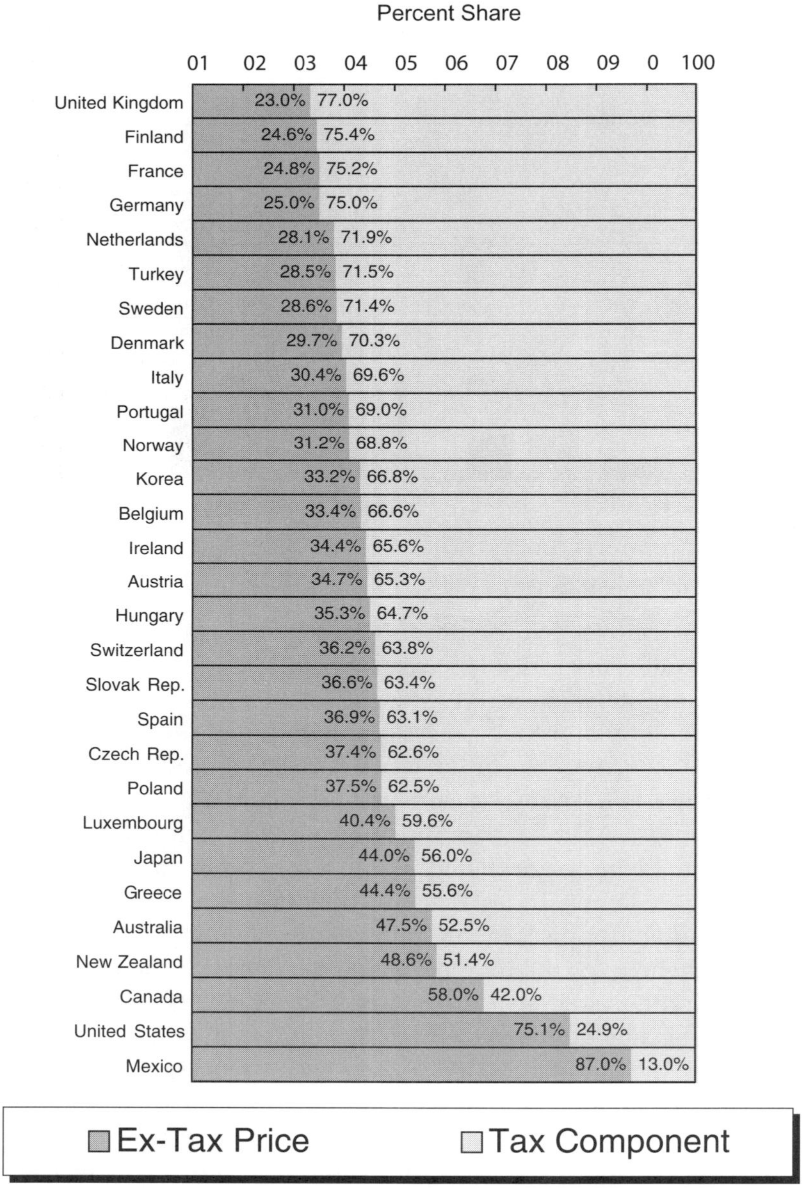

Source: International Energy Agency, "Energy Prices and Taxes," 1st Quarter 2004, p. xxxiv

Table 13-2: Unleaded Gasoline Prices and Taxes per Liter – 1Q2004

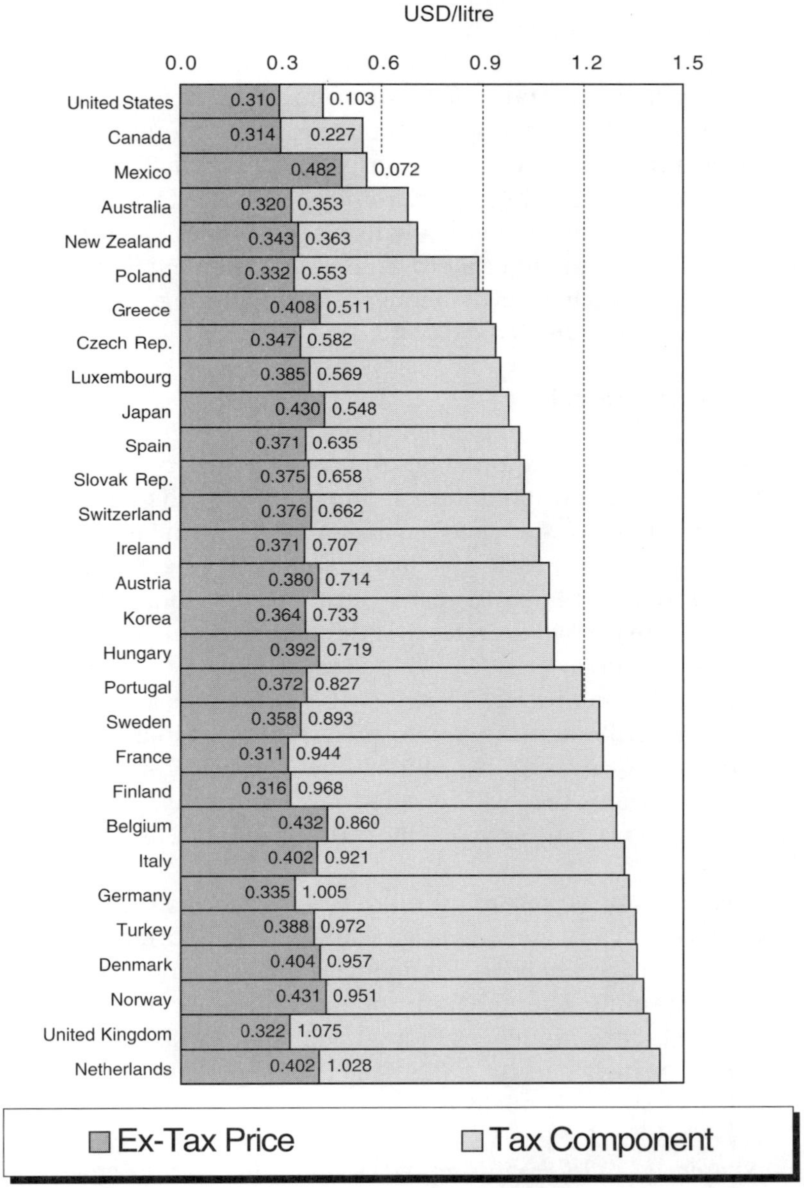

Source: International Energy Agency, "Energy Prices and Taxes," 1st Quarter 2004, p. xxxiv

With such relatively low motor fuel prices and taxation levels, the opportunity to generate resources for transport from this revenue source appears to be barely tapped in the United States.

The trends described in this section suggest that federal motor fuel and locally dedicated taxes will continue to play critical roles in the funding of public transportation. According to international benchmarks, considerable head room for future growth in motor fuel taxation is still available if the political consensus to act can be found. Beyond 2015, leveling or declining yields from federal fuel taxes, as well as expanding technology options, could increase adoption rates for pricing transport infrastructure in order to generate supplemental revenues, as well as to help balance travel demand. These longer-range pricing strategies are discussed in the next section.

Future Pricing Strategies

The opportunity to *supplement* fuel consumption-based revenue sources with innovative approaches to pricing road services is the subject of increased attention and experimentation in the United States and abroad. Public resistance to paying for road use that is already perceived to have been funded with taxes remains strong and is likely to continue for the next 10 to 15 years. During this period, ample capacity exists to increase fuel tax rates in order to improve revenue flows for investment, as well as to offset yield erosion arising from alternative fuel usage and rising fuel efficiency of the vehicle fleet. Critical technologies for implementing open road tolling systems are being deployed in a growing number of locations, but more universal applications face hurdles that will require an extended series of developmental steps for wayside systems, in-vehicle elements, and transaction processing.

Nonetheless, it is becoming more widely acknowledged that the continued growth in highway usage cannot be supported by massive expansion of the road network for financial and environmental reasons. Any long range outlook for the future of public transportation must consider the interactive influences of a gradual shift toward road pricing, particularly on high density, congested travel corridors. The implications of such a shift potentially involve:

- Shared costs to create limited access, high performance transportation corridors that can be used by single occupant auto travelers, carpools, and public transit vehicles;

- Evolution of dynamic pricing mechanisms that can help to balance loads on alternative modes for accomplishing the same trip based upon real-time conditions;
- Applying user-side subsidy mechanisms that ensure access to road and public transport networks to all groups within a market pricing environment; and
- Influencing future land development patterns by explicitly factoring transportation costs into the pricing of housing and employment centers.

The use of pricing to influence the timing and amount of road usage and mode choice is emerging as the "new frontier" of transportation finance for a fundamental reason:

> "The pricing of car use defies every rule of the free market – the low marginal cost of driving and the absence of charges for social costs give users the illusion that driving is virtually free."[121]

The nexus between road pricing and transit use is starting to be examined in a number of high profile examples. TCRP has studied the impacts of road pricing on traveler behavior and found the factors for elasticity of demand in the short term to be similar to those of public transit.[127] Longer term implications of changes in road pricing were found to include: decisions about trip-making, automobile ownership, and location choice for residences, employers, and activities.

FHWA is monitoring various road pricing experiments in the United States, several of which involve very large facilities, such as the New Jersey Turnpike and the Port Authority of New York and New Jersey's Hudson River crossings.[128] As noted in the TCRP research, many of these pricing schemes are yielding route shifts to non-priced or lower-priced road facilities, or temporal shifts in trip-making to periods of non-peak pricing.[129] However, a number of important cases explored below begin to examine mode shift behavior from highway to transit in response to value pricing.

In all cases, the experiments in road charging are being made possible by advances in electronic tolling technology that permit non-stop payment and avoid the congestion, air quality and safety concerns, and driver frustration associated with traditional cash transactions. As the connections between road pricing and public transit become more defined in the years ahead, the pace of evolution of road charging technology and the rate of its deployment are likely to emerge as significant forces in the future of public transportation.

Cordon Pricing in Dense Urban Areas

The universe of recent road pricing examples involves a variety of strategies depending upon the nature of the area affected. The London congestion charging scheme represents the impact of a cordon-type charging mechanism that tolls vehicles accessing a dense urbanized core with a significant transit mode share:

> The London program has reduced vehicle trips into the core by about 60,000 per weekday. Roughly 50-60% of these trips have been diverted to public transport, resulting in about a 2% increase in patronage levels since the start of congestion charging in February 2003, with about a 7% increase in bus ridership (15,000 passengers per weekday during the morning peak).[130]
>
> Another 15-25% of the forgone vehicle trips have shifted to other alternatives, such as walking, biking, motorcycle, car share, or taxi, or traveling during non-charge periods. Vehicle occupancies entering the charging zone have increased by around 10%.
>
> Bus operations have benefited from a 60% reduction in the scheduled service kilometers not operated due to traffic delays in the core charging zone compared to results for the same period of the prior year.[131] Average bus speeds in the charging zone increased by 7% during the morning peak[132], and additional waiting times at bus stops attributable to delays or missed trips declined by 33%.[133]

While $8.00 per day charges to enter the urban core of a metropolitan region with an 85% transit mode share may not be applicable in many U.S. cities, the London experience cannot be dismissed as unique or non-transferable. A similar scheme in Singapore has operated successfully for many years. A cordon toll of $8.00 must be placed in the context of existing toll and parking charges in a number of U.S. central cities, such as New York, Chicago, and San Francisco that range near or above $25 per day today.

A key factor in the public acceptance of the London congestion charging program has been the dedication of the incremental revenues to transportation improvements, particularly increased bus service. In addition, considerable resources have been devoted to traffic signal improvements within London and coordination of traffic management with public transit operations.

New York's Regional Plan Association (RPA) has tested four comparable schemes in Manhattan below 60th Street and found the potential for traffic reductions of 40,000 (5% in the morning peak) to 105,000 (17% in the morning peak) depending upon the pricing strategy applied.[134]The pricing strategy closest to London's would reduce traffic by about 73,000, or 13% in the morning peak. Significantly, transit ridership under the four test scenarios would grow from 94,500 to over 270,000 additional trips per day, with the "Like London" charging scheme generating about 170,500 new transit trips.

As noted above, other cities in the United States, many of which are highly congested, share similarities to London and New York in terms of very high daily parking charges, substantial existing tolls on bridges and tunnels leading into the downtown, relatively high transit mode shares for peak trips (particularly along fixed guideway corridors), and limited opportunities for additional road capacity.

In terms of finance, the implications of congestion charging are significant. London expects to generate 80-100£ million per year in new revenues that have been dedicated to transport improvements. These additional cash flows are subsidizing the expansion of bus service initiated in anticipation of the congestion charging program, as well as other improvements. In the New York City study, RPA estimated that the "Like London" congestion charging strategy would generate over $760 million per year in new revenues, with a potential for $1.7 billion annually under a full variable pricing regime.[135]

The London experience and the New York forecast suggest that the supply of public transportation can be readily expanded to meet the additional demands imposed by mode shifts induced by congestion charges for entry into dense urban cores. With a robust existing transport network already serving these urban centers, relatively modest increases in bus services may be the only requirement in the short term – particularly when the feedback effects of greater productivity from existing bus revenue hours are considered.

Longer term supply expansion from rail or road investment can be financed from the proceeds of congestion charges in these cases – a range of $8 to $20 billion of investment grade revenue bond capacity is indicated by the four strategies tested by RPA in New York City if the revenues generated by the various options are dedicated. This does not consider the cash flow benefits of roughly $65 million per year in additional farebox revenue under the "Like London" pricing scenario at the current New York City Transit average fare of about $1.25 (compared to the base fare of $2.00).

On the other hand, the potential implications of cordon pricing require extensive testing and evaluation. Political and institutional resistance is formidable and can be expected to remain so at least for the next decade or more. It is worth noting in this context that the Mayor of New York proposed a cordon pricing scheme as part of his current budget but abandoned the concept due to political resistance.

Other potential concerns include:

- Potential dispersion of economic activity away from the core
- Cost of collection / efficiency issues
- "Leakage" from evasion

Even though the eventual applications of cordon pricing 15 or 20 years from today may be limited to less than a dozen urban areas in the United States, the implications are potentially significant for the future of public transportation. For example, the highest density of urban development in the United States is often associated with the presence of heavy rail service. This single transit mode is present in only 11 metropolitan areas but accounted for over 27% of all weekday public transportation trips taken nationwide in 2001.[136]

The urban areas served by heavy rail account for the bulk of almost $40 billion of current "core capacity" investment needs identified in a 2002 survey conducted by APTA. These eleven metropolitan areas also represent large shares of the $37.5 billion of fixed guideway modernization requirements, the $75 billion in New Starts, and the $44.5 billion of bus investment reported in the 2002 APTA survey.[137]

Broadening the list of regions with potential to apply cordon pricing to include those with significant transit market shares but without heavy rail reinforces the conclusion that this congestion management mechanism could play a significant role in financing transit needs in the 2015-2030 time frame, even though only a handful of cities might decide to go forward with implementation.

As a consequence, examining cordon pricing options through experiments backed by incentive packages should be a near-term research and demonstration priority. Such experiments should focus on intermodal transportation planning and provide adequate lead time for technology development, deployment of transit alternatives, and stakeholder acceptance.

Corridor Pricing in Suburban Environments

How would road pricing interact with public transit use in the "new" urbanized areas of the South and West? These metropolitan areas typically include multiple activity centers and "Edge Cities" where traditional transit services do not have significant mode shares.

Numerous road pricing strategies are being examined by FHWA, and several of the most important operational cases point to a strong nexus between direct highway user fees and public transit, particularly when public transportation is viewed in a broader, mobility management sense to include all forms of shared ride activity (for hire taxi, carpool, vanpool). These research and demonstration concepts also incorporate innovations in bus rapid transit (BRT) service.

Examples of direct user fee charging concepts being tested by FHWA include:[138]

> **HOT lanes.** "HOT" is the acronym for "High Occupancy/Toll." On HOT lanes, low occupancy vehicles are charged a toll, while High-Occupancy Vehicles (HOVs) are allowed to use the lanes free or at a discounted toll rate. HOT lanes create an additional category of eligibility for people wanting to use HOV lanes. People can either meet the minimum vehicle passenger requirement, or they can choose to pay a toll to gain access to the HOV lane.
>
> **FAIR lanes.** "Fast and Intertwined Regular Lanes" or "FAIR lanes" involves separating freeway lanes, typically using plastic pylons and striping, into two sections: "fast" lanes and "regular" lanes. The fast lanes would be electronically tolled express lanes where tolls may change dynamically to manage demand. In the regular lanes, constricted flow would continue, but drivers with transponders would be compensated with credits. Credits could be used as toll payments on days when they choose to use the fast lanes, or as payment for transit, paratransit, or parking at commuter park-and-ride lots in the corridor.
>
> **Priced new express lanes** involve tolls on added lanes that vary by time of day and are collected at highway speeds using electronic

toll collection technology. Tolls may be set "dynamically," i.e., they may be increased or decreased every few minutes to manage demand so as to ensure that the lanes are fully utilized yet remain uncongested.

Queue jumps are roadway facilities that can be used by drivers paying a toll to bypass points on the transportation network where congestion is typically severe (colloquially, a "bottleneck").

Managed lanes is a term used to refer to HOV lanes, HOT lanes, or other types of restricted or special lanes such as truck lanes.

Value lanes is a term used to describe a concept that includes both HOV lanes and HOT lanes.

Variable tolls on toll facilities involve tolls on congested toll facilities that are varied by time of day with the intention of encouraging some travelers to use the roadway during less congested periods, to shift to another mode of transportation, or to change routes. With less people traveling during congested periods, the remaining peak period travelers will have decreased delays. To be eligible for the variable toll programs, vehicles must be equipped with transponders, which are read by overhead antennas.

Pay-As-You-Drive (PAYD) Automotive Insurance converts automotive insurance from a fixed to a per mile cost, providing a financial incentive to drive less.

Car sharing involves automated hourly neighborhood car rentals that substitute for car ownership. By sharing a neighborhood car, individuals eliminate their fixed monthly car expenses such as car loan and insurance costs, and instead incur a variable car payment based on usage.

Parking cash-out is a strategy that involves employers offering their employees the option of receiving taxable cash in lieu of free or subsidized parking provided by the employer. Employees may deny the cash and keep the tax-free parking subsidy or accept tax-free transit or vanpooling benefits in its place-with any balance in taxable cash. When people have a car readily available, they tend to think that using it is free, since the up front costs are already paid and each trip incurs few additional costs.

Car cash-out involves paying households to use one less car for a certain period of time. It helps people review their transportation choices and see how travel by foot, bicycle, transit, and ridesharing is competitive with the private automobile. The goal is to show people that they can save money and simplify their lives by not owning a second - or even first - car.

Initiated in 1999, San Diego's I-15 FasTrak Program generates approximately $2 million per year in net revenues that are applied to covering the cost of enforcement and to subsidizing two BRT routes known as the Inland Breeze. One of the BRT routes is a reverse commute service originating in downtown San Diego.

Car and vanpool riders and public transit patrons use FasTrak at no cost while single occupant auto travelers electronically pay variable tolls to enter the lane. Tolls can be adjusted every six minutes in order to manage the level of demand to maintain free-flowing traffic conditions.

Focus group and telephone surveys have been conducted in anticipation of an extension of the I-15 project. The results reflect support among both users and non-users:

- 66% approved of the HOT Lanes
- 71% agreed that tolls were an effective way to manage demand
- In response to the characterization of these facilities as "Lexus Lanes," 80% of the lowest income group supported the HOT Lanes compared to 70% of the highest income group.[139]

The number of daily carpools using the I-15 facility has increased from 7,700 to 17,600 under the FasTrak program,[140] and bus ridership in the corridor has grown 25%.[141] A similar experience with carpooling has been observed on SR 91, variable priced toll lanes in Orange County, CA that were privately built and financed but are now in public ownership and operation. Tempering these encouraging results is the reality that the project only generates about $2 million in net revenues – a very modest sum in relation to overall transport outlays in the corridor, let alone the metropolitan region.

In Houston, the QuickRide Program on I-10 (Katy Freeway) and US-290 (Northwest Freeway) permits HOV-2 users to "buy into" HOV-3 facilities that are operated by Houston Metro, for a $2 fee.[142] Future expansion of both the I-15 and Houston projects is under advanced study.

Many of the current ground-breaking road pricing experiences in both suburban environments and densely developed downtowns cited above share important characteristics with policy implications for the future:

- Intermodal planning and provision for single-occupant auto and shared ride modes
- Generation of new sources of dedicated, flexible funding for capital projects and future operating requirements outside of traditional silos
- Construction of intermodal linkages (park and ride lots, bus transfer facilities) at critical locations
- New roles for the private sector in development, finance, operations, and technology (SR 91, SR 125, Highway 407)
- Traveler information systems that convey pricing and performance information in real-time
- Use of pricing to both manage demand and generate additional revenues

In order to facilitate testing and adoption of road pricing schemes in the newly developing cities and major suburbs, near-term (present-2015) incentives will be needed to encourage demonstration initiatives. These demonstrations would have the following goals and objectives:

- Gradually introduce the public to the benefits of road pricing options
- Create incentives for multi-modal planning and investment using performance-based criteria to increase flexible funding commitments and break down modal funding silos
- Upgrade trip planning technologies to incorporate multi-modal alternatives and pricing information
- Test transit and road pricing strategies as a mechanism to balance demand and reduce congestion on both modes:

  ➢ Design, test, and refine targeted subsidy mechanisms, including requisite fare media and clearinghouse mechanisms, that will permit all users to equitably access value-priced transit and road alternatives

- ➢ Expand the limited experimentation in Washington, D.C., and other cities with distance, "peak period" and "peak of the peak" pricing in public transportation as mechanisms to balance supply and demand
- ➢ Test the extent to which mode choices are influenced by pricing strategies, and incorporate these parameters into travel demand models used to project capital investment "needs" as well as anticipated revenues
- ➢ Provide stronger incentives to upgrade public transportation fare collection systems in order to encourage market-oriented pricing strategies, provide multi-modal payment platforms, and enhance connections between regional public transit and private shared ride service providers
- ➢ Accelerate deployment of technologies that enable a single debit card/chip that can be used for road and transit travel
- ➢ Experiment with adjusting pricing based upon speed, predictability of arrival times, available space, comfort, or other consumer preference criteria, rather than simply modal differentiation

- Target locations for constructing intermodal connections that will integrate travel alternatives – parking facilities, transit hubs, BRT lanes, carpool formation stations, bike paths, and others
- Allow sufficient lead time to increase transit services and other shared ride alternatives in travel corridors planned for future value-pricing strategies
- Permit ITS and open road tolling technology to be tested, perfected, and integrated

  (Contrary to current policy that emphasizes "conversion" of free roads to tolled facilities, offer federal incentives for existing toll facilities to adopt open road collection technologies in order to accelerate the pace of deployment, prove the value of alternative technologies, drive down costs sooner, and encourage ITS systems integration)

- Stimulate a growth market for investment in ITS technology that will strengthen the supply industry and increase its stability, while providing incentives to integrate road and transit applications

- Test public/private partnership strategies for the development, finance, construction, and operation of value-priced facilities, services, and technologies

  (Provide incentives to test opportunities to overcome institutional barriers to provision of services by private providers; integrate private, public, and non-profit providers into a seamless network; and/or allow private infrastructure providers to cross-subsidize their own transit or quasi-transit services)

- Provide transportation planners with a tested toolkit of options to address specific congestion issues
- Develop a database of archival information to will help to pinpoint future investment needs
- Test mechanisms to integrate land use planning decisions with infrastructure development and pricing options in a value-priced context

These near term research and demonstration initiatives can facilitate the transition to a future that incorporates market pricing into both public transportation and road usage. In this future, philosophical differences over "collective" versus individual transport modes are transcended by a marketplace of travel options that offers consumers choices based upon individual preferences and real-time information regarding travel alternatives and variable pricing. Suppliers of road, public transportation, and other shared-ride modes (livery, taxi, and paratransit) are able to coordinate pricing and available capacity to transfer peak loads, dynamically balance demand and supply, optimize utilization of assets, and minimize investment in capacity expansion.

These capabilities are made possible by strategically located intermodal linkages that serve as "crossovers" between transport service networks. The same capabilities used to balance peak demands also are applied to manage surges caused by weather conditions, accidents, special events, and potential homeland security incidents. Distinctions between public, non-profit, and private owners, operators, and service providers are replaced by a marketplace driven by consumer preferences and pricing options.

Land Use Considerations

The implications of more extensive direct user charging for road access spill over into land use decisions, as does the prospect for tapping non-user benefits to pay for transport infrastructure.

"Value capture" methods have been extensively exercised in highway and transit construction, and this trend is now widespread. Incorporating the true cost of road or transit usage into direct user fees helps to offset lower land costs in outlying areas that lure development from higher density locations more easily served by public transit.

For example, developers outside of urbanized areas confronted with on-site or off-site costs for right of way donation, provision of facilities and/or services, impact fees, and special assessments, as well as having to count on access from value-priced facilities, will come to rely less on publicly subsidized infrastructure to make their subdivision investments profitable.

An important model is SR 125 in the San Diego area where local developers donated $35 million in right of way for a privately developed toll road that incorporates value pricing alternatives, a U.S.DOT TIFIA loan, and open access for carpools and public transit. Similar examples can be found in the $900-million Texas Turnpike Authority TIFIA loan transaction where tolls, public/private partnerships, right of way donations, and transit access are being integrated.

Public transportation's capacity to increase property values has been demonstrated in virtually every new system built in the United States. Along the future route of the Charlotte, North Carolina, South Corridor light rail system property values have jumped years in advance of actual construction. In Washington, D.C., transit has attracted the MCI Center back into downtown, dense clusters of development have sprung up in areas adjacent to previously suburban locations in Maryland and Virginia, and formerly depressed areas of Washington, such as Shaw, are being revitalized. Such trends are now being assisted by new mortgage lending practices that enable families to qualify for larger home loans for affordable housing located near public transit services because of lower car ownership costs.

Relationships between land use and transportation investment are examined in a large body of literature developed in recent years (for examples see Hudson's report *2010 and Beyond: A Vision of America's Transportation Future Additional Resource Materials*). In addition, sensitivity to transit oriented development, preservation of open space, and minimization of sprawl development have emerged as significant issues in Massachusetts, Maryland, Oregon, California, and other states. At the same time, a critical research need in testing road pricing schemes is to develop "best practices" that minimize the potential for cordon or corridor pricing strategies to encourage sprawl and shift economic activity away from the charging zones.

Future Funding Policy Issues

A work session of Hudson Institute's Project Advisory Group for public transportation was held on December 2, 2003 to gather input on policy issues. The discussion covered a broad range of topics that extended from policy concepts, such as viewing public transportation as a mobility broker, to specific ideas on fare collection, value capture, and marketing.

The issues and ideas have been sorted into three broad categories below. A technology "bridge" is often needed to advance current practices and realize future opportunities. These "bridge" requirements are designated by bold type.

Intermodal / Customer Focus:

- **End-to-end trip orientation – Mobility Broker; market-driven, customer service orientation rather than focus on asset ownership and service production; link to "New Paradigms" TCRP research**
- **Use of technology to connect modes and create market pricing mechanisms that boost usage – MetroCard example in New York, integrate monthly billing for toll accounts and monthly transit passes, use AAA or driver's license magnetic strip to pay for transit services**
- **Pricing and traveler information systems that link individual trips incorporating road (and parking) and transit components – who will create and manage these information and transaction systems?**
- Applications of package delivery paradigms – Are people packages? Is the package industry similarly regulated (vehicle safety, insurance, drug testing, vehicle specs, mandates, etc.)? What are the customer service/ preference parameters (speed, reliability, comfort, cleanliness, safety, security, privacy, trip chaining, special needs) that drive consumer choices in local travel compared to the package paradigm?

- Selection of routes and flexible array of services linked to alleviating congestion at specific choke-points or on entire corridors – coordinate investment in road and transit assets to facilitate crossovers between networks
- Family of services that can address needs in different land use environments to make transit more competitive with ubiquitous road network – fixed route, dial-a-ride, route deviation, ZipCar, carpool, guaranteed ride home
- Become market driven and recognize transit market segments are evolving over time – transit dependent, aging population, disabled services, immigrants, university students/faculty
- Respond to changing development patterns – suburb-to-suburb, reverse commute, inter-regional

Finance:

- Silos limit potential solutions to transport needs – inadequate level of transit funding in relation to need and demand
- In the mind of the public, transit is subsidized but road travel is not – not cost per new rider but investment per new rider
- Broader accounting of costs and benefits – public understands transit's costs but not its benefits
- Transit increasingly perceived as congestion solution in more diverse universe of communities – Edge Cities, Sun Belt
- Modify image of transit in public eye – moving the perception of transit forward from a social service for the needy to a high quality alternative serving a broad range of market segments
- Use of impact fees / development-related exactions to pay for transport infrastructure – recognize costs of sprawl, capture non-user benefits of transit, mechanisms to influence land prices in fringes relative to inner suburbs and urban core
- Diversity of funding needs requires flexibility – operating vs. capital, mega-projects, service expansion vs. asset replacement
- **Broader use of tolling / value pricing to manage demand and generate revenues for transit – balance competition of "free" roads and transit**
- Cost of federal mandates for planning, procurement, and services in relation to funding provided
- Federal role in establishment of local priorities – ranking projects through national competition for limited federal discretionary funding

Institutional Challenges:

- Role of the political process in transit – constraints on service delivery options, selection of routes (perception that transit may be causing congestion in some corridors), national and regional project selection priorities, funding allocation formulas, procurement limitations, unfunded mandates
- Legal and regulatory barriers to service integration with other passenger carriers limit efficiency, economies of scale, and customer service – school transport, taxi, and livery services, non-profit/social service providers.
- Integrate transport and land use planning – permit better integration of transit as a competitive alternative to road travel, recognize housing and travel cost trade-offs
- Employer and housing influences tend to bias against transit – "free parking," dispersion of jobs to locations difficult to serve with transit, mortgage economics subsidize dispersion of housing opportunities away from higher density locations into areas not well suited to transit.
- How to best select from a wide range of modal and carrier solutions to transit needs – rail, HOV/express bus, BRT/Curitiba, public or private service provider
- Possible roles for public/private partnerships
- **Transit agency procurement process is slow and highly regulated, which limits innovation and slows the rate of change – customer information, systems management and fare collection technologies; rolling stock (buses, railcars).**
- Transit market is relatively small, but specifications are often unique, driving prices and affecting supplier viability – need to buy items "off the shelf" and move toward performance specifications.
- Transit agencies as institutions are difficult to manage and change – public "fishbowl," management and collective bargaining factors, mandates, production/asset-management orientation.

Chapter 14

Scenarios for the Future of Public Transportation

If adequate resources are available to maintain a state of good repair, address capacity constraints, and provide for expansion where the matching resources have been committed from non-federal sources, a platform of stability for improving business processes in the public transportation industry can emerge.

Modifying business processes in public transit involves a multifaceted set of considerations that go to the heart of the industry's institutional structure, its core mission and function, its day-to-day applications of technologies, and its strategic alliances with public and private entities.

In recent years, considerable energy and resources have been devoted to study of both the larger context and the underlying trends influencing public transportation. A glimpse of this work is provided in Hudson's report, *2010 and Beyond: A Vision of America's Transportation Future Additional Resource Materials.* The report includes NCHRP and TCRP topical areas, as well as web links to the executive summaries of selected research in subject areas identified as "driving forces" in the public transit's evolving role in the transportation sector.

Extensive thought has been devoted to the analysis of "new paradigms" in public transportation.[143] Concerned that the historic business model of the public transportation agency as a supplier of services using its own assets and employees is not sustainable, TCRP has sponsored a series of studies highlighting future directions for change.

The resulting framework for a "paradigm shift" in public transport is drawn from experiences in related businesses, such as intermodal freight and package shipping, as well as innovations at public transit entities in the United States and abroad who are attempting to redefine the mission and functions of their organizations.

The conclusions of this research emphasize the use of technology to focus on the customer's requirements for a door-to-door travel experience that is capable of incorporating multiple modes and service providers.

The "new paradigm" studies identify six dimensions of change that collectively define a future vision for public transit agencies:[144]

1. Mission Shift	A change in the strategic mission of the organization from a "provider of capacity" and "an operator of owned assets" to a "manager of mobility," regardless of whose assets might be used to provide capacity.
2. Customer Focus	A change in the measures of success from service *outputs* to measures of the *quality of the customer experience* and *outcomes* of service investment and use across the community.
3. Collaboration	An expansion of sustained relations and communications across modes, agencies, organizations, and jurisdictions with responsibility for mobility and community quality of life.
4. Integration	An expansion of formal and informal arrangements that integrate facilities, equipment, systems, services, functions, and resources across agencies and organizations with a responsibility for mobility and community quality of life.
5. Information Technology	Full-scale introduction of state-of-the-art information technologies to support customer focus and integration across organizations – that is, universal fare media; real-time, on-street customer information; shared dispatching and scheduling systems; and so forth.
6. Organization Structure	Introduction of new or altered functions, business units, skills, support systems, and so forth to support the new strategic mission.

The implications of the "new paradigms" research are far-reaching in terms of the definition of public transportation, the interests of transit's stakeholders, and the industry's strategic relationships with other service providers – non-profit and paratransit entities, taxi and livery organizations, private operators, and for-profit businesses capable of delivering critical functions (bus services, taxi and limousine services, telecommunications, fare collection, maintenance services, equipment leasing).

Through transformation into mobility brokers whose primary mission is to serve as the customer interface, public transportation agencies will require a new framework for tracking revenues and expenses, setting priorities for capital investment, and measuring performance.

An interesting side-note to the TCRP research relates to the discussion of FedEx as an example of a "new paradigm" organization embodying the six dimensions of change described above. The recent acquisition of Kinko's by FedEx for $2.4 billion represents further evolution of the "new paradigm" wherein a company built around handling physical objects may now be able to incorporate an electronic "leg" in the chain of moving material from "Point A to Point B." This direction has efficiency implications (why move the package at all if you don't have to?) as well as business development opportunities (adding value by taking over document production as well as shipping).

The concept of "mobility management" advanced in the TCRP research was first explored in the late 1980s under FTA's Advanced Public Transportation Systems Program in collaboration with the International Taxicab and Livery Association (ITLA).[145] This study developed approaches to using technologies considered innovative at that time to integrate prior demonstration efforts in applying market mechanisms to public transportation services under the principals of "consumer choice" and "user-side subsidy." The summary concept that emerged more than 15 years ago defined the "new paradigm" investigated by Stanley and Coogan for TCRP:

> The Mobility Manager is a mechanism for achieving the integration and coordination of transportation services offered by multiple providers – public, private for-profit, and private non-profit – involving a variety of travel modes – bus, taxi, vanpools, rail, etc. – and multiple sources of funding. This integration is accomplished through electronic technologies, allowing the programmatic integrity of all participants to be preserved, while

> at the same time automating most of the transactions – financial and otherwise – which occur in the system. The Mobility Manager's function resembles that of a travel agency and a financial clearinghouse. Through a single point of contact it offers information to tripmakers on all relevant travel choices and their price-service characteristics. It can make trip reservations directly or refer prospective users to a service provider for this purpose. It also handles most or all of the financial transactions in the system, aided by software designed for this purpose. Various hardware and software technologies, such as magnetic or electronic fare media, in-vehicle card readers which can communicate with computers, computer-assisted vehicle scheduling and dispatching, and computer database systems would be used in such a system.
>
> The Mobility Manager is in many respects analogous – within the urban travel context – to airline reservation systems, as well as the systems of large package delivery firms such as Federal Express and UPS.[146]

The *Mobility Management* study identified three enabling technologies: computer assisted scheduling and dispatching; electronic fare collection; and customer databases.[147] Integration of these technologies in support of a customer service orientation was considered the next level of innovation required for implementation.

As part of the study effort, FTA and ITLA held a series of workshops and identified potential sites for demonstration efforts. The strongest initial applications for the concept were found to exist in the paratransit arena, where high costs per trip could justify the investment in technology and provide incentives for efficiency. Paratransit came to be viewed as a potential platform to design and implement new service strategies and technology applications that could be scaled-up to the larger public transportation sector.

Follow-up demonstration efforts were conducted, and a research report was prepared that identified requirements for a successful transition to a mobility management business model and noted the institutional barriers to accomplishing change.[148]

The notion of organizational transformation in the context of a large, multi-modal public transit system was explored in an FTA-funded research project conducted through the Institute for Transportation

Systems at the City University of New York under the guidance of Milton Pikarsky.[149] The project suggested new business models and organizational strategies for the New York Metropolitan Transportation Authority (MTA).

A series of change models for adapting the organizational structure and practices of the MTA toward improved efficiency and greater customer service orientation were identified. These models included examples also cited in the later "new paradigms" research and were based upon turnaround initiatives at CSX and Conrail, as well as innovations at the MTA and the New York City Transit Authority that were capable of being applied more broadly within the organization. The CSX and Conrail examples were intended to demonstrate how capital intensive organizations in the transport sector with similar cultures, and labor relations climates could be transformed in response to crisis, as well as rapid deregulation.

The 1988 CUNY study also suggested an organizational restructuring that created three new subsidiaries under the MTA Board – a customer service company, a technologies company, and a stations and properties company. It was recommended that all transit services be delivered through the customer services subsidiary. The customer services organization could act as a broker to reach outside of the MTA for service providers needed to meet customer requirements. In addition, options to reorganize the existing operating subsidiaries to increase sensitivity to customer service and to realize efficiencies from public/private collaborations were suggested. The organizational change model was based upon strategies that had been applied at CSX to facilitate a customer service, intermodal perspective within the company.

The CUNY research anticipated current mobility management models with a scenario describing how an MTA Customer Service Company might operate:

An Expensive Commute to Manhattan

> A commuter subscribing to the transportation service calls a destination and departure time into the Customer Service Company's Trip Planning Center from his home computer. The subscriber's Preference Profile for cost, speed, comfort, privacy, access to a mobile phone, intermediate stops, or other requirements is retrieved automatically.

Travel alternatives meeting the Preference Profile are planned, and total trip prices calculated for each option. Alternative routings are based on the existing status of the transportation system – breakdowns, traffic jams, capacity conditions at parking lots and transit routes, etc. The Preference Profile is used to establish priorities among the options. Pricing is based upon time of day, capacity conditions, and time of the year.

The subscriber selects the desired travel alternative, and the Customer Service Company's Trip Planning Center (TPC) arranges the trip, updates capacity counts, and charges the customer's account.

Since the subscriber has just made a killing in the stock market, he refuses his usual shared-ride trip on the 8:05 AM Manhattan Express Bus. The computer knows he does not like vans and won't pay for a helicopter. Its back-up alternative involves driving to a commuter rail station (a station further down the line is offered because the parking lot at the closest stop is filled) and connecting for a reserved seat on the 7:55 AM to Grand Central. The subscriber accepts the commuter rail option.

At the commuter rail station, the car's transponder identifies the vehicle to the parking lot gate where the TPC had reserved a space. The reservation is verified, the car is permitted to enter, and a parking charge is sent to the TPC for part of the quoted trip price.

The subscriber passes his travel card through a turnstile which verifies the seat reservation and applies to the TPC for payment on the rail portion of the trip. Aboard the train, the subscriber remembers he has an early meeting on the West Side and will have to change his destination. He is presently scheduled to take the Lexington Avenue Local to his office.

Using his travel card, he logs into the TPC via the train's on-board trip computer, and requests a new routing. Since the destination is on the West Side, the TPC suggests the subway shuttle at no change in trip price. Wanting to impress his neighbor who is on the train, the subscriber requests that a stretch limo meet him at Grand Central.

> The TPC replies that the limo can be arranged, but 42nd Street is jammed, and he will miss his appointment by using surface transportation. In addition, the "through-price" would be broken, and he will have to pay premium charges because of the limo leg. Caught between impressing his neighbor and paying extra to be late for his meeting, he selects the limo.
>
> The TPC contacts private limo companies it has qualified for service, finds one with a car already at Grand Central, and provides the subscriber's information for transmission to the driver. The subscriber is given a description of the car and hands the driver his travel card. The card is passed through a hand-held computer, and later that evening the data is transmitted to the TPC so the private limousine service can obtain a portion of the new, premium billing rate for the trip.
>
> The subscriber impresses his neighbor, arrives late for the meeting, and decides that next time he will take public transit. At the end of the month the TPC bill arrives, and his wife underlines the $68 charge for a premium trip to Manhattan."[150]

The public/private partnership concepts in the 1988 CUNY report were the subject of a follow-up study that emphasized the potential for strategic alliances with the private sector in broadening the range of service options and increasing efficiency.[151] Again, significant regulatory barriers were identified in creating a unified, multi-modal transportation network in New York City.

Related research on Mobility Management and paradigm shifts has focused on the larger conceptual issues, as well as particular travel market niches, such as suburban mobility, reverse commute, rural transportation requirements, demand response, services for the elderly, and car sharing (see "B" series project codes in NCHRP and TCRP listings in Hudson's report *2010 and Beyond: A Vision of America's Transportation Future Additional Resource Materials*).

Perhaps the greatest indicator of the need for incentives to initiate demonstration efforts is the 15-year period that has elapsed since the "mobility management" concept was recognized and the lack of subsequent progress in advancing these ideas into practice.

Over the next six years, adequate resources for the development and deployment of technologies essential to advancing mobility management strategies will be required and incentives will be needed to encourage experimentation with new business models. Inducements are necessary to offset risks, encourage senior management to invest the time, attention, and political capital to initiate difficult negotiations with stakeholders to effect change, and to encourage regulatory adjustments at the state and local levels necessary for successful implementation.

Essential aspects of mobility management that must be proven or developed in order to advance this strategy include:

- Real-time vehicle location, dispatching, and passenger information systems
- Intermodal passenger information and trip planning systems that can link legs of a single trip involving multiple modes or carriers and calculate a single through price
- "Back office" transaction clearing that can allocate fares among carriers or service providers
- Fare collection systems capable of smart-card applications with potential for corporate alliances with banks, credit card merchants, and, potentially, retail locations
- Software and cooperative linkages between public, private, and non-profit carriers to locate vehicles and dispatch and price rides
- Capability to link road pricing, parking, and transit components into a single trip
- Real-time capability to reconfigure services and pricing in response to travel conditions
- Direct linkages to social service providers for shared resources in delivering paratransit rides and providing targeted subsidies
- Collective bargaining and gains-sharing arrangements that permit new types of job assignments and migration between public, private, and non-profit service providers
- Regulatory adjustments that allow taxi, livery, and transit services to be more closely integrated
- Construction of intermodal facilities that permit crossovers between shared ride alternatives, HOV/park-and-ride opportunities, and traditional transit services

Given this background, how might public transit appear in 2010?

Being only six years off, there is insufficient time for profound change; however, important trends are emerging that suggest a longer range "vision" for public transit. A "vision" for public transit in 2020-2030 is outlined below. The intervening years will be crucial for the development and deployment of the requisite technologies, as well as the gradual introduction of new funding mechanisms and institutional changes.

The most critical period for transformation is the next six years. During this time the seeds for change must be planted. Existing infrastructure must be brought to a state of good repair. Congestion along critical travel corridors must be relieved through capacity expansion. Enabling technologies must be advanced. New business models for public agencies and public/private partnerships must be tested. Best practices must be brought forward and incentives offered for broader application. Intermodal passenger and freight connections must be established. Incentives also will be needed to demonstrate the benefits of changing institutional relationships between land use and transportation, and between public, private, and non-profit transportation providers.

As discussed in the previous, curing the backlogs of deferred maintenance on existing road and transit networks and relieving critical capacity constraints will require considerable expenditures in the near term. Maximizing the potential of existing revenue sources, primarily by increasing motor fuel taxes, will be necessary to achieve these near-term objectives – the supplemental funding concepts of the future described in the value pricing section above are not ready for "prime time" technically or politically.

Gradual exposure of the public and other stakeholders to alternative mechanisms for pricing and delivering transport services through test cases backed by incentives to offset risks can guide the path to 2020 and beyond. Some experiments over the next few years will fail, others will prove viable only in limited applications, but the general knowledge base will expand, and successes gradually will be replicated. Most importantly, the markets for enabling technologies can be established over the next six years to justify private research and development expenditures, several generations of advances can be deployed, and the integration of current stand-alone systems will be encouraged. All of these steps are needed to advance new public transit business models.

A Transit "Vision" for 2020 - 2030

Organizational Transit organizations will be the customer interface for multi-modal trip planning, service delivery, and payment. Models of marketplace providers such as Travelocity, Orbitz, Hotels.com, and Amazon will be adapted to offer travelers similar information and booking options for local trips. Itineraries customized to consumer preferences will be created, priced, and, when necessary, modified in real time based upon actual travel conditions. Public transit organizations may or may not be the actual provider of services. Door-to-door trips will involve mode changes to satisfy customer preferences for speed, comfort, reliability, safety, status, multi-destination trip chaining, and cost. Private and non-profit service providers, infrastructure owners, maintenance contractors, or vehicle lessors will be integrated with public and non-profit entities.

Technology

Heavy technology inputs will permit advanced mobility management functions to be performed seamlessly. Critical functions will include: integration of performance data on road and transit network conditions for real-time trip planning; vehicle location and dispatching in real time; automatic passenger counting; linkage of multi-carrier/multi-provider networks; through-trip arrangement, and fare collection covering road usage, parking, and transit/shared ride options; universal smart card fare collection capable of receiving targeted subsidies; dynamic segment-by-segment trip pricing in response to real-time travel conditions; full vehicle diagnostics via telemetry; on-vehicle and facility security, and safety systems for surveillance and detection; advanced train controls allowing bi-directional operation at high speeds and close headways to maximize throughput of fixed facilities; advanced customer information networks on and off-system with "push" capabilities.

Infrastructure

Transit infrastructure will be a blend of dedicated transit facilities and shared-use rail and road facilities. Rights of way will be heavily automated to maximize through-put, provide failsafe public safety protection, and meet high security requirements. Mainline bus routes will apply advanced in-vehicle and wayside BRT concepts while lower density services will rely more heavily on real-time dispatching, route deviation, livery, and car-sharing alternatives. Transit stations and shelters will be advanced customer information centers and serve as intermodal connection points. Extensive construction of intermodal linkages will knit old infrastructure segments into a robust transport network capable of balancing peak loads between modes in real time and reconfiguring "best routes" for individual trips in response to demand peaks, special event surges, weather conditions, accidents, or terrorist incidents.

Pricing

Road and transit trip pricing will be integrated. Advanced payment technologies will allow modal boundaries to fade from the customer's perspective with a single price charged for multi-leg, multimodal trips. Time and distance-based pricing will be applied universally, and pricing will be used to allocate capacity during peak demand periods on transit as well as roads. Transit fares will be value-based and market driven, permitting higher levels of service to command premiums over other modes or other public transportation options. Targeted subsidies will be used to ensure access to needed services for all population groups.

Market

The aging of America, continuing immigration, and population shifts to urban areas are indicators of growth in public transit markets. Uncertainty regarding fuel prices and supplies, higher fuel taxes, more extensive application of road pricing, better linkages between land use and transportation, new service strategies tapping advanced technological capabilities, and increasing congestion will increase transit's market share. Greater attention to customer service, extensive product differentiation offered by multiple service providers, and market pricing will increase the penetration of public transportation into a broader spectrum of trips.

Funding

Transit finance will continue to involve a blend of dedicated state and local taxes, federal support, and internally generated revenues from user fees and ancillary sources; however, funding silos separating the modes will weaken, cross-subsidies from user fees will become typical, and internally generated income from fares, transaction fees, brokerage fees, and corporate alliances will reduce public transportation's appetite for operating subsidies. Higher levels of motor fuel taxes will prevail in order to generate revenues, and to fulfill a variety of social, national security, and environmental objectives. Value capture techniques will play an increasing role in transit finance as communities adopt land use policies that link property values and accessibility.

Near-Term Considerations

The pace of change toward the 2020-2030 vision for public transit will be influenced by background events over the relatively near term with regard to the nation's economy, the ability to develop a consensus on transportation policy, international events, the availability of public resources for transportation, and the character of state and local institutional arrangements.

As noted at the outset, the most important factor influencing the shape of events in 2010 will be the ongoing debate over reauthorization of TEA-21. The level of federal resources provided for transit and highway investment over the next six years will drive the pace of change. Post-TEA-21 funding levels will reflect the degree to which a national policy consensus can be achieved in transportation, the level of capacity that can be created in all modes to meet increasing demands, the balance between federal and non-federal funding partners, the capability to sustain a state of good repair in transport infrastructure, and the ability to deploy new technologies that will permit changes in public transit business models. Opportunities for expanded private sector roles in the development, construction, finance, operation, and maintenance of transit services and infrastructure also will be a function of demonstration initiatives under consideration at this time.

Three background scenarios have been developed by the Hudson Institute research effort to examine the likelihood of progress by 2010 toward a longer-range vision for public transit and the transport sector in general:

Hard Times A recessionary economic environment in the United States and abroad produces above-average unemployment, growing budget deficits at the federal, state, and local levels, and widespread voter initiatives to reduce tax burdens. Funding for government programs declines in real terms, and in many cases in current dollars. National policy direction is mired due to lack of political consensus, pre-occupation with electoral politics, general distrust of government, special interest lobbying, and lawsuits. The business outlook is negative due to governmental rules and a climate of uncertainty. Terrorism events occur periodically in the United States, and considerable fiscal and human resources are devoted to stabilizing international "hot spots." The Middle East remains volatile, resulting in periodic disruption to worldwide oil markets.

Status Quo A relatively flat economic environment in the United States and abroad produces moderate unemployment, large but static budget deficits at the federal, state, and local levels, and scattered voter initiatives to reduce tax burdens. Funding for government programs declines in real terms and, in many cases in current dollars. National policy direction is mixed with agreement in some areas but conflict in others due to lack of political consensus, underlying distrust of government, special interest lobbying, and lawsuits. The business climate is moderate, with some bright spots in a few sectors of the economy. Terrorism events occur periodically outside the United States, and while fiscal and human resources continue to be devoted to stabilizing international "hot spots," some successes are achieved. The Middle East remains volatile, but results in only minor disruption to worldwide oil markets.

Good Times Modest growth characterizes the economic environment in the United States and abroad reducing unemployment, narrowing budget deficits at the federal, state, and local levels, and permitting increased funding for a few government programs. National policy direction is mixed due to lack of political consensus on energy, environmental, and health care issues; however, underlying distrust of government has gone down due to government responsiveness to voter concerns. The business climate is generally positive due to overall economic conditions. Terrorism events occur rarely outside the United States, and while fiscal and human resources continue to be devoted to stabilizing international "hot spots," success is being broadly achieved. The Middle East enters a peaceful era, and worldwide oil markets function predictably.

Public Transit Responses to Hudson Background Scenarios

How will public transit respond to these near-term scenarios? How will these circumstances influence progress toward the future vision of public transportation? The following matrix examines the alternative outcomes for 2010 along the dimensions for change described above.

The state of public transportation in the United States in the future will reflect the level of resources available for investment over the next six years, as well as the incentives available to encourage innovation and best practices. The ability of public transit to advance innovative technologies, test new organizational strategies, acquire innovative funding sources, establish strategic alliances with other modes and private entities, and grow its markets in the longer-term future will require substantial commitments in the near term. The benefits of reduced congestion and a smooth transition to a "new paradigm" for public transportation will yield handsome returns on this investment.

	Hard Times	Status Quo	Good Times
Organizational	As a result of budget cuts and pressures on wages and benefits, special interests retrench to limit further erosion of their economic position. Consensus to make institutional reforms is lacking. Crowding and ridership losses result from service reductions, breakdowns, higher fares, and lack of new capacity on publicly operated mass transit. Experimentation with new institutional arrangements is discouraged by adversarial relationships among stakeholders brought on by competition over inadequate funding, as well as lack of interest in providing incentives to test new organizational possibilities.	Building on a stable economic and political environment, a few public transit systems are able to forge the necessary coalitions with labor, community groups, elected officials, regional planning organizations, private providers, and non-profit organizations to test new organizational and service delivery strategies. Despite continuing budget pressures, priority is given to creating incentives to encourage experimentation, and resources are earmarked to promote the deployment of emerging technologies. Adequate research and development funding is provided to document and disseminate the results of these test cases.	Policy consensus, adequate funding levels, and favorable economic conditions allow key stakeholders in metropolitan areas around the country to test new strategies for providing public transit services. These efforts have been facilitated by incentive grants and strong public interest in transit alternatives for addressing congestion arising from expanding economic activity. A number of agencies have successfully transformed themselves into customer-service organizations that have taken the initial steps to link public, private, and non-profit providers through shared information, rate-setting, and fare collection systems funded by incentive grants. Multi-provider dispatching and vehicle locator systems have been integrated in some cases, allowing the initial testing of new service options. In a limited number of cases, these early stage efforts have been supplemented by intermodal alliances with state DOTs, regional expressways, and the private sector to test service and pricing packages involving managed lanes, park-and-ride, HOV, and BRT.

	Hard Times	Status Quo	Good Times
Technology	Reduced budgets, lack of consensus on future direction, and a high risk business environment slow the pace of technology development and deployment, limiting options for introducing new business models, safety devices, and service delivery strategies. Suppliers exit the market.	The consensus for a stable funding base for transportation includes provision to target investment in customer information, fare collection, and dispatching systems. Research and demonstration projects involving real-time system performance are advanced, and limited applications involving intermodal trip planning are tested. Important platforms for new technologies are found in paratransit and rural transit applications where the resulting efficiencies are reducing trip costs and increasing productivity. Encouraged by modestly growing markets for fare collection, vehicle locator, and customer information systems, private research and development initiatives begin to attract risk capital. Homeland Security considerations encourage traveler information, vehicle location, and trip planning advances in order to facilitate responses to potential terrorist incidents. These improvements find applications in the day-to-day service environment.	Policy consensus on the broad outline of the future of the transport sector permits targeting of public resources to deployment of enabling technologies. Integration of the transport policy consensus with Homeland Security initiatives leverages available funding. More certain deployment commitments encourage investment of risk capital for research and development. Start-up firms enter a growth market, and successful ventures are the subject of acquisitions and public stock offerings. Targeted investment areas include: fare collection, real-time multi-modal system performance, traveler information, trip-planning, vehicle locator, dispatching, and integrated service opportunities with roadway service providers (HOV, park-and-ride, managed lanes, and BRT). In some cases, larger public transit agencies join with technology partners in new ventures that yield innovative revenue sources. Important test-beds for new technologies are found in paratransit and rural transit applications where the resulting efficiencies are reducing trip costs and increasing productivity.

	Hard Times	Status Quo	Good Times
Infrastructure	Crisis atmosphere builds as investment in new and existing assets declines. Deferred maintenance increases, and vehicle replacement cycles are stretched-out. The supply industry is weakened by lay-offs, and firms exit the market. Road congestion increases as transit usage falls. Few incentives exist to modify traditional approaches to infrastructure development, while lack of political consensus results in deadlocks over environmental issues, adequate funding levels, and potential roles for the private sector.	Stable investment in transit infrastructure permits some progress toward a state of good repair, but capacity constraints limit public transit's ability to contribute further to alleviating congestion. Safe, clean, reliable service encourages additional ridership, but crowding is an increasing problem, and new service initiatives are limited. Local and regional land use policy changes encouraged by federal requirements for discretionary grants result in greater developer and private sector involvement in the design, construction, and funding of transit-related infrastructure. Intermodal initiatives such as BRT, shared right of way use, managed lanes, and park-and-ride are encouraged by flexible funding and federal policy. Some experimentation with private sector initiatives is facilitated by experimental programs and limited incentives. More robust infrastructure investment and fleet modernization levels create opportunities for technology deployment and updates. The supply industry consolidates but market leaders are able to improve returns as a result of stable demand. Homeland Security requirements result in additional costs that are not offset by increased funding.	Federal leadership in dedicating meaningful increases in resources leverages state and local matching funds to allow progress in bringing the public transit network to a state of good repair and begin clearing the backlog of expansion and new capacity projects in the pipeline. Policy consensus on managing growth reduces implementation delays caused by environmental concerns. Ridership maintains steady growth, justifying continued capacity expansion and relieving pressure on highway facilities. Requirements for land use planning adjustments as a condition precedent for receiving discretionary federal funding increase the number of capacity expansion projects and accelerate the trend toward building more transit-friendly environments and leveraging private sector resources. Innovative collaborations among transit and highway stakeholders result in multimodal investments encouraged by federal demonstration initiatives aimed at improving regional transportation system performance according to broadly defined congestion and capacity parameters. Private sector initiatives in the development, construction, and operation of transit infrastructure are facilitat-

	Hard Times	Status Quo	Good Times
Infrastructure (cont.)			ed by market growth and favorable policy conditions. Demand for new technology deployments accelerates in response to requirements arising from state of good repair investment, fleet renewals, expansion projects, and retro-fits required to maintain compatibility between new and existing infrastructure. Suppliers improve margins and justify needed investment in modernization and product innovation, resulting in higher quality and increased competition. Modest increases in funding cover Homeland Security features that are incorporated into modernization and new capacity projects.
Pricing	Transit fares increase faster than the rate of inflation as subsidies erode, and dedicated tax revenues stagnate. Lack of national consensus on health care issues results in continued escalation of the operating costs of public transit, while eroding equity values trigger increased exposure for pension fund liabilities and escalating fuel costs limit new and existing services.	Stable subsidy levels provide operating support that limits pressures on fares; however, pension and health care obligations and escalating fuel costs increase deficits at rates in excess of inflation. A movement toward consensus on national health care issues brings some relief for operating budgets, while an upward trend in the financial markets limits the growth in pension liabilities. Transit fares continue to be benchmarked against the ability of those least able to pay. Pressures to generate revenues internally, and some demonstra-	Strong economic growth, a policy consensus on transportation futures, and enhanced federal discretionary funding for capacity expansion projects yield successful dedicated tax initiatives that boost sources of operating subsidy and reduce pressures on the farebox. In order to maximize the capital investment potential from expanded dedicated revenue sources, experimentation with new fare strategies built around innovative organizational and institutional arrangements occurs in several major metropolitan areas. In some cases

	Hard Times	Status Quo	Good Times
Pricing (cont.)		tion funding incentives result in limited receptivity to considering experimentation with new fare strategies that are more market-driven. Enabled by organizational shifts toward customer service, as well as innovative fare collection and clearing-house technologies, there is a growing capability to target subsidies to those most in need.	these initiatives are developed in concert with highway stakeholders as part of coordinated investment strategies or road pricing experiments along specific corridors. Deployment of advanced trip-planning, trip-pricing, and fare collection technologies facilitates experimentation with new pricing policies and allows targeted subsidies for those most in need to be applied more transparently. Operating deficits are restrained by revenue growth from more intensive ridership, a consensus on national health care strategies that slows public transit cost escalation; a growing stock market that shrinks pension fund liabilities; and a stable international environment that keeps fuel costs manageable.
Market	Customer satisfaction levels erode as service frequency and reliability decline. Demand is negatively influenced by unemployment and service reductions, while unmet needs of elderly and low income riders increase. Those with other transportation choices opt out of a public transit system that can no longer fulfill modern expectations for service quality, comfort, and reliability. In response to declining transit services, rising gasoline prices, and periodic	Stable economic conditions produce gradual increases in transit markets, while usage generated by elderly riders, immigrants, and higher population densities in urban and suburban areas add to employment-driven demand. The ability to keep pace with state of good repair requirements allows safe, reliable service, but crowding is a growing concern. Resumption of economic expansion and episodes of international stress cause spot fuel shortages and price spikes	Economic growth, consensus on national policies and regional development, as well as a variety of public transit capacity expansion projects broadly distributed across the nation, result in strong ridership demand. New systems and modernization investments in existing bus and rail services raise customer service levels to equal or exceed modern expectations for speed, comfort, and reliability. The improved pace of regional growth also accelerates opportuni-

	Hard Times	Status Quo	Good Times
Market (cont.)	fuel shortages, there is an influx of informal, unregulated, shared-ride service providers that soon compromise public safety. Economic pressure reduces the pace of development in transit-served areas and limits the ability of localities to impose transit-friendly design criteria on the dwindling number of suburban development projects.	that trigger surges in demand for public transit. Consensus on housing and growth management issues in a number of metropolitan areas results in greater transit market penetration in the suburbs and also reinforces traditional markets in built-out urban cores. While transit and roadway markets operate independently in most regions, limited experimentation is initiated to create a more integrated transportation marketplace. These efforts are enabled by investments in advanced traveler information systems offering real-time information on system performance. In addition, isolated experiments with value pricing trigger mode shifts along affected corridors that are the subject of intensive research and documentation. Technological and customer service advances also result in broadening public transit markets to include shared ride options offered by private providers in a few jurisdictions.	ties to integrate transit infrastructure and services into new markets through transit-friendly land use and comprehensive intermodal planning. Consensus on a future vision for the transport sector results in funding and policy support for enabling technologies that enhance public transit's customer service capabilities in a variety of non-traditional geographic environments. These initiatives are driven by experimentation with new organizational approaches to mobility management and efforts to promote more seamless integration of highway and transit services for customers. Various roadway value pricing arrangements are tested in several metropolitan areas that include transit elements. Private and non-profit providers are able to tap into public mobility management technology infrastructures to offer an expanded array of services to elderly and disabled users. Incentive grants are offered to test integrated mobility management systems that include real-time trip planning and traveler information systems in tandem with advanced fare collection and dispatching systems.

	Hard Times	Status Quo	Good Times
Funding	The federal role is increasingly questioned as locally enacted dedicated taxes are less able to leverage New Start match, the relative costs of federal mandates increase, and essential local services are either discontinued or funded by states or localities. Ability to use "carrot" approach to encouraging positive change through grant incentives is lost, and progress to advance best practices slows. Restricting the flow of new projects through the New Start pipeline generates delays that drive up project costs. Economic decline and lack of consensus limits the ability of localities to impose new exactions on real estate development, and voter resistance defeats most dedicated tax measures including several crucial renewals of levies subject to sunset provisions.	Modest increases in federal support for transportation are realized, leveraging larger increments of matching funds at the state and regional levels. The added funds permit state of good repair improvements to continue. The funding is derived primarily from fuel-tax sources, with limited additional general fund and user fee (tires, batteries, vehicle registration fees, etc.) revenues. Firewall protection raises public acceptance of gradual increases in the level of indirect user fees, while a limited number of metropolitan areas are able to secure sufficient regional consensus to enact new dedicated revenue streams for public transit. Existing dedicated tax collections increase in response to economic stability, permitting limited construction of expansion projects temporarily shelved during the recent recessionary period. Modal funding silos continue to soften through extension of federal flexible funding provisions. Modest increases in discretionary federal programs for capacity expansion and demonstration initiatives provide incentives to improve best practices in the introduction of new technologies, organizational structures, public/private	Sufficient increases in federal funding are realized to permit all public transit providers to achieve a state of good repair and to reduce the backlog of expansion projects in the "pipeline." The increment in federal funding is leveraged through new state and local revenue boosts triggered by the matching opportunity, as well as consensus on transportation priorities. Federal funding is derived from fuel-tax sources, with limited additional general fund and user fee (tires, batteries, vehicle registration fees, etc.) revenues. Firewall protection raises public acceptance of gradual increases in the level of indirect user fees. A broad range of metropolitan areas are able to secure sufficient regional consensus to enact new dedicated revenue streams for public transit. Existing dedicated tax collections increase substantially in response to economic expansion, permitting accelerated construction of expansion projects temporarily shelved during the recent recessionary period. Higher ridership levels increase farebox collections, freeing more dedicated tax revenues for capital investment. Modal funding silos continue to soften through extension of

	Hard Times	Status Quo	Good Times
Funding (cont.)		partnership arrangements, and strengthening the linkages between transportation, housing, and land use. Encouraged by generous incentives, a handful of innovative highway and transit value-pricing experiments are undertaken and expose the public and political leaders to potential opportunities and constraints to generating new resources for transportation investment. Homeland Security grants are used to introduce technologies and physical improvements that are integrated with state of good repair and capacity expansion work programs.	federal flexible funding provisions. Expansion of discretionary federal programs for capacity enhancement and demonstration initiatives provides a stimulus to improve best practices in the introduction of new technologies, organizational structures, public/private partnership arrangements, and strengthening the linkages between transportation, housing, and land use. Encouraged by generous incentives, a geographically diverse set of innovative highway and transit value pricing experiments are undertaken and expose the public and political leaders to potential opportunities and constraints to generating new resources for transportation investment. Homeland Security grants are used to introduce technologies and physical improvements that are integrated with state of good repair and capacity expansion work programs. Private sector initiatives to develop transit infrastructure are tested in a limited number of experimental projects.

	Hard Times	Status Quo	Good Times
Bottom Line	Public transit enters a spiral of decline and loses much of the ground gained under ISTEA and TEA-21. The impact ripples through urban cores dependent upon quality transit services and puts increasing pressure on suburban road infrastructure that is similarly under-funded. In desperation, public receptivity to privately funded road expansion schemes increases, but inability to achieve policy consensus limits experimentation, market user fees set by firms generate political backlash, initiatives are delayed by environmental challenges, and congestion grows worse.	Economic stability, modest funding increases, and growing consensus on future transport sector priorities permit continued progress toward achieving state of good repair objectives, although capacity constraints become more severe in a growing number of metropolitan areas. Sufficient federal funding is provided to attract modest increases in matching funds from dedicated taxes and to create incentives for testing new technologies, business models, multi-modal infrastructure solutions, and public/private partnership options.	Economic growth, funding increases, and a consensus on future transport sector priorities permit accelerated progress toward achieving state of good repair objectives. Capacity constraints are slowly being addressed in several metropolitan areas. Federal funding attracts increases in matching funds from dedicated taxes and creates incentives for testing new technologies, business models, multi-modal infrastructure solutions, and public/private partnership options.

Chapter 15

A Vision of America's Transportation Future

Great interest exists in the future of transportation in the United States. Growing population, record freight movements, safety concerns, and burgeoning demands for increased mobility for people and goods all motivate a desire for change, improvement, and a more effective national transportation system. If the United States continues on its current course, the future is predictable: further growth in congestion, tragic mortality and injury levels, and inability to compete in the global marketplace. If industry leaders and public policy makers could influence transportation's future, what then would it look like? Would consumers have choice in transportation decisions? Would financial investments reflect sound business practice? And, perhaps most importantly, would transportation become a transparent element of our existence and not the current drain it is on our quality of life?

Virtually every man, woman, and child is affected every day by transportation systems at the national, state, and local levels. Whether commuting to work on a freeway or light rail, going to school on a bus, or traveling around town on errands, transportation is always present in our lives. Some would argue that a person confined to a retirement home might not depend on transportation because they never venture beyond the confines of their care facility. On the other hand, an argument could be made that the cost of this person's food, prescriptions, or their ability to go to a physician for healthcare are all influenced by the effectiveness and efficiency of the transportation system.

This chapter considers some large-scale factors affecting transportation, and presents a vision of the future of transportation in the United States.

Freight

A change in the way information is gathered, handled, and distributed will mark one of the major changes in freight transport. Real-time data will optimize handling and movement, diminish costs, increase service, and meet regulatory requirements. In the future, data collected by shippers and carriers would be combined with data collected by public agencies, such as weigh-in-motion, ITS-CVO (Intelligent Transportation Systems-Commercial Vehicle Operations) monitoring, travel time, and volume, and would be accessible to use from a clearinghouse.[152] Data must also be gathered and shared on an international level in order for freight to flow with optimal levels of efficiency.[153] This data will allow freight transportation customers to make more informed decisions about alternatives and require freight transportation to meet higher standards.[154] Information-sharing at all steps in the manufacturing-distributing process will allow for reduction in inventories and for operation integration between companies.[155]

In "Freight Transportation Planning and Logistics," by the Transportation Research Board, the researchers stated that domestic and international freight demand will grow because of an increase in consumption of goods and a growth in the world economy conducive to producing goods.[156] Freight planners will have to account for an increase in consumer service demands as well as a decrease in available infrastructure capacity. The future will require existing infrastructure to be used more efficiently and new infrastructure to be carefully developed. E-commerce will result in a decrease in shipment size and an increase in shipment frequency. Because of an increase in the complexity of global supply chains, there will be an increased use of third-party logistics providers.

In another Transportation Research Board report, "Intermodal Freight Transportation," one researcher states that the focus of transporting freight should be changed from containerized shipments to all multi-modal, single-bill transports.[157] Challenges facing the system include a lack of physical and technological growing room, demands by consumers for products which may be obtained at any time and are delivered faster and cheaper, and a lack of recognition for needed changes by the transportation industry. Both the transportation industry and regulatory officials must consider the supply chain in connection with global transport efforts and understand how competition and technology changes will affect this chain.

Another report notes that there has been a resurgence in rail-freight transport.[158] Small, local service is as important as national, Class 1 systems. Infrastructure, equipment improvement, and updating are needed. Relationships between small carrier and Class 1 systems are varied, yet crucial. Competition from other modes, especially trucking can be challenging. The public sector affects the industry through regulatory efforts, financial assistance, safety requirements, and corridor maintenance by planners.

Social Issues

The Federal Highway Administration estimates that 1 in 11 people in the United States are employed in transportation. Some studies indicate that up to 50% of transportation workers may be eligible to retire by 2010. These are the workers who have spent their careers building the current transportation system, and with them will go the built-up institutional knowledge of these many decades of experience. The next generation of workers will have different ideas of the ideal job and will be willing to change jobs more often. This requires a change in recruitment strategies by transportation industry leaders. Transit industry recruiting is also important to the future viability of that mode.

The social and economic impacts of transportation projects should be studied so that decisions will result in the most effective and efficient solutions for all customers. New technology should be used for impact assessment, and external costs should also be evaluated. Transportation must evolve and find solutions to environmental, injury/fatality rates, and congestion concerns in order to be sustainable.

The changing nature of our society will surely affect transportation in the future. The aging population will affect all aspects of life in the United States, including transportation. As the population grows older, population growth will occur mainly in suburbs and in the West and South. Telecommuting is a trend that will continue into the future and will be joined by other work-from-home arrangements. Additionally, planners must also account for the growing trend of city dwellers working in the suburbs, creating a reverse-commute effect.

Changing Technology

Changing technology also will impact the future of transportation. New technologies will influence every aspect of transportation, from safety to environmental impact to economic and social aspects. The influences technology will have on the future of transportation have been explored throughout this book. However, a summary of past research is appropriate here.

Researchers are working on the technology of highways. Using nanotechnology, they have the potential to make concrete and pavement last longer, as well as making steel stronger and more durable. They can also use sensors imbedded into roadways and bridges to find early signs of weakness. Sensors could also be used to alert responders to incidents on the highways and alert drivers to quickly changing weather conditions. The future may hold highways that are able to correct cracks and potholes on their own, self-cleaning metal that doesn't corrode, automatically realigning guardrails, and bridges able to adjust their shape to wind conditions.

In "Transportation in the Twenty-First Century," researchers said that transportation would advance because of current trends in smart growth, high-speed trains, outsourcing, intelligent transportation systems, road pricing, and advancing technology in automobiles.[159] Americans will continue to utilize motor vehicles, but will also begin to make transportation choices that will relieve traffic congestion. New automobile technology will be a primary means of addressing environmental concerns. Outsourcing will increase, and private-sector companies will continue to consolidate.

Currently, 97% of the fuel used by the transportation sector is oil. According to one researcher, that must change. Alternative fuels will have specific requirements to meet before they can replace petroleum. These include sustainability, minimizing their contribution to greenhouse gas emissions on a life-cycle basis, contribution to emissions of criteria pollutants, toxicity, effect on land use and damage, cost competitiveness, and infrastructure requirements. Natural gas and electrical energy from fossil sources, ethanol or methanol from biomass, hydrogen, and electrical energy from biomass are possibilities although each has significant hurdles to overcome. Unless stringent policies are developed to implement low CO2 fuels such as hydrogen, natural gas-derived fuels will probably see a marked increase in use in the twenty-first century.

Another emerging technology is GIS-T (Geographical Information Systems for Transportation): "GIS-T is interconnected systems of hardware, software, data, people, organizations, and institutional arrangements for collecting, storing, analyzing, and disseminating information about areas of the earth that are used for, influenced by, or affected by transportation activity."[160] Whereas now GIS-T is now in its infancy, the technological and institutional communication systems necessary for GIS-T to be a major factor will continue to grow. In many cases the technology already exists for this type of network, and the challenges lie in improving the types and levels of communication between the many public and private entities that will be involved in a robust GIS-T system. In addition, it will also become more usable by the average consumer. Decisions made now about the direction GIS-T is taking will regulate the viability of this system as a force in the future.

Intelligent transportation systems also will be integral to the future. The goals of the Intelligent Transportation Society of America are: to decrease accidents by 15% and save 5,000-7,000 lives a year, protect the transportation system against natural and man-made threats, save $20 billion a year through better management of information and congestion, allow information to be universally available, save one billion gallons of gasoline per year, and reduce emissions. These objectives can change the direction transportation takes in the future.

Economic Change

Solutions that worked in the 1970s or even the 1990s will not work in the future because we are going through a major transition period.[161] Companies of the future must be global. No matter what the industry, everyone doing business in the twenty-first century will function on a global level. We are also going through a period of mergers and acquisitions. In the end, three large companies usually will have a significant portion of the market share, and a few niche companies will have a smaller share. Technology is increasing so rapidly that the next ten years will bring innovations allowing companies to solve problems they have not been able to in the past. The supply chain will have to become less disjointed for transportation to progress (22).

Institutions must change to account for that which is occurring in the external environment. The difference between changes in agencies and institutions that have occurred in the past and what will happen in the future is that they will have to focus on the external environment to facilitate the type and extent of their adaptation instead of the internal environment. The same types of tools will apply though: "internal restructuring, resizing, public-private partnerships, performance-based planning, and information sharing," but institutions must use these tools along with new technologies and new partnerships to progress in the twenty-first century.[162]

In "Trends We Cannot Afford to Miss," researchers predict an increase in the affluence of our society, which will affect both passenger travel and freight movement.[163] Also, specialization will increase, and demographic changes will occur, affecting the economy. The authors conclude that efforts made to improve safety, international competitiveness, operations, job access, and metropolitan capacity will have significant long-term effects on our society.

Another report predicts that environmental law will change in response to transportation concerns.[164] Because of the length and complexity of rules regarding transportation plans and programs in relation to Statewide Improvement Programs (SIP), Congress and the EPA will have to simplify them to allow projects to proceed more efficiently. Although the Kyoto Protocol would limit the amount of greenhouse gasses allowed in the future, there is little political support for its ratification in the United States. Mitigating methods suggested include taxation-induced driving reductions and changes in land use density or developing new technologies to use non-petroleum-based fuels. The authors contend that NEPA and related laws will continue to grow in strength because of the strong environmental lobby and because congressional committees overlap on environmental issues. Confusion will reign in the area of waste management until federal laws are reformed, although clean-up costs and liability risks should continue to decrease because of state laws.

Three main issues are at the forefront of global transportation at the beginning of this millennium: oil dependence, air pollution, and greenhouse gas emissions. Although running out of oil is not a worry – researchers estimate the supply will last 1,500 more years – it is not economically advisable to remain dependent on oil because of the potential for continually rising costs and global instability. Carbon dioxide emissions have decreased by 25% in the last 30 years, but they must fall still further to decrease the damage to humans and the ecosystem. It will be important to implement these changes in the rest of the world.

Communications can also affect transportation. Against expectations, improved communications has not reduced travel. Three communication modes exist: face-to-face, transfer of information objects, and telecommunication. Studies differ about whether telecommunication replaces or complements travel. Future research should focus on this as well as "mobile work"— the home-based consultant. E-commerce (virtual supply chain) and teleshopping should be studied so that planners will fully understand and account for it in the future. The effects of telecommunication changes on office space and form also need additional research.

Demographics and Transportation

Changing demographics are a major area of influence on transportation needs and resources. Considerable research on demographic trends and workforce issues that will affect employment, societal inclinations, and economic performance has been conducted by private and public entities alike. In the end, no vision of the future would be complete without a thorough examination of these other influences.

Hudson Institute's defining work, *Workforce 2020,* explored the myriad of issues relating to demographics in our nation and their influence on our future workforce.[165] It notes four powerful trends that planners must consider in relation to the workforce and which ultimately will have an impact on demographics and transportation. They are:

- The pace of technological change in our society has never been greater
- The rest of the world matters
- America is getting older
- The U.S. labor force continues its ethnic diversification

The challenge of transportation planners is to understand how each of these factors will influence the systems they are envisioning today and ensure that which they develop truly meets the needs of our society 20 and more years into the future.

The U.S. labor force is becoming very diverse in its makeup and communications. The Asian and Hispanic workforce will grow faster than other segments, increasing to 6 and 14 percent respectively in the next 20 years. The African American element of our workforce will remain the same, with white non-Hispanics replacing themselves and not adding to the overall increase in total workers. Most of this influx in diversity of the workforce will occur in the South and West with less impact in other parts of the country.

No one will dispute that technology is changing our lives. Yet, try as we may, our projections are often far from accurate. In the early '70s, few predicted how important the personal computer would be. Fiber optic communication was still in development. Cell phones and other telecommunications devices were the stuff of science fiction. Can anyone really predict what will happen when nanotechnology is fully deployed throughout the world, forever changing manufacturing activities, medical practices, and other critical areas of our lives? The object of the planner is to foresee what is unseen and build a transportation system to meet the mobility needs of the future generation—no small task. Perhaps the best advice to planners is to ensure that no option is ignored, permitting the system to adjust and even rapidly "morph" as necessary in the coming years.

The United States is not an island in the sea but an integral part of the global community—coordinated, related, and otherwise connected to the rest of the world. A discussion of U.S. demographics or workforce cannot be credible without incorporating elements of the global workforce and its related demographics. The U.S. workforce of the future will be more mobile and willing to change domiciles at rates unheard of in the past century. Small and medium size businesses will outperform larger counterparts who are less nimble and less able to respond to changing markets. Job volatility will be a major issue, with traditional efforts to outsource causing many jobs to go overseas (*Workforce 2020*, pp. 1-4).

It's no secret that America is getting older. The Baby Boom brought many millions of our citizens into the world between the years of 1945 and 1965. By 2010 the first of the Baby Boomers will begin to retire, leading to a 20% segment of the U.S. population being over 65 years of age by the year 2020 (*Workforce 2020*, p. 5). These aging citizens will affect the labor market, the economy, political issues, and society as a whole. Medical advances will allow this group to work and play longer in life, spawning new and different trends to accommodate this emerging lifestyle of the "healthy and active senior." Our aging society will stay in the workforce longer, recreate differently, and in general be unlike any former group of retirees.

Transportation must accommodate this important segment of society, their living habits, and their quest for quality of life. In the end, technology may also influence how much longer they are able to retain their driver's licenses and safely operate a vehicle. Those who choose not to drive, but who are still healthy enough to get out and about will also put different demands on our nation's transit systems. The whole array of transportation services from automobiles, to transit, to ship and air will slowly evolve in response to what will be a more affluent, demanding, and active group of consumers.

Distribution of population will influence how transportation will operate and provide mobility in the twenty-first century. Shifts from the Northeast to the Southwest are well known and expected. The depopulation of rural states like South Dakota and the general depopulation of rural America to urban areas also will occur. Eastern seaboard states will experience different transportation impacts due to demographics than their west coast counterparts. Thus, one solution truly isn't going to fit every challenge that lies ahead.

Assumptions about fertility rates and mortality rates have been rather stable and predictable. What has been challenging is that the levels of immigration, which have been much higher than anticipated by the U.S. Census Bureau, don't fit the traditional models for forecasting population change. Increasing immigration has been a pattern for U.S. population growth for over 20 years. For example, in 1980 the net migration into the United States was 500,000. Ten years later it had grown to 650,000. By the year 2000 it had increased to 1.5 million. By the year 2050 the majority of our population growth will be from immigration and not from organic growth.[166]

All told, demographics and the changing workforce will create change in significant ways. Transportation planners and policy makers would be wise to account for these changes as they prepare for the future.

The Global Economy

How will the global economy impact our twenty-first century transportation system? This question is fundamental to addressing the future in a responsible way. In 1999 Thomas L. Freidman, foreign affairs correspondent for *The New York Times,* wrote a telling book on the global economy, *The Lexus and the Olive Tree.*[167] In it he expounds on the impact the global economy is having on the United States and nations throughout the world. He summarizes as follows:

> Globalization is not just a phenomenon and not just a passing trend. It is the international system that replaced the Cold War system. Globalization is the integration of capital, technology, and information across national borders, in a way that is creating a single global market and, to some degree, a global village. You cannot understand the morning news or know where to invest your money or think about where the world is going unless you appreciate this new system, which is influencing the domestic policies and international relations of virtually every country in the world today.

U.S. manufacturing firms have long looked to overseas markets for more economical production activities. For years, white-collar employees in U.S. companies felt assured that their positions were not at risk. Today, with software, engineering, and a myriad of other non-blue collar positions being outsourced to Asia and the Near East, these workers are facing as much risk as any other segment of the workforce.

For years, Wal-Mart touted their "Made in America" origins for the products they sold. In 2003 even they succumbed to the need to provide goods at the lowest possible price—generally manufactured overseas. In an article published by *The Washington Post* this point is driven home with finality.[168] It noted that Wal-Mart reported that its imports from China exceeded $15 billion in 2003—placing the firm at number five in the list of China's largest trading partners, ahead of France and Britain.

The U.S. consumer is now caught in a conundrum of economic policy and customer choice. Will they choose lower prices, which are often provided by offshore labor, or will they be willing to pay a little more for domestically provided products? In spite of their feelings towards protecting domestic labor, the trend appears to be towards a choice for lower prices, as evidenced by the fact that Wal-Mart is America's largest retailer with sales of more than $245 billion a year. One of the key differentiators will be the available transportation system and how it will be used by consumers and retailers: transportation can serve to reduce the marginal cost of goods. Improved transportation systems, borne out of transportation policies and improved efficiencies, can and will have an impact on the price competitiveness of goods manufactured and sold in the United States.

Irwin Stelzer, director of Economic Policy Studies at Hudson Institute and a noted economist in the United States and in Britain, offered many insights into the global economy during a presentation to Hudson in the fall of 2003. He stated that five principal policy areas will affect America's twenty-first century transportation system. They are:

- Macroeconomic and microeconomic policy—the mixture of monetary, fiscal, and microeconomic policies that affect economic growth and the wealth of nations
- Individualism vs. collectivism—the decisions of various societies concerning the scope of individual freedom, which will play out as a battle between the automobile and public transport
- Tax policy—the power not to tax is the power to stimulate. The future of our transportation network will be determined by how we deploy the power to tax.
- Homeland security and defense policy—increasing security results in additional costs for every transportation system in the world. How security and defense interact in the future will have a major impact on our nation's economic vitality and transportation system.
- Environmental policy—how nations develop environmental policy will affect transportation systems in the future. One should

consider what safety objectives may be sacrificed to reach these environmental objectives.

He concludes that: "In the battle over transport policy, politics will trump economics. Prices that internalize the social costs and benefits of various modes of transport will remain of interest to economists and think tanks, but prove of little interest to politicians more interested in creating construction jobs, responding to . . . lobbyists, preserving uneconomic air and rail service to small communities in their states and districts, catering to the not-in-my-backyard crowd that abhors airports, and otherwise responding to political, rather than economic pressures."

Perhaps one of the most vivid reminders of the global economy and its influence on the U.S. business market is the steel crisis of 2004, where demand for steel in China affected price and availability in the United States. *Engineering News Record* reported in its March 22, 2004, issue that prices for scrap steel had increased by 20-60% in the first quarter of 2004 due to the huge demands placed on the market by work in China.[169] Ten years ago, who would have thought that rebar prices in Duluth would be influenced by projects in mainland China? Today it is a reality of the global economy.

The global economy is real and without borders. It makes possible a "call center" in India providing services to clients in America. Software engineers write code for clients thousands of miles away. Jobs of all types are at risk. Transportation systems become facilitators as well as elements of this global economy. Transportation planners and policy makers can't deliver on the future without an appreciation for this important part of the overall picture of our nation and world.

Many factors will force decisions about our twenty-first century transportation system. Safety, congestion, demographics, and the global economy are just a sampling of those factors that must be considered when making strategic transportation decisions. There will be many routes and directions to choose from in determining our future system. Transportation leaders would do well to choose wisely.

Transportation Security

Transportation security is a high-priority element of the twenty-first century transportation system as a consequence of the changing environment in our world today. Even before the tragic events of 9/11, transportation systems were vulnerable to terrorist events as evidenced by repeated terrorist activity in Israel as well as the nerve agent attack a number of years ago in a Japanese subway. In spite of these past occurrences, transportation security in the Unites States prior to 9/11 was largely focused on modest efforts in the airline industry and general security measures at ports and other freight terminals. Today much has changed, requiring professionals and policy makers to view their future through the "security lens," in order to have a full vision of the twenty-first century transportation system.

The Threat

The threat to transportation security is rooted in the airline hijackings of the 1960s, with spectacular and tragic incidents occurring over a number of years and involving various perpetrators with and without political motives. Implementing modest counter-measures in airport terminals as well as deploying sky marshals mostly eliminated hijacking as an issue. However, in the ensuing thirty years, isolated incidents served to remind us of our vulnerabilities. The downing of Pan Am Flight 103 in Lockerbie, Scotland, was foreign-generated with direct transportation links. Others, like the bombing of the Murrah Federal Building in Oklahoma City in 1995, originated domestically and had a transportation connection solely as a function of weapons conveyance.

Today, the array of threats to be considered by transportation professionals is much more complex and multi-dimensional. Origins may be foreign or domestic. Perpetrators may live in the United States or enter temporarily for the purpose of causing harm. Virtually any mode of transportation is a possible target as are citizens of every walk of life.

A variety of threats must be considered when designing and operating the twenty-first century transportation system. In the recent years much media attention has been given to weapons of mass destruction (WMD). Certainly, from a national security standpoint, WMD must be dealt with and considered. However, the March 11, 2004 train bombings in Madrid, Spain, revealed a new dimension to the linkage between terrorism and transportation. This incident illustrates how a series of bombs, carefully coordinated in areas where large numbers of citizens have congregated, can also result in a high loss of life, cause psychological turmoil, and ultimately sway political processes. Thus, security in the twenty-first century must address events both large and small.

The types of threats for causing harm are now varied and further complicate the transportation security issue for a transportation professional and policy maker alike. These include:

- Nuclear, including dirty bombs
- Biological
- Chemical

Each of these poses a threat to the safe conveyance of persons or goods on our nation's transportation system.

Transportation Vulnerabilities

Transportation systems are particularly vulnerable targets. In 2002, the National Academies of Science published a report entitled *Making the Nation Safer, The Role of Science and Technology in Countering Terrorism.*[170] This comprehensive work considered a wide array of homeland security measures including those particularly relevant to transportation. In this report it is noted that transportation systems are vulnerable due to some of their inherent characteristics. Those listed are:

Openness and Accessibility—Most systems are designed to be efficient, easily accessed by users, and in many ways unrestricted. Even airport ticketing and baggage claim areas are still open to the public. Transit facilities and highways are also notably open and easily accessed by user and perpetrator alike.

Extent and Ubiquity—Transportation assets tend to be characterized by their high numbers. With almost 600,000 bridges, a 160,000 mile National Highway System (NHS), a freight-rail network of over 300,000 miles, and 10,000 miles of commuter and urban rail systems, the size and extent of the overall network is a major vulnerability.

Emphasis on efficiency and competitiveness—The emphasis we place on being price and performance competitive in the services we render and receive impacts security measures in a number of ways. The foremost one is the pressure to move consumers through the system with as little delay as possible while balancing the impediments inherent in a competent security system.

Diversity of owners, operators, users, and overseers—In nations that have nationalized transportation modes and networks, the coordination activities that are part of a transportation security system are eminently easier to implement as opposed to the diverse nature of the U.S. system. Coordinating security practices among a variety of public and private sector entities is always challenging.

Entwinement in society and the global economy—Our economy and way of life are inseparable from transportation. Whether commuting, shipping, recreating, or engaging in any other activity, almost every element of our daily lives is influenced by transportation. Our vulnerabilities are many and the potential consequences significant. For these reasons, transportation security is a major issue with no single solution.

Each mode has its own specific vulnerabilities. Not all components would have the same levels of exposure or consequences stemming from a violent event. A brief listing is provided below:

Air
- Aircraft
- Terminals
- Freight operations

Ports
- Ships
- Cargo containers
- Transfer facilities
- Intermodal terminals

Highways
- Bridges
- Lifeline facilities
- Tunnels

Pipelines
- Terminals
- Pipelines
- Valves
- Booster stations

Transit
- Vehicles
- Terminals
- Underground stations

The depth and breadth of the challenge may seem overwhelming given the array of transportation elements listed above. However, transportation professionals and policy makers must aggressively plan and execute security measures appropriate to the feature and threat level.

The Response

Transportation security involves identifying risks and managing them in the context of the operational requirements of the network in question. It takes many forms. Transportation security includes protection of cargo and its conveyance systems, of passengers in automobiles and on transit systems, of the infrastructure itself, and of course adjacent people and facilities, which might be in danger from a security event involving transportation. Each has its own set of vulnerabilities and requirements for ensuring security.

In the wake of 9/11 the U.S. response to the threats to transportation security were heavily focused on the airline industry and passenger travel. Heightened security measures were immediately implemented and have continued to evolve in sophistication and practice. The U.S. DOT established the Transportation Security Administration (TSA) to staff and manage this key element of our nation's domestic defense. Eventually, TSA was consolidated into the Department of Homeland Security (DHS) along with other federal agencies focused on various elements of national security. In addition, the Patriot Act and many other state and federal actions worked to provide greater protection for our infrastructure and citizens.

In the war on terrorism, there is no place for complacency. Yet, with extensive security measures in place in the airline industry, attention is now turning to other transportation modes. Transit operators have long felt exposed to the threat of terrorism. The Madrid bombings brought this mode to the forefront of the discussion on transportation security. In addition, other modes including freight, inland waterways, ports, and other critical transportation links are being scrutinized.

In the twenty-first century, transportation planners will have to add additional elements to the normal process for planning and delivering projects to their customers. These elements include a comprehensive process of risk analysis and management based on specific project needs and issues. There are four steps in managing risk:

- Identification of risk elements or features
- Assessment of risk levels including human and infrastructure exposure
- Identification of mitigation strategies
- Implementation of mitigation measures

This chapter is not intended to provide detailed tools for addressing each of these elements of risk but to identify this process as a new requirement for our nation's twenty-first century transportation system.

Funding

Many analysts believe future funding will be earmarked for security at state transportation agencies for a variety of purposes. These individuals originally saw this heightened interest in security as a possible means for expanding infrastructure beyond what traditional funding sources would provide. Unfortunately, indications are that any funding directed to state DOT's will probably be focused on specific security measures and not for meeting infrastructure needs and not on capacity expansion. Several examples illustrate this point.

During the 2002 Winter Olympic Games in Salt Lake City, Utah, a heavy emphasis was placed on security for this post-9/11 event. Congress provided federal funds to assist federal, state, and local law enforcement agencies in meeting the security needs of the games. The Utah Department of Transportation (UDOT) worked hand in hand with these agencies and provided an important dimension to the overall efforts to thwart potential terrorist events. Pertinent to this discussion is the fact that virtually all efforts and resources employed by the Utah DOT were staffed and funded using existing appropriations from the legislature, with no additional funding with security origins going to the agency or its infrastructure.

In the wake of the Madrid bombings, many analysts have had raised expectations that the transit industry will experience a funding windfall to assist with security, critical capacity requirements, and operational needs. To be sure, transit properties seem poised to receive funding to address these marked security needs. However, every indication is that funding received will be strictly a reimbursement of expenses incurred and not a contribution to system expansion or enhancement. To date, funding for port security measures has also followed this pattern of attending to the newly implemented systems and not the capacity concerns which impact freight operations on a daily basis.

Transportation leaders should move cautiously on the matter of funding and security. It would be unwise to say that state transportation agencies, transit properties, or port authorities would never receive funding under the auspices of transportation security. Nor should efforts to secure funding be curtailed. However, two points seem clear. First, transportation security funding, if provided at all, will probably be reimbursement funds based on expenditures already made or anticipated by the agency or operator. Second, substantial infusions of funding for capacity purposes will not be a goal of federally provided transportation security funds.

The security issues surrounding our transportation systems are significant and must be addressed. This is a dynamic area for transportation professionals and policy makers alike to consider thoughtfully. It will not go away but rather must become an integral part of all planning and operational consideration for transportation policy makers into the future.

Transit in the Twenty-First Century

The history of transit usage in the United States can best be described as cyclical. From 1900 until the beginning of the Great Depression in 1929, ridership grew steadily. During the Depression years, poor economic conditions, unemployment, and differing travel patterns resulted in a decrease in overall usage. As a consequence of World War II, American society was forced to substantially change its travel patterns. Fuel rationing, among other things, created an environment for increased transit usage, with peak ridership experienced in 1946 at 23.4 billion trips on trains, buses, and trolleys.

Another cycle began after World War II, when fuel prices dropped, postwar suburban sprawl took hold, cross-country travel was romanticized by Route 66, and a new interstate highway system was born. Within15 years of the end of World War II, ridership dropped from a high of 23.4 billion trips to 9.3 billion in 1960 and a low of 7.3 billion in 1972. Since that time, ridership has again increased to 9.7 billion trips in 2001. The indications are that trend will continue and that transit ridership will continue to grow in the future.

Transit Today

Transit usage continues to expand as systems around the country mature and new investments take hold. The ridership numbers reported in 2001 at 9.7 billion trips represent a 3% increase over the previous year with a net increase of 24% for the last six years. Several factors are behind this growth in transit usage:

First is choice. Consumers are exercising freedom of choice and using transit in lieu of other transportation modes. This choice allows stress-free travel to and from work or other destinations on safe, clean, and reliable public transportation.

Second is availability. With increasing investment and property upgrades in transit systems within many communities, users are finding a greater range and convenience in service, which influences their choice of mode.

Third is the environment. More and more riders are using transit as a way to help both community and environment as we become more conscious about health, quality of life, and environmental issues.

Transit service is provided by approximately 6,000 public transportation agencies representing every state, cities like New York and Chicago, and towns, down to very small townships or rural counties. These agencies operate a variety of modes including buses, commuter rail, light rail, bus rapid transit, subways, and others. It is a complex network often taken for granted until it is not available.

Further Growth Needed

The transit industry is changing, becoming once again a meaningful contributor to the overall mobility of our nation. Moreover, there is substantial opportunity for additional growth. One of the main issues to be addressed by the transit industry will be sustainability, which hinges on creating a variety of services with reliable and meaningful funding sources. Other issues include the needs of various groups who use transit such as the elderly and those with disabilities, as well as funding, environmental, and safety concerns. Some past researchers suggest goals for the transit industry including using new technology, improving flexibility, training employees in customer-first service, considering new ventures, expanding research and training, gaining more information about current markets, sharing information, continuing research, maintaining customer satisfaction, increasing an awareness of customer communities, and flexibility.[171]

In John A. Harrison's report, "Intercity Passenger Rail," the author notes that transit has a huge opportunity for growth in the coming years.[172] He states that in Asia and Europe intercity passenger rail is far advanced beyond that in North America, but certain challenges must be faced before a viable intercity passenger rail exists in all major metropolitan areas of North America. For example, technology needs to be developed or acquired from other countries, infrastructure must be put in place, and funding sources must be found. Although high-speed rail has a nearly unblemished record, room for safety improvements exist. There are also environmental concerns for high-speed rail including noise and vibration, and electromagnetic interference/electromagnetic field effects.

In a 1999 report, "Public Transportation Marketing and Fare Policy," the researcher addressed the issues of marketing transit and fare collection.[173] He found that people are motivated to use public transportation for various reasons. Marketing involves addressing these "value" issues. Target groups must continue to be identified and customer loyalty maintained. Marketing efforts may target neighborhood transit efforts, alternative modes, clean fuels, and transit safety. He believes commuting patterns and practices will also change in the future. Suggested improvements include fare payment enhancements, use of a universal smart card, cross-industry marketing, and imbedded uniform product codes (UPC).

Another author has made the case that in the New Millennium, transit must be more focused on the needs of the elderly and those with disabilities.[174] It will be important to create Trip Chains, which make every part of the trip accessible and therefore possible. Improving transit so that it will allow access to all, including those with children, language barriers, luggage, or unfamiliarity with the local area, will make transit more useable for those with disabilities as well. It will also be important to build a family of services which include accessible road and rail transit, routes near housing areas used by elderly or disabled persons, accessible taxi services, and door-to-door services. For the whole system to be accessible, it must also have equally accessible pedestrian infrastructure, terminals, stations, and stops, and travel information available for those with cognitive, sensory, or linguistic impairments.

The future practices of transportation planning also are influenced by changes relating to transit usage in America. Future planning changes include renewed focus on neotraditional development patterns, demographics, public transit shaping development, increased multi-municipal planning and cooperation, research in new techniques, and outreach plans. Future transit growth and development will also be impacted by global issues such as technology, the global economy, our aging population, economic disparity, and environmental concerns. Local issues will also affect transit and influence transit planners. These issues include changing demographics and business development, technology, customer attitudes, finance, infrastructure, environment, and as yet unmet needs.[175]

Transit Funding

Transit system growth is a function of funding availability. Requests for federal funds are at record levels as more and more communities seek to build new systems or expand existing networks. The Transportation Equity Act for the twenty-first century (TEA-21) provided a significant boost to overall transit funding with a 2003 level of $7.2 billion. But federal funding paints only part of the transit investment picture. Local and state funds have become a principal source for the needed monies to meet the requirements of transit properties across the country. Chapter 12 of this book noted the disparity between the level of federal investment in transit and that of local or state government. The author expresses concern about this growing gap and its public policy implications.

Transit officials face many constraints as they seek additional funding. Fare box revenues have upper limits, and increasing the basic fare in communities is challenging. The portion of the federal fuel tax that goes to transit is fixed in law, with increases coming only with a commensurate increase in fuel consumption or the fuel tax. Specialized and general taxes represent efforts by states and local communities to tap their own scarce resources to find sufficient money beyond federal funds and the fare box. Those familiar with sales tax initiatives and other local funding sources will understand the challenge of increasing these revenue streams sufficiently to achieve desired funding levels.

Failure to adequately invest in infrastructure is not only a problem in building and maintaining highways. Underinvestment in transit has caused critical needs to be unmet year after year. In its Bottom Line Report, AASHTO notes that to maintain the current system would require an investment of almost $19 billion per year from 2004 through 2009, assuming a ridership growth rate of 1.6% per year. [176] Contrasting this need with the current funding level of $9.5 billion makes it clear that transit maintenance is in a downward spiral that will reduce available service levels when riders are demanding increases.

Truthfully, the funding discussion shouldn't focus on the basic cost to maintain the system. A system that is an integral part of our overall transportation network is an investment, and simple maintenance should not be a long-term management strategy. The same AASHTO report indicates that "an annual capital investment of $43.9 billion will be required to improve the current physical condition and service performance of the nation's transit system," assuming a 3.5 % growth rate of ridership.[177] This ridership growth rate is more in line with actual experience as opposed to the 1.6% level mentioned in the previous paragraph. In summary, a critical need exists for additional transit funding, but only limited funding sources are available.

Transit projects are criticized for their highly subsidized nature and the fact that they are not self-sustaining through fares. It is true that no transit agency is able to meet all of its financial obligations through the fare box. It is also true that state and local funding sources must pay the difference in operating costs less the amount collected from riders. However, to say that transit is a subsidized mode of travel and highways are not is false. Roads and highways are also heavily supported through fuel tax revenues, sales taxes, user fees, and other general revenue. Finding a balance between available funding, modal requirements, and transit/highway interrelationships will be influential in resolving financial issues for both modes. Any analysis must include methods of procuring a substantial increase in available funding for transit properties to maintain, improve, and even expand their systems.

Twenty-First Century Transit

Transit's future will be defined by two specific elements—money and mobility. Previously, the need to change the level of investment in our transit systems was mentioned. There is a related need to integrate transit systems into the national transportation network through a new vision of mobility.

A sense of future demand for transit service may be gained from a review of the status of requests to the federal New Starts program. AASHTO reports that currently 78 projects in 26 states and the District of Columbia are included in the New Starts program—projects which have moved beyond the initial study stage. These projects carry an estimated aggregate value of $47 billion. In addition, over 150 other projects across the country are in the preliminary study stage, the majority of which will ultimately vie for funding through the New Starts program. The 78 projects currently in the pipeline for New Starts funding represent years of available federal money. This makes prospects for the other 150 projects bleak unless transit funding improves substantially. Clearly, finding a way to enhance the revenue streams available to transit properties across the country must be a principal goal for achieving the vision of transit in the twenty-first century.

Perhaps the most exciting prospect in transit arises from the concept of mobility management, mentioned in chapter 14 of this book. This is an emerging idea that reflects a possible vision of our future transportation system and can create an environment where transit again provides a substantive contribution to mobility.

As noted in chapter 14, mobility management is about a system of modes, operating as a seamless unit, where transportation decisions are made by consumers based on travel time, cost, routing, schedule, and convenience. The environment is totally integrated so that travelers can make choices based on performance and reliability and not by chance.

Twenty-First Century Transportation

As chapter 1 of this book demonstrated, perhaps the most important factor in determining what the vision of our transportation future will be is finance. Where does the money come from to pay for the maintenance, capacity improvements, and operational aspects of our future transportation system? Ideas are powerful. Vision is wonderful. It can be a future where technology and transportation are joined in a seamless system offering safety and lifestyle value to our everyday pursuits. All of the concepts presented in this book lead us to a future mobility that would ensure America's role in the global economy and provide us with transportation choices to not only preserve but also enhance our quality of life. However, none of this will be possible without financial support. In short, bringing to life the vision of the year 2010 and beyond for transportation will depend on our nation's ability and willingness to invest in all of its transportation modes.

The most important point to make in the discussion of finance options for transportation is the need for net new revenue. Transportation will continue to have a major influence on our daily lives in the years to come. It will determine our mobility and affect our professional lives, and it may persuade us to live in a certain community or part of the country, or control how we allocate our precious discretionary time. This system will be a significant factor in how competitive the United States is in the global economy and in the vitality of the domestic business environment. Transportation will be just as important in the future as it has been at any point in America's history.

The challenges that lie ahead may seem overwhelming. Congestion is growing at alarming rates, with vehicle-miles-traveled projected to increase by 50 percent in the next 20 years. Mortality on our nation's highways is still at an unacceptable level, consistently exceeding 40,000 per year. Inefficiencies are too common as freight moves around the country with the prospects of higher levels being experienced as freight tonnage is projected to grow by 67% by 2020. The different modes still don't work well together. The funding gap seems to grow on a daily basis. Even conservative estimates peg the gap between needs and funding at values in excess of $1.5 trillion between now and 2025. Sometimes it seems that we are impossibly far away from the vision of the twenty-first century transportation system presented in this book.

In the next few years transportation leaders and policy makers have to make some of the most important decisions that have ever faced the industry. The good news is that these issues have been thoughtfully considered by the publications and documents referred to in this book and in others not presented. The research performed as a consequence of this joint Hudson Institute, AASHTO, APTA, and TRB effort has provided even more insight into appropriate solutions.

The network we know today will be substantially different from the one that will serve this nation in the future. Solutions won't be easy to find or to achieve. They will require new public-private relationships never before used in the transportation community. Technology will need to be deployed and accepted at a faster pace than ever. All modes must unite into a seamless transportation system. Laws will have to be changed, procedures modified, and major new funding sources will have to be developed in ways unknown at this time. Failure to take on "hard" issues like tort reform, public-private partnerships, and other thorny and complex problems will impede the realization of this vision.

Leaders throughout the country, representing all elements of the transportation community, are engaged in deliberate and thoughtful activities regarding the future of the U.S. transportation system. The sophistication found in these agencies, groups, associations, and companies is at its highest level ever. These leaders understand the economics of our transportation system and are well schooled in many of the areas discussed in this book. They have taken the time to gather the facts and understand the issues.

The time to act on that knowledge is now. None of the conditions described in this book will improve in the absence of action. For this vision of America's transportation future to become real, public policy makers and transportation leaders will have to step up and make it happen.

Summary

Revolutionary changes in the financing, technology, and management of the nation's surface transportation system must be made. These changes are essential if the American economy isn't to become bogged down by the last-century's transportation inadequacies as the role of transportation becomes increasingly vital. Since these changes are likely to take a generation to work their way fully through the surface transportation system, the time to begin is now.

Hudson commissioned five technical papers detailing key issues confronting the nation's surface transportation modes. The main body of the book consists of chapters derived from those papers, while stressing the importance of integrating what have traditionally been separate travel modes into a smoothly functioning system that concentrates on service to the customer rather than on engineering processes.

Finance

The most serious financial challenge facing the nation's transportation system involves the nation's roadways: existing methods of funding highways and streets have broken down. The American Association of State Highway and Transportation Officials (AASHTO) estimates that \$5.3 trillion will be needed during the first quarter of the twenty-first century to prevent further deterioration of the nation's highways, to overcome the effects of past underspending, and to keep pace with growing transportation demand. The present federal motor vehicle fuel tax and appropriations from state and local government budgets are projected to meet less than two-thirds of these needs. Similarly, Cambridge Systematics, Inc., the author of the technical report on transportation finance, estimates that \$44 billion dollars a year will be needed for transit expenses going forward.

The solution to this funding shortfall is to end the traditional practice of regarding access to highways as "free." Instead, motorists should be charged reasonable user fees for using the highways, based on the miles they travel, the kind of vehicles they drive, the amount of pollution they generate, and the levels of traffic demand in effect when they choose to make their trips. New technology now makes it feasible to retrofit the nation's existing highways to collect such fees without affecting traffic flow. This makes it possible to deliver highway access to motorist customers through the marketplace in the same manner that we deliver access to seats in movie theaters and a host of other goods and services where allocation has always been governed by price. Highway fees should be accompanied by money-back performance guarantees so that each motorist can make meaningful tradeoffs between travel-time savings and how much they pay to use highway lanes.

To fund what could be a lengthy transition to a fully user-supported highway network, index the federal motor vehicle fuel tax to track rising construction costs. This would provide funds for attacking the backlog of highway repairs and overdue capacity increases that too many decades of revenue-starved underspending have made the nation's highway system increasingly dysfunctional. The tax initially should be indexed back from 2005 to 1995, which would result in an immediate—but temporary—increase in the tax. Revenue from the fuel tax would be lock-boxed to avoid any questions in the minds of motorists about any of it being "borrowed" by other branches of the federal government to fund non-transportation activities.

As increasing portions of the highway system became retrofitted to generate user-fee revenue, the fuel tax would be phased out. The fuel tax would disappear entirely when the system became completely user-supported through fees. During the interim, the fuel tax would provide the funds needed to restore the highway system to a state of good repair.

Technology

Hassle-free collection of user fees is only one of the benefits that new technology offers the surface transportation system. Equally important are the many ways in which technology can help smooth the flow of people and goods, as savings in travel time and cost are becoming increasingly vital components for achieving economic prosperity.

For example, technology already available or being developed can greatly reduce the incidence of motor vehicle accidents on crowded highways and limit the personal injuries and property loss from crashes that can't be avoided. This would save lives, prevent injuries, reduce the increasing financial burden that such events impose on American society, and minimize the travel time delays they cause. The same technology can also work around the clock to optimize vehicle spacing, speeds, and routing so that a given number of highway lane miles can move more vehicles in less time.

More effective technology will help to break down the artificial barriers between surface transportation modes so that people and goods move expeditiously door-to-door through a properly integrated system.

Management

Superior technology is not enough to make the necessary difference by itself. More important is how intelligently the use of technology is managed to produce desirable results. Transportation system managers must change their traditional focus from engineering-oriented performance measures, such as pavement condition and vehicle-miles-of-travel, to customer-oriented measures that emphasize reduced door-to-door travel time, greater reliability, and smoother interfaces between transportation modes. With improved customer service as their primary goal, transportation managers will find new uses for technology as it becomes available, and new ways to make existing technologies work together.

Consequences

The most radical concept may be to convert what are now disconnected groups of separate surface transportation modes into a fully integrated system that travel customers perceive as virtually seamless and transparent. A key element for accomplishing this is to have the national, user-fee-supported highway network become a major funding source for all surface transportation modes, not just for roadways. This can include using user-fee revenues to support a larger network of freight railroad lines so that more goods can be moved by rail rather than by road, which will reduce highway congestion and collisions. The same approach can be applied to public transit in large metropolitan regions to avoid clogging highways with single-occupancy work trips that can be handled more efficiently by properly funded transit systems.

This use of cross-subsidies is consistent with the contemporary business portfolio management concept used in multi-product corporations such as the automobile and pharmaceutical companies, where various product lines reinforce each other rather than operating in entirely independent worlds. It will prove especially important in the strengthening of public transit, which will be a necessary component of the long-term process of upgrading and integrating the nation's transportation system into a coherent, logical structure that moves people and goods with the greatest possible efficiency and lowest costs. Currently, the public correctly sees transit as subsidized, but often believes that road travel is not, and it typically understands transit's costs but not its benefits. Transportation policy must correct this impression through broader accounting of the costs and benefits of all its modes. In addition, the emphasis should not be solely on cost per new rider but also on required investment per new rider. Policy makers must modify the image of transit in the public eye, moving the perception forward from its current image as a social service for the needy to that of a high-quality transportation alternative serving a broad range of market segments.

Indeed, transit can and should be increasingly perceived as a solution to traffic congestion in a far more diverse universe of communities, including edge cities and the Sun Belt. Use of impact fees and development-related exactions to pay for transportation infrastructure will enable taxpayers to recognize the costs of sprawl, capture non-user benefits of transit, and create mechanisms to influence land prices in fringe areas relative to those in the inner suburbs and urban core.

Hudson's visionary approach for creating an integrated surface transportation system poses major new financial, technological, and management challenges for the United States. These challenges, however, will arise anyway, and answering them will be a necessary element in maintaining national economic competitiveness in a world where the value of saving time and money in moving people and goods is growing by leaps and bounds.

Appendix A

Freight Transportation through Pipelines

Pipelines carry crude oil, petroleum products, and natural gas. Due to the differences in the physical properties of these commodities, different pipeline systems are involved in transporting them from production/refinery sites to end users.

As depicted in Figure A-1, oil pipeline traffic volumes declined modestly (1.4 percent) from 1990 to 2001–although volumes were above the 1990 level throughout most of the decade. Natural gas pipeline traffic (measured in millions of cubic feet), however, increased by 7.6 percent from 1990 to 2000, at an annual growth rate of 0.7 percent.

As also shown in Figure A-1, both oil and natural gas pipeline traffic are expected to grow steadily over the next 15 to 25 years. Combined, volumes (ton-miles) are anticipated to grow by 1.4% annually from 2003 to 2014.[178] Alternatively, the Bureau of Transportation Statistics predicts that volumes (in tons) will grow at an annual rate of 0.9% from 2002 to 2025.

Figure A-1: Trends and Forecasts Relevant to Oil and Natural Gas Pipeline Traffic

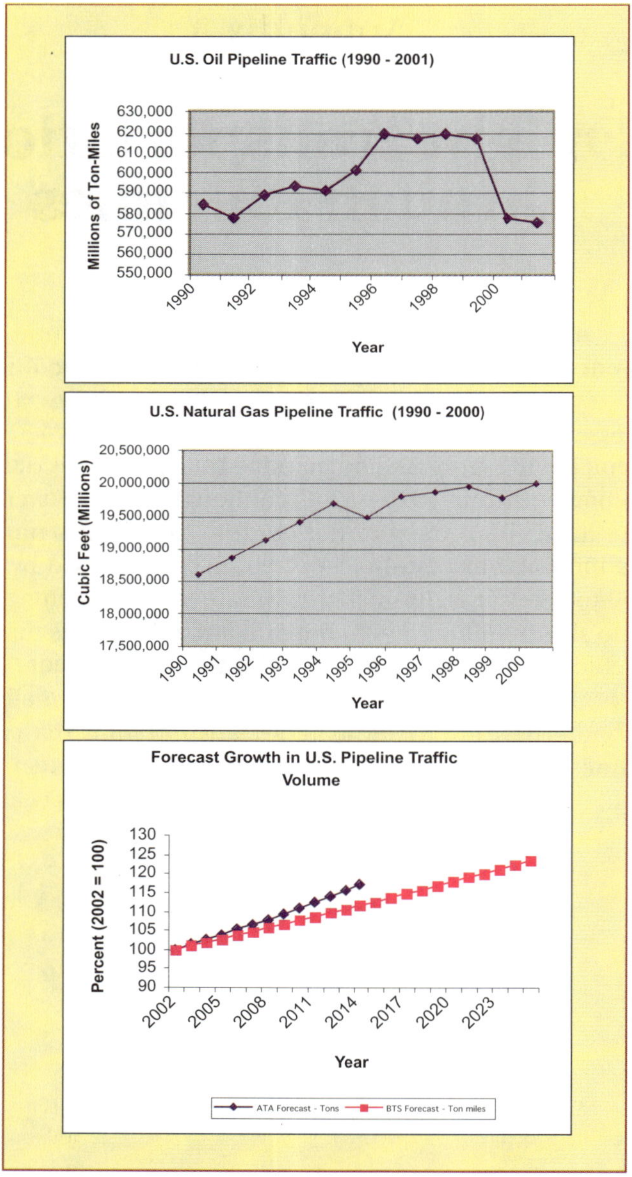

Appendix B

Freight Policies and Policy Research

Overview of Existing Laws, Regulations, and Financing Mechanisms

The following discussion briefly summarizes the laws, regulations, and financing mechanisms that currently guide investment in and the operation of our nation's freight transportation system. It is organized by mode (trucking, rail, waterway, and air). The summary of each mode is further divided among economic regulation, other regulation, and financing mechanisms.

Trucking

There is no longer any significant economic regulation of the trucking industry, but the federal government continues to regulate the industry with regard to safety and the environment. For example, the new hours-of-service (HOS) rule specifies ten hours of rest for truckers between work periods, two more hours than before. This rule is intended to improve safety on the highways, but it could lower the productivity of truckers. Truck size and weight regulations also affect the productivity of the trucking industry by limiting the amount of freight that each truck can carry. Customs requirements and border-crossing procedures affect the flow of freight between the United States and its neighbors, Mexico and Canada.

Federal surface transportation laws provide the basic structure of financing for the nation's major highways. Federal excise taxes on fuels and taxes on trucks, truck tires, and trailers are deposited into the Highway Trust Fund. A portion of these proceeds are dedicated to funding mass transit programs, but the bulk of the funding is distributed to states through a number of programs and formulas. As depicted in Figure B-1, states and localities provide the majority of funds for highways (79 percent of highway expenditures in 2001), which they raise through their own fuel taxes, other user-based fees, and from other sources.

Figure B-1

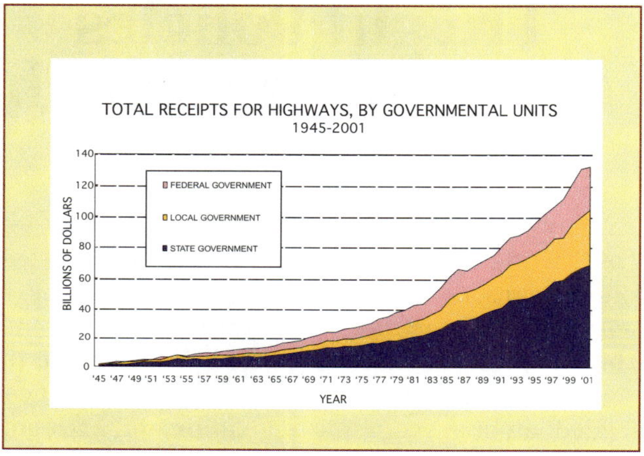

Although the trucking industry is highly dependent on the condition and performance of the highway system, until recently trucking concerns have not been featured prominently in state and local highway-planning processes.

Rail

Economic regulation of the rail industry is largely a thing of the past, although some price regulation still applies in areas when a single railroad dominates a market; this situation is most likely to arise in coal and grain markets. Some observers believe the recent mergers and consolidations in the rail industry have increased market power for the remaining companies. As a consequence, there have been some calls for more economic regulation of industry.

The Federal Railroad Administration (FRA) is responsible for regulating the rail industry with regard to safety-related operating practices, transport of hazardous materials, signal and track controls, and grade crossings. Collectively, these regulations affect the productivity of the rail industry and its ability to compete with other modes of freight transportation. Also crucial to the rail industry's productivity are federal labor laws and regulations and the labor agreements that rail companies make with their union work forces. These labor agreements affect the industry's productivity by dictating such things as crew sizes and operating practices.

The freight-rail industry is for the most part privately financed, although the federal government does provide some financial assistance to the industry. FRA administers the Rail Rehabilitation and Improvement Financing (RRIF) program, which provides direct loans and loan guarantees to acquire, improve, or rehabilitate intermodal or rail equipment and facilities. FHWA also administers the Transportation Infrastructure Finance and Innovation Act Program (TIFIA), which is available for some rail-related projects.

Some of the federal funding provided to states through the federal-aid highway program can be used for projects that benefit the rail industry. Within the Surface Transportation Program (STP), a portion of the funds that a state receives must be set aside for improving rail-highway grade crossings. Federal funds distributed to states for the National Highway System (NHS) can be used to improve intermodal connectors, the routes that connect major freight centers such as ports and rail terminals to the National Highway System. Finally, intermodal freight facilities are eligible for funding provided by the Congestion Mitigation and Air Quality Improvement (CMAQ) program.

Waterways

The Jones Act is the federal cabotage law that requires that vessels transporting goods between U.S. ports be owned by U.S. citizens, built in U.S. shipyards, and manned by U.S. citizens. The federal government also regulates waterborne shipping with regard to customs, environmental protection, and homeland security. For example, the Coast Guard requires double hulls on tankers in order to prevent environmental damage from oil spills. The Department of Homeland Security (DHS) now houses the Customs Service, which issues requirements concerning waterborne imports. DHS, through the Coast Guard and the Transportation Security Administration, is primarily responsible for port and cargo security.

Federal funding for operation and maintenance of the nation's waterborne transportation network is focused primarily on maintaining channels, aiding navigation, and monitoring the entry of ships into the nation's ports. The U.S. Army Corps of Engineers maintains more than 12,000 miles of inland waterways, operates over 200 locks, and maintains channels in roughly 300 commercial harbors. State and local governments generally finance landside infrastructure such as terminals, berths, piers, and freight-transfer facilities.

Roughly 80 percent of federal expenditures for the commercial waterborne transportation system come from general funds. The remaining 20 percent come from the Harbor Maintenance Trust Fund and the Inland Waterways Trust Fund. These trust funds receive receipts from fees on users of the waterway system.[179]

Air

Aside from antitrust regulation in the case of mergers, the only remaining economic regulation of air cargo transportation concerns the right of foreign-flag carriers to operate between U.S. airports. The Federal Aviation Administration (FAA) is responsible for regulating the safety of air passenger and air cargo transportation. Air freight transportation is also subject to the security requirements of the Transportation Security Administration (TSA). In addition, international air freight shippers must comply with applicable customs requirements.

The national air traffic control system is the responsibility of the federal government. The federal government also provides funding for airport infrastructure through the Airport Improvement Program. This funding, as well as most of the operating funds of the FAA, comes from the Airport and Airway Trust Fund. Federal user fees on air passengers and cargo are deposited into this trust fund. Separate security fees pay for TSA's activities at airports. Hub airports are largely self-financing through gate leases, landing fees, and payments from concessions such as parking lots and restaurants. State and local governments provide a significant portion of funds for infrastructure and operations at smaller airports.

Recent Policy Recommendations and Developments

There have been a number of important reports, recently produced, that have approached the freight industry from different angles and have developed guiding principles for government action or sets of specific policy recommendations. The following are brief summaries of four of the most important reports that were reviewed as part of this study.

TRB's* 21st Century Freight Capacity *(2003)

In its 2003 report, a committee of the Transportation Research Board (TRB) considered the long-term implications of trends in freight transportation markets and how government policies could produce a more efficient level of freight transportation system capacity. The report recommends four principles to guide decisions about using, enlarging, funding, or regulating the freight transportation system:

1. Economic efficiency ought to be the primary goal of transportation policy.
2. Government involvement should be limited to circumstances in which market-dictated outcomes would be far from economically efficient (e.g., monopoly power, non-market costs).
3. A government responsibility to provide facilities or leadership in developing a project does not necessarily justify government subsidy of the costs.
4. The government should rely on revenue from users and on local matching funds to increase the likelihood that worthwhile improvements will be made and that facilities will be operated and maintained efficiently.

TRB's *21st Century Freight Capacity* report also delineates a number of recommendations for moving forward with surface transportation policy, port development, harbor maintenance, inland waterways, and regulation. Overall, the report recommends that state and local governments should routinely conduct evaluations to quantitatively test the economic rationale for government involvement in freight transportation infrastructure projects, and that federal rules should require such evaluations.

As for mode-specific suggestions, TRB's report presents the following considerations:

TEA-21 Reauthorization

The report argues that any programs created during TEA-21 reauthorization to encourage states to select freight-related projects should: 1) sustain the user-pays principle of the federal-aid program, 2) fund projects that have the broad support of fee payers, 3) maintain the competitive balance between trucking and other modes by adjusting user fees, not by supplying offsetting subsidies to the competing modes, and 4) require ongoing and retrospective evaluations of the performance of projects. In general, TRB's report provides the following guidance for TEA-21 reauthorization:

- Maintain and reinforce the principle of user financing by aligning fee structures more closely with the costs each highway user imposes (e.g., Value Pricing Pilot Program, user fee financing).
- Support improved operation and maintenance of existing highway facilities.
- Provide funding adequate to ensure that states have the resources to maintain the overall performance of the highway system.
- Require DOT to study the costs and market potential of exclusive truck facilities (i.e., truck-only roads).

Port Development

With respect to port development, the report recommends that Congress and the president consider the following reforms:

- *Deauthorization Reviews*—reviews of all authorized harbor and waterway projects, considering commercial, defense, and environmental criteria,
- *Regional Planning*—regional decision-making for port investment decisions,
- *Cost-Sharing and Fees*—greater reliance on local cost-sharing and user fees,
- *Outside Reviews*—stronger requirements for independent review of the economic and environmental evaluations of large or controversial projects.

Harbor Maintenance

As for harbor maintenance, the report recommends the development of a new revenue source for maintenance dredging of navigation channels, preferably tying channel capacity expansion and maintenance to project-specific user fees.

Operation and Management of Inland Waterways

The report also makes specific recommendations on how to improve the performance of our inland waterways. The authors suggest the following:

- The U.S. Army Corps of Engineers should improve the efficiency of congested locks on inland waterways through demand management.

- Congress should begin to rely on revenues from user fees to fund operations and maintenance as well as capital expenditures.
- New institutional arrangements should be sought for management of inland waterways (e.g., regional authorities) that would require less federal subsidization of waterway operation and expansion.

Air Transportation

With respect to air freight, TRB's report recommends that the federal government pursue multilateral agreements as well as bilateral agreements to liberalize the international air freight market.

Decision-Making Processes and Planning

TRB's *21st Century Freight Capacity* report also investigates needs associated with the transportation decision-making process. Specifically, the report investigates options for better mainstreaming freight needs into the process, and recommends the following:

- *U.S. DOT Data and Analysis Programs*–Congress should give continued support to the development of U.S. DOT's capabilities for economic analysis of the federal-aid highway program and federal highway user fees and to the application of this analysis in support of decisions. Congress should support joint state-federal efforts to transfer and adapt these tools to state and local needs.
- *Evaluation Method*–Congress should create a clearinghouse within the U.S. DOT devoted to evaluation methods in which the U.S. DOT and state and local agencies can share and compare methods and examples of evaluation.
- *Reducing Project Delivery Time*–The U.S. DOT should implement a streamlined environmental review process. Congress should consider allowing federal agencies to accept funds from non-federal public agency applicants to pay for expedited project reviews.

GAO's Freight Transportation: Strategies Needed to Address Planning and Financing Limitations _(2003)_

In December 2003, the General Accounting Office (GAO) issued a report regarding the challenges facing the freight transportation industry and strategies that could help the country overcome those challenges. GAO found that congestion problems are common across the country but are particularly nettlesome at freight-specific "chokepoints" such as entrances to port facilities, at-grade highway-rail crossings, and roads linking Interstate highways to ports and other intermodal facilities.

GAO concluded that the fundamental limitation on maintaining and improving freight mobility is that the public planning and financing processes are not well suited to addressing freight concerns. GAO recommended two strategies for remedying this situation. First, the agency argued for a more system-wide perspective in the transportation planning process. Second, GAO advocated a wider range of financing options for projects that enhance freight mobility.

Specific recommendations included the following:

- ➢ Improve the collection and sharing of freight-related data with state and local planning organizations.
- ➢ Develop consistent and sound analytical methods and evaluation approaches for freight-related projects.
- ➢ Expand the eligibility criteria for existing programs to cover a broader range of freight projects.
- ➢ Use low-cost alternatives to expand capacity through more efficient use of existing infrastructure.

AASHTO's Freight-Rail Bottom-Line Report *(2002)*

In 2002, the American Association of State Highway and Transportation Officials (AASHTO) issued a report to present its views concerning the capacity of the nation's freight transportation system, especially the freight-rail system, to keep pace with the expected growth of the economy over the next 20 years. The report describes the freight-rail industry, estimates investment needs and the capacity of the industry to meet these needs, and quantifies the consequences of not investing in freight-rail, including the impact on highway congestion and condition.

The AASHTO report points out that in the recent past, public investment in the rail sector has focused on the bottom of the rail system, such as grade crossings, branch lines, and commuter rail services. According to the report, the need today is to address key elements of the national rail network, including nationally significant corridors, urban rail interchanges, and intermodal terminals and connectors.

The report concludes that the rail industry will be unable to invest enough in its infrastructure to keep up with the growing demand for freight transportation over the next 20 years. The report explores a number of options for public investment, such as:

- ➢ Allowing highway funds to be used for freight projects that have benefits for highway users and the general public,
- ➢ Creating a separately funded federal rail program,
- ➢ Expanding federal loan and credit enhancement programs for the rail industry,
- ➢ Utilizing innovative financing, such as tax-exempt or tax-credit bonds, and
- ➢ Developing multi-state partnerships such as infrastructure corporations or banks.

TRB's* Policy Options for Intermodal Freight Transportation *(1998)

This TRB report was motivated by the fact that intermodal freight transportation is one of the major technological and organizational trends affecting the performance of the freight transportation industry. In the report, the authors set out guiding principles for public investment in intermodal transportation and make policy recommendations.

In general, the report sounds a cautionary note about public investment in intermodal facilities, noting that these facilities have usually been financed exclusively by the private sector. The report concludes that introducing public funds into this mix could undermine the "user pays" principle of highway finance, fuel interstate rivalries, and build expectations in the private sector for continuing public subsidies.

As part of this cautionary stance, the report recommends that government agencies develop and apply standard analysis tools to estimate costs and benefits and winners and losers of any public investments. The report also recommends that the public role in financing major facilities should receive close scrutiny to ensure that public benefits (e.g., congestion relief or reduced pollution) justify the expenditure of public funds and that users pay to the extent that they benefit.

Among the report's specific policy recommendations are the following:

- ➢ Seek ways to increase the involvement of freight interests in the public process of selecting infrastructure projects.
- ➢ Ensure that the federal government's information systems in areas such as customs, enforcement, and the military are interoperable with those of private industry.
- ➢ Undertake research on standard methods for evaluating freight infrastructure investment proposals and on defining, measuring, and forecasting the performance of the national freight system.

Recent Legislation

The Transportation Equity Act for the 21st Century (TEA-21) was the law that authorized federal surface transportation programs for fiscal years 1998-2003. In the spring of 2003, the Bush administration submitted its reauthorization proposal (known as SAFETEA) to Congress. Due to significant disagreement over the appropriate overall funding level for the bill, Congress was unable to pass a reauthorization bill before TEA-21 expired in September 2003 and has had to pass two short-term extensions. The following is a description of the major freight-related components of the Bush administration's proposal and the House and Senate bills:

All three of the bills are focused on highway safety, and, as part of that focus, they include provisions to improve the safety of rail-highway crossings, which would benefit freight as well as passenger traffic. In addition, all of the bills amend the environmental review process for infrastructure projects in an effort to shorten the time devoted to that process. If successful, this reform would result in faster timelines for new highway capacity, with obvious benefits for the trucking industry. Finally, all three bills include provisions intended to advance the use of information technology and intelligent transportation systems, which could increase the productivity of the freight sector.

The Bush Administration's Safe, Accountable, Flexible, and Efficient Transportation Equity Act of 2003 (SAFETEA)

The Bush administration's reauthorization proposal contained little new funding specifically for freight-related concerns, but it did contain a number of new set-asides and eligibility changes to increase the availability of funding for freight-related infrastructure. The administration referred to these changes collectively as the "Freight Gateways Program." The main features of the administration's proposal were the following:

- Dedicating a portion of NHS funds for highway connections between the NHS and intermodal freight facilities such as ports and freight terminals;
- Allowing STP funds to be used for publicly owned intermodal freight transportation projects that address economic, congestion, security, safety, and environmental issues associated with freight transportation gateways;
- Allowing private freight rail projects to qualify for TIFIA credit assistance;

- Expanding the availability of tax-exempt private activity bonds to include highway projects and freight transfer facilities; and
- Requiring states to designate a freight transportation coordinator and to integrate intermodal freight transportation needs into the planning and project development processes.

Senate Bill (S.1075)

The Senate-passed reauthorization bill mirrors the President's proposal in many ways. The Senate bill also creates a "Freight Gateways Program" consisting of many of the same set-asides and eligibility changes that were in the President's proposal. However, since the Senate bill contains significantly more overall funding than the President's proposal, the amount of funding generated by these set-asides is much larger in the Senate bill. The Senate bill does differ from the President's proposal in some key respects, such as:

- The Senate bill does not expand the use of the TIFIA program or private-activity bonds for rail or other freight facilities;
- The Senate bill creates a non-governmental, non-profit corporation to issue bonds for certain infrastructure projects, including freight-related infrastructure such as freight corridors, intermodal freight transfer facilities, border crossing facilities, freight rail facilities, and port and airport facilities;
- The Senate bill contains rail-related provisions not found in either of the other two reauthorization bills. The Senate bill would create two new rail-related grant programs, one for improving the tracks of Class II and III railroads and another for relocating rail lines.

House Bill (H.R. 3550)

As originally conceived, the bill put forward by the House Transportation and Infrastructure Committee contained $375 billion for the period 2004-2009 and therefore could accommodate several new, ambitious programs that would have benefited the freight transportation industry (primarily trucking but to some extent the rail industry as well). However, the version of the bill passed by the House contained less than $300 billion for the six-year period, so these initiatives were trimmed back.

The bill's major freight-related provisions are:

- New funding for improving intermodal connectors, public roads that connect major intermodal facilities to the national highway system,

- New funding to improve the flow of traffic across the borders with Mexico and Canada,
- New funding for "projects of regional and national significance" that will improve the flow of traffic beyond the immediate area of the project (includes freight railroad projects),
- A National Corridor Infrastructure Improvement Program to fund regional and multi-state corridor projects,
- A new pilot program for truck-only lanes, and
- A new requirement that states obligate a certain portion of their highway formula funds for congestion relief activities in urbanized areas of 200,000 people or more.

Appendix C

Current State of In-Vehicle Technology

Advanced technology in the 21st century vehicle will have the ability to provide standalone processing to assist the driver in both day-to-day driving and in extreme situations such as automobile crashes and emergency evacuations.

As the infrastructure is developed for communications from a vehicle to other vehicles and to information and emergency services, advanced onboard electronics and internet accessibility will provide the means for drivers and passengers to access a wide array of information and service providers as well as to supply data that will help make driving safer, more productive, and more comfortable for everyone.

This appendix provides a summary of the safety-oriented technology that is currently available on vehicles or that is scheduled to become available in the very near future.

The safety technology described here is available mainly on high-end vehicles. One way to make highways safer is for these safety features to be implemented on a far wider range of automobiles.

Currently Available Safety Features

Automotive safety is a high priority for most car buyers. It is also a high priority for governments and ITS industry associations worldwide. This has resulted in a large number of significant safety innovations in vehicles. Just three years ago, most the safety features in this section (except airbags) were listed as "future developments" in ITS articles and documents. There has indeed been significant progress in the area of in-vehicle safety technology.

Safety devices lie in a continuum that goes from protection to information to warning to control. Some of the offerings appearing in 2004 begin to cross into the "control" category. For example, adaptive cruise control that maintains a following distance is, within limits, in the control category. Ford/Volvo's active rollover prevention system for SUVs is strongly in the control category.

Driver Assistance

Driver assistance features help drivers and vehicles perform better. Vehicle manufacturers have been billing these features as "comfort and convenience" to avoid making claims for ensuring safety and taking on the corresponding liability. However, each feature can be reasonably regarded as contributing to the safe normal operation of the vehicle. These functions generally fall into:

- Warning the driver of an developing problem (e.g., tire pressure monitor)
- Giving the driver additional information (e.g., backing assistance)
- Amplifying the driver's actions in an emergency situation (e.g., microprocessor-controlled braking assistance)
- Allowing the driver to focus more completely on the task of driving (e.g., hands-free cellular phone dialing)

Warning Features

Tire pressure monitoring

Tire pressure monitors can detect if a tire is significantly underinflated and alert the driver.

Tire pressure monitors are available on a few high-end automobiles. They have been common in the trucking industry for some years.

Parking assistance

Parking assistance systems use sensors to alert the driver to obstacles at the front, rear, and corners of the vehicle.

A few high-end automobiles offer this feature as an option. These sensors have been available on buses for some years.

Information Features

Backing assistance

Backing assistance provides the driver with the ability to see behind the vehicle with a rear-facing camera. This is most helpful for large vehicles like SUVs and minivans.

A few high-end vehicles offer backup assistance as an option. As an example, Lexus's Rear Backup Camera uses a real-time video camera mounted near the top of the rear license plate. When the vehicle is in reverse, the image from the camera is displayed on the navigation screen.

Auto-aiming headlights

Auto-aiming headlights adjust their angle based on the steering motion of the vehicle to better illuminate the road around curves and corners.

Many high-end automobiles now offer auto-aiming headlights. Future generation auto-aiming headlights may use the navigation map database to anticipate curves and hills, keeping the headlights on the curving road ahead even before a turning maneuver begins.

Night vision systems

Night vision systems use infrared heat-sensing cameras to provide better visibility of roadway hazards at night. In particular, the camera can "see" animate objects (people and animals) and other cars at night before they are in visual range. The infrared image appears on a heads-up display on the windshield.

Cadillac and Ford both offer night vision systems. GM states that Cadillac's night vision allows drivers to see three times farther than low-beam headlights and two times farther than high-beam headlights.

Driving Action Amplification

Enhanced braking

Electronically enhanced braking improves driver braking performance. Electronic brakes often work in conjunction with other car systems such as stability control to provide safer stopping and shorter stopping distances.

Enhanced braking systems are available on a number of high-end cars with a variety of implementations.

Lexus's Brake Assist system is integrated with its antilock brakes to help the driver in emergency situations. Brake Assist determines if the driver is attempting emergency braking and, if the driver has not applied enough brake pedal pressure to activate the antilock brakes, Brake Assist applies maximum non-skid braking pressure until the driver lets up on the pedal.

Mercedes' SBC™ electro-hydraulic braking system uses a combination of microprocessor and sensors to reduce stopping distance in emergency situations. This system detects an emergency stop based on how fast the driver moves his foot from the accelerator pedal to the brake. The system begins braking before the brake is engaged by the driver and, if it determines that the driver is depressing the brake pedal, it amplifies the driver's actions. SBC works with Mercedes' Electronic Stability Program so that a quick stop does not cause the vehicle to lose traction.

Drive-by-wire

Drive-by-wire systems connect human controls directly to a computer over a vehicle databus. The computer interprets the action and directly controls the vehicle system (brakes, steering, etc.). Drive-by-wire, already common in airplanes, improves vehicle reliability while reducing reliance on mechanical linkages.

Drive-by-wire systems are just starting to appear in production automobiles. Several Lexus models have a drive-by-wire system called the "Electronic Throttle Control System with intelligence" (ETCS-i), which connects the gas pedal directly to the engine's computer for smoother acceleration.

Driver Focus Features

Cell phone integration and hands-free operation

Hands-free cell phone use has become important as more states and localities pass laws banning hands-on use of cell phones while driving.

Hands-free cell phones are frequently built in on high-end vehicles and are also available in the aftermarket. To enhance the safety of cell phone use, some vehicle manufacturers offering built-in cell phones limit the functions that are accessible when the vehicle is in motion and provide steering wheel controls to answer calls, end calls, and adjust call volume.

Driving style adjustment

Driving style adjustment uses sensors to determine the driving style of the current driver and adjusts the suspension accordingly.

Mercedes offers a system that electronically adjusts the suspension from standard/comfortable to sporty. In manual mode, the driver can choose between these settings.

Crash Mitigation

Crash mitigation products help to minimize the consequences of crashes, reducing deaths and injuries. Crash protection in the form of airbags and collision anticipation systems were among the earliest automotive safety devices to gain wide public acceptance. These products have undergone a number of enhancements in recent years based on experience with previous implementations.

Airbag improvements

Airbags have been a standard part of the safety equipment in automobiles for over a decade. All new vehicles sold in the United States now come with at least a standard airbag for the driver and the front seat passenger.

Recent airbag improvements have come in two varieties: refinement of basic airbags and additional airbags to mitigate injuries in a wider range of crash situations.

Variable force airbags are now available on many models. These airbags deploy at a different velocity depending on the weight of passenger and the speed of the vehicle at the time of a crash. This improvement was created to avoid injuries to small-framed adults and children from the airbags themselves.

A number of automakers are also introducing auxiliary airbags. For example, Lexus has implemented knee airbags for the driver and front passenger as standard equipment. Many manufacturers have introduced side curtain airbags on some models. On Ford SUVs, side airbags are used in conjunction with horizontal vehicle roll information that anticipates a rollover.

Collision anticipation

Collision anticipation systems detect an impending crash and take action to safeguard vehicle occupants, generally by activating seatbelt pretensioners to tighten occupants' seatbelts. Some collision anticipation systems work in concert with airbags or computer-controlled braking systems to provide additional crash protection or mitigation.

These systems are found on a few high-end vehicles. Lexus and Mercedes have each implemented collision anticipation, but in different ways.

Lexus is introducing the Pre-Collision System (PCS) in 2004. PCS uses millimeter-wave radar to detect obstacles in front of the car and a pre-collision system computer that makes use of vehicle speed, steering angle, and yaw rate. PCS works in conjunction with Lexus's Brake Assist.

Mercedes E-Class vehicles are equipped with a rollover sensor that helps minimize the effects of rollovers by triggering occupant protection systems.

Crash Avoidance

Crash avoidance products shift the paradigm from minimizing the consequences of crashes to preventing crashes from occurring. A number of new capabilities have recently appeared that provide automated crash avoidance support.

Rollover anticipation and protection

Rollover anticipation and protection systems monitor vehicle dynamics. If the system detects a danger of rolling over, it activates the electronic braking system and electronic stability program to keep the vehicle upright.

This feature is available on the Volvo XV90 SUV.

Stability control – Correcting loss of control by the driver

Electronic Stability Programs (ESP) provide automated vehicle control when the vehicle is in danger of skidding or losing lateral traction when cornering. ESP works with other systems in the vehicle – the brakes, the transmission, and the throttle – to take corrective action to prevent a skid.

Virtually all high-end automakers have implemented ESP. In addition, ESP is now appearing on some mid-range vehicles such as the Ford Explorer SUV and Freestar Minivan.

One objective of the European Commission's E-Safety initiative is to have ESP in all vehicles sold in Europe by the end of 2005. The Commission believe that ESP is proven as a significant accident prevention technology.

ERTICO (ITS Europe) quotes statistics which show that from 2000 to 2001 an overall 4% reduction in accidents was directly attributable to ESP. The reduction of rollover accidents resulting from the use of ESP was estimated to be about 12%. A Mercedes study indicated that vehicles equipped with ESP were involved in 15% fewer accidents than unequipped models.

Adaptive cruise control

Adaptive cruise control (ACC) adds ranging technology (radar or lidar) to standard cruise control. The radar monitors the distance to the vehicle ahead and maintains a driver-selected following distance. ACC detects when the vehicle ahead slows down, or when another vehicle enters the lane at less than the set following distance, and takes corrective action. This corrective action is modest, simply slowing the vehicle. In current implementations, hard braking or lane change action must still be done by the driver.

ACC is available on virtually all high-end vehicles.

A number of vehicle manufacturers indicate that an advanced stop-and-go version of ACC is included in their concept cars. This advanced version allows use of ACC in heavy traffic.

The CHAUFFER project in Europe plans to combine ACC with experimental lane-keeping technology to reduce rear-end collisions.

Comfort and Convenience Features

Comfort and convenience features help drivers get to their destinations more efficiently and more comfortably.

Navigation systems

Navigation systems help plot an efficient driving route and guide the driver to a specified destination. The key internal components are a map database, positioning sensors (typically GPS-based), and software for route planning and guidance. At present, routes are based on static (predefined) roadway network information. Future navigation systems will incorporate real-time and predictive information about traffic and road conditions to plan optimal routes based on the best information then available. The map database may also play a part in safety-related features such as adaptive cruise control and curve warnings.

Although navigation systems are not usually characterized as safety products, they can improve safety by helping the driver to avoid sudden maneuvers and by relieving driving stress.

Navigation systems are available in virtually all high-end automobiles, in an increasing number of mid-market automobiles, and in the aftermarket, including hand-held versions. Map databases for navigation systems now provide nationwide or continent-wide coverage.

Personalized climate control and air filtration

This feature allows the driver and passengers to control temperature and humidity and helps protect them from mold and other air pollutants.

Personalized climate control has been available for some time on most high-end vehicles. The air filtration feature is newly available on some high-end automobiles.

Satellite radio

Satellite radio offers a wide range of radio stations, most without commercial interruption and without having to re-tune as the automobile moves from one area to another.

Satellite radio is currently offered by some automakers and in the aftermarket. At present, the radio costs about $150 and the service is about $10 a month. The two leading providers are XM Satellite Radio and Sirius Satellite Radio. At present, XM and Sirius collectively have about two million subscribers following an investment of over $3.4 billion.[180] Collective losses in 2004 are expected to be about $550 million. XM has a marketing partnership with and is partly owned by General Motors and Honda. Sirius has marketing partnerships with DaimlerChrysler, Ford, and Volkswagen. Both companies are forecasting positive cash flow in 2005 and more than 23 million collective subscribers by 2009.

Rain-sensing wipers; automatic headlights

Rain-sensing windshield wipers and automatic headlights switch these components on and off based on sensed environmental conditions.

Lexus, Honda, and Cadillac all offer rain-sensing wipers. Automatic headlights are widely available down through mid-market automobiles.

Stolen vehicle tracking

Stolen vehicle tracking systems help assist the rapid recovery of vehicles reported stolen, by providing authorities with the location and travel path of the vehicle. Some stolen vehicle systems include the ability to remotely disable the vehicle or shut down its engine.

Stolen vehicle tracking is available as a commercial aftermarket product from LoJack and others, and is a component of some telematics services (e.g., OnStar).

Telematics

Systems have arisen to assist drivers in various ways using wireless communications between a land-based infrastructure and the vehicle. Such communications-based information and service applications are called telematics.

Three businesses offering Telematics are the BMW (Driver Assistance system), Mercedes (TeleAid system), and OnStar. OnStar was initiated by GM, but is now a separate company. OnStar is currently licensed to Acura, Audi, Isuzu, Lexus, Subaru, and Volkswagen in addition to GM. In the Lexus, OnStar is called Lexus Link, and is available in only some of its models. ATX Technologies provides the telematics service for Mercedes TeleAid and for other vehicle lines.

For many telematics offerings, the typical arrangement is that the first year of service is "free" (i.e., included in the purchase price of the vehicle). In subsequent years, the vehicle owner must pay a subscription fee to keep the service running. Based on statements by the companies and on a small independent survey, it appears that fewer than 50% of owners continue the service after the introductory period.

Services offered by all telematics providers are:

- Airbag deployment detection and automatic crash notification
- Emergency assistance on request
- Roadside assistance
- Tracking of stolen vehicles
- Driving directions
- Remote door unlock for equipped vehicles
- Information services
- Personal calling via an included cellular phone
- Concierge services

Many telematics services require the use of a cell phone. In the OnStar implementation, this is a separate cell phone from the driver's personal cell phone, which has generated some customer resistance.

Driver assistance software including remote diagnostics

The OnStar system provides remote diagnostics. This allows a technician at a remote site to determine whether a driver's car is safe to continue driving in case of certain failures. The primary failure noted in the literature is the check engine light, though it is noted that some other remote diagnostics can be performed.

Driver assistance software including breakdown assistance, directions to destination, traffic information

BMW Driver Assistance service is available in Germany, Japan, the UK, and the United States. It works with BMW's in-vehicle navigation system and cellular phone to provide location-based services. Services include directions to destination, hotel and restaurant information, and car trouble assistance. If the driver requests telephone numbers, they can be transmitted directly to the onboard cell phone.

Internet connectivity

Internet connectivity provides vehicle occupants with much the same range of information available to users of desktop internet. There are many ergonomic and safety hurdles to overcome before the internet can be used widely in vehicles.

BMW currently offers BMW Online, which allows the driver to access the internet. The service is presently available in Germany and the UK.

Expected Future Developments

Driver Assistance

Lane keeping

Lane keeping warns the driver if the automobile leaves its current lane.

This feature is not yet available on production vehicles although Nissan recently announced its near-term intention to make the feature available. Almost all automakers have a lane-keeping feature on their concept cars. BMW's Heading Control will help a driver stay in the current driving lane.

Curve warning

Curve warning systems use the navigation map database to determine the curvature of the road ahead and gauge whether the curve can be negotiated safely at the vehicle's current speed. If the speed is too high, a series of visual and audible warnings are issued. In future versions, the automobile will be slowed automatically if the driver does not take responsive action.

Although not yet offered commercially, both DaimlerChrysler and Toyota are developing systems that provide warnings if a curve is being approached too fast.

Digital maps for enhancing safety

The information available in digital maps has the potential to significantly increase the accuracy of in-vehicle safety systems and reduce their computational load. Digital maps can act as predictive sensors.

On its website, Mercedes indicates its plan to implement digital map enhanced safety systems. A number of other automakers are testing safety applications using digital maps as electronic driving aids. The aim of the tests is to establish the safety-relevant information that might sensibly be included in navigation systems and to find ways of presenting the great variety of information without distracting the driver.

Table of Features by Manufacturer

The table below provides a sampling of the advanced technology features which automobile manufacturers indicate they have implemented. This is not intended to be a complete listing of all features offered by all manufacturers, but rather to provide an idea of the breadth and depth of currently available technology.

	BMW	Toyota/ Lexus	Daimler Chrysler	Ford/ Volvo	GM	Acura/ Honda	Infiniti
Driver warnings							
Tire pressure monitor		X	X		X		X
Parking assistance	X	X	X	X			
Driver information							
Backup assistance	X	X	X				X
Auto-aiming headlights	X	X	X				
Night vision		X		X	X		
Driver action amplification							
Enhanced braking	X	X	X	X			X
Drive-by-wire		X					
Driver focus							
Cell phone integration and hands-free operation	X	X	X	X	X		
Driving style adjustment	X	X	X	X			
Crash mitigation							
Airbag improvements	X	X	X	X	X	X	X
Body structure reinforcement	X	X	X	X	X	X	X
Collision anticipation	X	X	X	X			
Crash avoidance							
Rollover anticipation and protection				X			
Electronic stability control	X	X	X	X	X	X	X
Adaptive cruise control	X	X	X	X	X		X

	BMW	Toyota/ Lexus	Daimler Chrysler	Ford/ Volvo	GM	Acura/ Honda	Infiniti
Comfort and convenience							
Personalized climate control and air filtration		X	X	X		X	
Satellite radio		X			X	X	
Navigation systems	X	X	X	X	X	X	X
Rain-sensing wipers	X		X	X	X		
Automatic headlights	X	X	X	X	X		X
Stolen vehicle tracking					X		
Theft deterrent		X			X		
Telematics							
Internet connectivity	X						
Traffic info	X						
No hands unlock		X	X	X	X	X	X
Personal phone-book integration with cell phone		X	X				
Driver assistance – remote diagnostics					X		
Driver assistance – directions, breakdown, traffic	X		X	X	X	X	X
Future							
Lane positioning assistance	X						
Curve warning		X					

Appendix D

Demographic Considerations for the Early Twenty-First Century

Population Change

Total Population: The Central Consideration

As we begin to think about the transportation infrastructure necessary to support the U.S. population, the first question concerns how big or small, how quickly or how slowly growing, the population will be. We will use the U.S. Census Bureau data here for population projection figures. This data brings its own issues and uncertainties, which we will examine and account for.

In the aggregate, the general frame for understanding future U.S. population growth is "steady but slower." The Census Bureau's Middle Series projection forecasts absolute growth that is fairly comparable to our recent experience. The United States added 55 million people in the last two decades of the twentieth century (see Table D-1). It is projected to add 54 million people in the first two decades of the twenty-first century. Of course, the relatively diminished absolute growth translates into a slower rate of growth:

Table D-1: U.S. Population, 1980-2000

Year	U.S. Population	Decennial absolute growth	Decennial growth rate
1980	227m	24m	12%
1990	249m	22m	10%
2000	282m	33m	13%

The difficulty with the projections shown in Table D-2 is that they are likely to turn out wrong and under-predict the true extent of population growth in the United States. For example, if we go back to the projections made after the 1990 Census, the July 2003 population figure of 291 million exceeded its Middle Series projection by some 8 million people. The Census Bureau publishes other projections series— "Low," "Middle," "High," and "Zero Migration" series—but all these missed the mark as well. Even the "High Series," which predicts faster population growth as its name would suggest, projected a figure less than the eventual outcome, falling 6 million people short.

Table D-2: Census Bureau Population Growth Projections for 2010-2050, Middle Series

Year	U.S. Population	Decennial absolute growth	Decennial growth rate
2010	309m	27m	9%
2020	336m	28m	9%
2030	364m	28m	8%
2040	392m	28m	8%
2050	420m	28m	7%

This under-prediction by the Census Bureau has been a fairly continuous problem and has a clear culprit: exploding immigration that cannot be totally accounted for in statistical models. As the next section will detail, immigration into the United States is occurring at unprecedented levels. Immigration will of course be subject to the domestic and international policy, economic, and security landscapes. There is no guarantee that it will continue at its current astronomic pace. However, it is likely to. This suggests that while it is best to use the Middle Series as a guide, faster growth, as detailed in Table D-3, is important to keep in mind as an alternative for the medium- and longer-term.

Table D-3: U.S. Population, 2010-2050; Middle Series vs. High Series[181]

Year	Middle Series	High Series
2010	309m	311m
2020	336m	355m
2030	364m	410m
2040	392m	476m
2050	420m	553m

The Immigration Factor

In 1980, yearly net migration to the United States was 500 thousand. In 1990, the number had climbed to 650 thousand. By 2000, the figure was 1.3 million, three times the level of 1980 and twice the level of 1990.

That type of trend line creates difficulty in predicting the future, as suggested by Figure D-1.

Figure D-1: Periodic Annual Net Migration to the United States, 1980-2050[182]

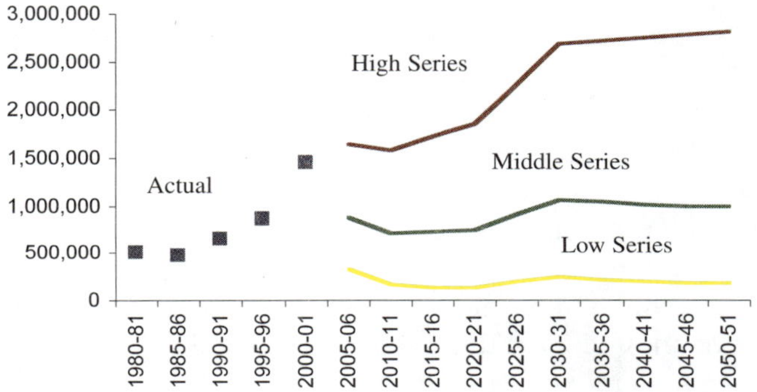

The Census Bureau's Middle Series assumes that the yearly net migration rate through 2020 will be at 700 to 800 thousand. However, this rate has been at 1.3 million for most of this decade. At such a rate, total immigration is likely to be much higher than Middle Series Projections. Through 2020, immigration is likely to produce a population size (and immigrant pool) somewhere in between the Middle and High Series forecasts, as described in the previous section.

However, immigration levels are at least partly a function of very malleable policy. The United States could possibly force immigration down near the range of the Census Bureau Middle Series assumptions or lower if desired. Yet, there is little in the present policy context that suggests this is likely to happen. Neither the Bush administration nor the Congress introduced any legislation to limit or restrict immigration in the last four years. Instead, in 2004 President Bush proposed immigration reform that would grant legal status to immigrant workers for three years and thus would bring even more foreigners to America for work.

As we begin to think about the implications of sustained high immigration levels for issues like transportation, the effect on changing the character of the U.S. population is important to consider. Immigration does not just swell the overall size of the U.S. population; it creates a foreign-born population different in its racial, ethnic, and linguistic profile. The cumulative effects are astonishing, as shown in Table D-4.

Table D-4: Total U.S. Population and Foreign-Born U.S. Population, 2005-2020

	Middle Growth Series			**High Growth Series**		
Year	Total U.S. Population	Foreign-Born Population	Percent Foreign-Born	Total U.S. Population	Foreign-Born Population	Percent Foreign-Born
2005	288m	30m	10	292m	33m	**11**
2010	300m	33m	11	311m	40m	**13**
2015	312m	36m	12	332m	47m	**14**
2020	**325m**	**38m**	**12**	**355m**	**54m**	**15**

Of course, data like these are the very sources of opposition to the recent size of immigration. Forty to 50 million foreign born persons walking around the United States could not help but alter almost every facet of public and economic life. Still, the likelihood is that the United States will continue to tolerate or encourage the influx of high numbers of foreign-born persons. To grasp this likelihood, it is necessary to examine the impact of native population trends on the labor force. From that perspective, immigration looks less like an optional determinant of population change and more like an inevitable economic lifeline to stagnating labor force rolls.

The Labor Force Factor

The United States will need more foreign-born workers in the upcoming decades to compensate for much slower growth in the native-born labor force. The ultimate production of America's workers is obviously determined by both the number of workers and the amount each worker can produce. Economic growth is thus a function of the increase in size of the labor force and the increase in productivity. Some argue that the population effects described above, and their impact on labor force size, can be overcome by focusing on the productivity side of the economic production ledger. Thus, augmenting the labor force side of the ledger through immigration would be unnecessary.

One cannot totally discount such a possibility, of course. The world is in the midst of an historic technological revolution. Yet, there is a wide gap between possible and probable in this case. Consider the future growth of the labor force as shown in Table D-5.

The United States is in the midst of a massive slowdown in the rate of labor force growth, as well as the absolute size of the increases it will experience. This problem will get much worse before it gets better, and even then, better is a relative concept. The absolute increase in the labor force in the ten years between 2015 and 2025 will be only 3.8 million. In the 1980s, it took less than two years to reach this level of growth. At the present rate of growth, that level will require a little less than three years.

Table D-5: Absolute Growth and Growth Rate in the 25+ Labor Force, United States, 1980-2050

Decade	Absolute Growth	**Growth Rate**
1980-90	22m	**27%**
1990-2000	15m	**14%**
2000-10	17m	**11%**
2010-20	7m	**6%**
2020-30	4m	**3%**
2030-40	8m	**6%**
2040-50	**10m**	**6%**

Again, it would seem optimistic in the extreme to expect that productivity changes can completely compensate for this kind of slowdown in the number of new workers added to the economy. Absent a miracle in productivity growth, it would seem injudicious in the extreme to expect policymakers to tolerate slower economic growth in favor of smaller immigration.

Aging

The primary cause of the acute and sudden reduction in labor-force growth is of course the retirement of the Baby Boomers, one expression of the aging of the population. The first Baby Boomers will reach the official age for retirement, 65, in 2011. This process will continue into the 2030s. It is difficult to overstate the changes that the size of this retirement cohort will bring about on nearly every aspect of American public and economic life. To get a sense of this, consider the basic data described in Table D-6.

Although the official retirement age is in the mid-60s, the choice to retire occurs much earlier for some. Hence, it is convenient to segment the population into those who are younger than 60 and those who are 60 and older, as in Table D-5. The growth of the latter group is stunning. Between 2005 and 2030, its size will almost double. The cohort will swell by 10 million over the current decade, by nearly 20 million in the next decade, and by 15 million in the decade after. Essentially, the process will change the composition of the American population from the recent point when about 1 in 7 Americans were 60 or older to a point where 1 in 4 are 60 or older.

Table D-6: The 60 and Older Population in the United States, 1980-2050

	Population 60 and Above	**Percent of Total Population**
1980	36m	**16**
1990	42m	**16**
2000	46m	**16**
2005	49m	**17**
2010	56m	**19**
2015	64m	**21**
2020	74m	**23**
2030	89m	**25**
2040	96m	**25**
2050	**103m**	**26**

The chief problem with this generational shift as it impacts the labor force is that there are really two problems. If there were no public costs associated with retirement at all, Boomer retirement would slow labor force growth and probably economic growth, compared with past experiences. Since there are public costs, and quite significant costs at that, associated with retirement, the repercussions will be enormous: increasing public commitments squeezing a labor force with growth dynamics that make it ever harder to pay for those commitments. All expenditures in the public realm will come under pressure.

In addition to the labor force and entitlement effects, it is always important to keep in mind that an older population, from the perspective of "the norm," is a more diverse population. Moreover, as we begin to segment the older population further, an important general conclusion arises: the older the cohort, the faster the growth. In other words, the 80 and over population will generally grow faster than the 60 to 70 year old population. This diversity relative to the historic profile of the United States will place different demands on public systems and private markets. This group will have different preferences that may frustrate policy solutions that would otherwise be considered optimal. As an example, consider the technological complexity inherent in the personal transportation systems envisioned by some forward thinkers. There is no guarantee that a population in which a quarter came of age long before the basis of the technology will embrace such technological immersion.

Regardless of the countless considerations one could pose about an aging population, the repercussions of anemic labor force growth, particularly in the face of massive entitlements owed to the retirees who bear much of the responsibility for the growth collapse, are enormous and countless, and the government will be forced to address the changes this demographic shift will bring. Allowing immigration of foreign laborers into the United States would be one of the clearest solutions to satisfy the American labor shortage. From the standpoint of future transportation needs, population change will put continue to put larger numbers of people and goods on the various facets of America's transportation infrastructure. Perhaps just as importantly, the character of the population will change, as well. It will be older. It will be increasingly foreign-born, and this has important implications for the racial and ethic make-up of the United States.

Diversity

Although diversity was a word that took on a number of meanings in the 1990s—not all of them welcome by some—it is an apt description of the changes occurring in the U.S. population and workforce. Usually connoting race or ethnicity, though more usefully broadened to include age as above, the diversification of the United States has its roots in immigration.

The U.S. population includes far more foreign-born people today than in the past. As Table D-3 showed, the foreign-born population in America may range from 38 to 54 million people by 2020 and may make up 11 to 15 percent of the general population. Along with additional immigration, certain ethnic groups will grow more quickly than others in the next fifty years. The Hispanic and Asian populations are expected to experience the largest absolute increases (see Table D-7).

Table D-7: Composition of American Population by Race/Ethnicity, 1980-2050

Year	Middle Growth Series					**High Growth Series**				
	White	Hispanic	Black	Asian	Other	White	Hispanic	Black	Asian	**Other**
1980	79	6	12	2	1					
2000	71	12	12	4	1					
2025	62	18	13	6	1	58	20	13	8	**1**
2050	**53**	**24**	**13**	**9**	**1**	**47**	**27**	**13**	**13**	**<1**

The High Series projects that whites may lose majority status as early as 2042; the Middle Series date is at 2060. The notable growth of the Hispanic population in the United States is due to increased immigration from the countries of Latin America. Indeed, over half of the foreign-born legal citizens and permanent residents in the United States in 2002 were born in Latin America, totaling 16 million (see Figure D-2). Half of the 16 million were born in Mexico, and it is estimated that there are an additional 2 million illegal Mexican immigrants living and working in the United States. This number is also expected to increase, although it is a more likely suspect for reduction through policy change than legal immigration is.

Figure D-2: U.S. Foreign-Born Population by Region of Birth, 2002

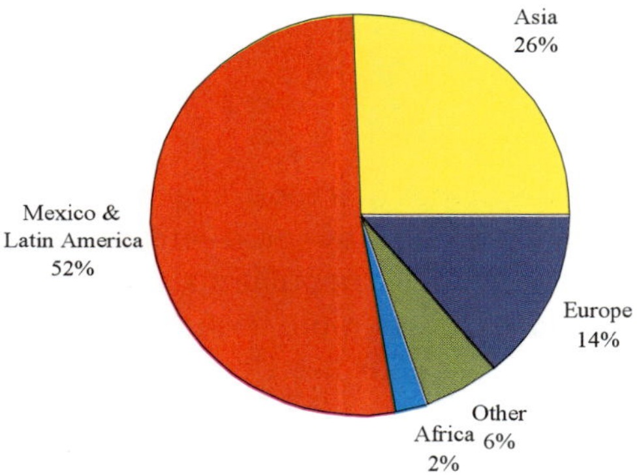

Although persons of Hispanic ethnicity currently dominate the immigrant pool, it is important to consider that this may not always be so. There are a number of obvious factors such as proximity that contribute to the size of the Hispanic share of the immigrant population. Yet, the propensity of a nation to be a source for an emigrating population is partly a function of that nation's internal population dynamics. In this respect, the current state of Latin American populations is not a permanent one. After 2030, the population growth rates are expected to decline in the countries of Latin America. As the following table shows, Latin America's growth rate can be expected to fall from 30% in the 2000-2025 period to 12% in the 2025-2050 period, while Sub-Saharan Africa and the Middle East will have the highest rate of growth in the second period. East Asia's population growth will begin to slow down as well, but its sheer size, as well as the growing East Asian population already in the

United States, make it a likely candidate to fill any vacuum that would be left by dwindling stocks of Hispanic immigrants.

Table D-8: Global Population and Growth Rate by Regions/Continents, 2000-2050

Region	2000 Population	2025 Population	2000-2025 Growth Rate	2050 Population	**2025-2050 Growth Rate**
Sub-Saharan Africa	657m	1,039m	58%	1,537m	**48%**
Middle East	316m	473m	50%	600m	**27%**
East Asia	3,443m	4,392m	27%	4,869m	**11%**
U.S. & Canada	313m	388m	24%	462m	**19%**
Latin America	522m	680m	30%	766m	**12%**
Oceania	31m	40m	30%	45m	**12%**
Europe	729m	715m	-2%	654m	**-9%**

Thus, with the international demographic shifts of the twenty-first century, it seems likely that the profile of the immigrant population in the United States will change as the century wears on. All these demographic changes in age-based and ethnic/racial diversity suggest that future transportation system design considerations will be significantly different from those of the past. The United States will be required to put forth policies to accommodate larger numbers of the elderly and the foreign-born on the roads, as well as to address the changing needs and characteristics of both groups.

Urbanization and Suburbanization

With the coming waves of immigration and population growth in the United States, it is necessary to analyze where the new millions of Americans will live in the coming decades. We have to address whether population trends will favor urban, suburban, or rural environments, and we also have to look at which regions of America will have the highest population increases in the future.

The death of distance may have been a mantra of the 1990s, but the decade did nothing to slow the de-ruralization of the U.S. population. Quite the opposite. As we enter the twenty-first century, the information networks and multidisciplinary intellectual work demanded by the knowledge economy is placing great value on geographic proximity and sustaining a preference for metropolitan labor networks.

The Census Bureau definitions of urban and rural areas are based on population density figures. Unfortunately, these definitions make it difficult to separate suburban areas from urban (or central-city) areas. Here we will instead use the Census Bureau definitions of metropolitan and non-metropolitan areas for data, which will allow us to distinguish the central city and the suburbs that together make up the metropolitan area. The 2000 Census figures put the rural population at 59 million and the non-metropolitan population at 55 million. The difference of 4 million indicates that about 2% of the metropolitan population is rural. For the sake of brevity, we will use the term "rural" to mean "non-metropolitan" in the following tables.

Table D-9: Percent of the U.S. Population that Is Urban and Suburban, 1960-2002

Year	Central City Population	Growth Rate	Suburban Population	Growth Rate	Metropolitan Population	**Percent of Total Population**
1960	58m		55m		113m	**63**
1970	64m	10%	75m	36%	139m	**69**
1980	68m	6%	101m	35%	169m	**75**
1990	77m	13%	120m	18%	197m	**79**
2000	85m	10%	141m	18%	226m	**80**
2002	82m	-4%	148m	5%	230m	**82**

High population growth in metropolitan areas and urban settings in the last 40 years has resulted in four out of every five Americans today living in metropolitan areas. While today many central cities are filled to capacity, suburban population is increasing everywhere. Suburban growth contributed to over 75% of metro area growth for cities as different as Denver, Indianapolis, Las Vegas, and New York City from 1990 to 2000. The 2002 U.S. metropolitan population of 230 million is equal to the entire American population just 20 years ago.

With continued suburban growth, the boundaries of most metropolitan areas will expand away from the central city—the Census Bureau diameters of many metropolitan areas are now as great as 40 miles. Much of the suburban growth will be a result of increased immigration and the higher numbers of foreign-born people it will bring to the United States. The growth of the foreign-born population in U.S. metropolitan areas has been conspicuous, especially since 1990 (see Table D-10).

In 2002, 94% of the foreign-born population in the United States lived in metropolitan areas. With current trends likely continuing, immigrants in the coming decades will mostly settle in metropolitan areas, bringing about even higher rates of suburban growth. Foreign-born population growth in central city areas will also be significant as the foreign-born will make up a larger percentage of central-city populations in the future. This will aid the recovery of central cities across America, which suffered net population losses in the 1970s and in the 1980s but have resumed growing in population since 1990. Today, many central cities across America are healthier than in decades past, but suburbanization is still the major source of population growth in the United States.

Table D-10: Foreign-Born Population in U.S. Urban, Suburban and Rural Areas, 1990 and 2002

Area type	1990			2002			**Absolute increase**
	Pop.	% of area population	% of f-b population	Pop.	% of area population	% of f-b population	
Central city	9.5m	12.2	47.8	14.0m	17.2	43.3	**4.5m**
Suburban	9.3m	7.8	47.2	16.6m	11.2	51.1	**17.3m**
Rural	**1.0m**	**1.9**	**5.0**	**1.8m**	**3.4**	**5.6**	**0.8m**

The average population growth rate per metropolitan area in the United States from 1990 to 2000 was 14%, and many areas experienced much higher growth rates. Among the top 10 metropolitan areas in the United States, southern cities Dallas, Houston, and Miami had the fastest growth rates, above 20%.

Table D-11: Population Growth in the 10 Biggest U.S. Metropolitan Areas, 1990-2000

Metropolitan Area	Population Increase	**Growth Rate**
Detroit, MI	0.2m	**5%**
Philadelphia, PA	0.2m	**5%**
Boston, MA	0.3m	**6%**
New York City, NY	1.5m	**9%**
Los Angeles, CA	1.1m	**10%**
Chicago, IL	0.9m	**11%**
Washington, DC	0.7m	**18%**
Miami, FL	1.0m	**24%**
Houston, TX	0.9m	**25%**
Dallas, TX	1.2m	**29%**

The high growth rates in Dallas, Houston, and Miami hint that future population growth will preference the southern and western Sun Belt region of America. Indeed, the highest population growth rates between 1990 and 2000 were in the southern and western states of Nevada, Arizona, Colorado, Utah, Georgia, Florida, and Texas, greatly outpacing the overall growth rate for the United States. More American population has been added in the states of the South and the West in the past 20 years than in any other region in the country. If we look at large metropolitan areas with the highest growth rates between 1990 and 2000, we again see that southern and western cities are growing the fastest, indicating the likelihood of more major population growth in those regions in the coming decades. Atlanta, Georgia, experienced the largest absolute population increase among these remaining cities, at 1.2 million, while Las Vegas, Nevada, had the greatest growth rate among all metropolitan areas with population over one million (see Table D-12).

Table D-12: Metropolitan Areas of Population over a Million with Highest Population Growth Rate, 1990-2000

Metropolitan Area	Population Increase	**Growth Rate**
Indianapolis, IN	0.2m	**17%**
Seattle, WA	0.5m	**19%**
Jacksonville, FL	0.2m	**21%**
Sacramento, CA	0.3m	**21%**
San Antonio, TX	0.3m	**22%**
Nashville, TN	0.3m	**25%**
Portland, OR	0.4m	**26%**
Riverside, CA	0.7m	**26%**
Charlotte, NC	0.3m	**30%**
Denver, CO	0.5m	**31%**
Orlando, FL	0.4m	**34%**
Atlanta, GA	1.2m	**38%**
Phoenix, AZ	1.0m	**45%**
Austin, TX	0.4m	**48%**
Las Vegas, NV	0.6m	**86%**

Only six of the sixteen large metropolitan areas with growth rates over 20% are located east of the Mississippi River, and all six are in the southeast states of Florida, Tennessee, North Carolina, and Georgia. The 10 American cities with the highest growth rates from 2000 to 2003, led by Gilbert, AZ, are all located in the far west or in Florida. In the same period, California, Texas, Florida, Georgia, and Arizona experienced the largest absolute population increases. The Census Bureau projects population growth to stay in the South and West through 2025, with over three-fourths of the new American population living in the West, the South, and the Southeast in 2025. Table D-13 reveals that the Middle Series projections of the Census Bureau put the absolute growth in the Far West at 20.3 million from 2005 to 2025. The High Series projections put this number near 30 million, though the relative share of U.S. population and share of population growth stay close to the Middle Series predictions. Returning to our earlier hypothesis, it is likely that true population growth will be a little above the numbers offered by the Middle Series projections of the Census Bureau.

Table D-13: U.S. Population by Region, Share, and Absolute Growth, 2005-2025

Region	2005 Pop. Share	2025 Pop. Share	Absolute growth, 2005-2025	**Share of total growth, 2005-2025**
New England	18%	17%	4.6m	**9%**
Midwest	19%	17%	3.1m	**6%**
Plains	7%	7%	2.5m	**5%**
Southeast	25%	25%	11.5m	**23%**
South	10%	10%	6.9m	**14%**
Far West	21%	24%	20.3m	**41%**
U.S. Total			**49.1m**	

We should not forget that regional population growth can be highly variable and sensitive to economic conditions, so these projections may change dramatically. It is still likely that in the near term, the most growth will occur in the Far West, much growth will be in the South and the Southeast, while there will be steady, low growth in the other regions of the country. Actually, if all regions of the United States maintained the growth of the Northeast, Midwest, and the Plains through 2025, the country's population would only increase by 25 million, to 320 million in 2025, a number much lower than that given by the Middle Series projections.

It is likely that in the near term Hispanic immigration will add significantly to the populations of the states bordering Mexico in the west and south. In 2000, 40% of the foreign-born population in America lived in California, Texas, Arizona, and New Mexico—12.6 million people. The same states contained 56% of America's Hispanic population. However, Census results also showed that growth of the Hispanic population has accelerated in states far from the Southwest. This migration of the Hispanic population caused large population increases in states such as Florida, Georgia, Illinois, New Jersey, New York, North Carolina, and Virginia. The growing Hispanic presence in the interior regions may signal an accelerating migration there in the future.

While the South and the West will grow at the highest rates in the coming years, the recovery of the "Rust Belt" region, centered in the Midwest, should not pass unnoticed. The Rust Belt, stretching from Iowa to the Great Lakes, had seen many of its major factories close down because they were unprofitable in the 1970s and 1980s. As a result, Rust Belt cities suffered high unemployment, high crime rates, and population declines due to migration of residents to other parts of the country. However, the Rust Belt cities started growing again in the 1990s due to the rise of new market-oriented companies in areas such as business services, high technology, light manufacturing, medical research, and pharmaceuticals. In addition, lake cities such as Detroit and Cleveland have used their strategic locations to increase the shipping of goods and the distribution of raw materials. Whereas the growth rate was negative for most Rust Belt centers in the 1980s, the 1990s brought renewed growth to the region, with notable population rises in the Detroit, Cleveland, and Louisville metro areas. The recovery of the Rust Belt hints that the Midwest may again attract workers and have significant population increases. The presence of many major research universities in the Midwest offers significant advantages in the new knowledge economy and may play a role in increasing Midwest population growth beyond what is currently projected.

The Impact on Transportation

General population growth and especially suburban growth will put more pressure on both public transportation and automobile transportation. However, with the continuing population growth, the number of registered vehicles is steadily increasing, while little new public transportation is being offered. In 2000, 88% of American workers used a private automobile to get to work, 5% used public transportation, 3% walked or cycled to work, and the remaining 4% worked at home. The figures were quite similar to those from 1990, with the biggest change being in the growth of Americans who work at home. Table D-14 shows the great changes in transportation that occurred between 1990 and 2000.

Table D-14: Selected Transportation Statistics, 1990-2000, Census Bureau and *Statistical Abstract of the United States*

Statistic	1990	2000	Change	**Growth Rate**
U.S. Population	249m	282m	33m	**13%**
Registered vehicles	188m	221m	33m	**18%**
Vehicles per 1000	755	783	28	**3%**
Trucks, vans, and SUVs	55m	87m	22m	**58%**
Auto accidents	6.47m	6.28m	-0.19m	**-3%**
Total U.S. road mileage	3.88m	3.93m	0.05m	**1%**
Miles traveled per vehicle	11,100	12,300	1,200	**11%**

There are more vehicles on American roads today than ever. In particular, there are more trucks, sports utility vehicles, and vans. Average annual travel mileage per vehicle is the highest it has ever been. Surprisingly, the number of auto accidents has actually decreased. Much of the increased travel mileage is due to suburban growth. Living away from the city offers the benefits of space and privacy, but it also requires long commutes to work. The time for the average American worker to get to work was at an all-time high of 26 minutes in 2000 (see Table D-15).

Table D-15: Travel Time to Work, Share in 1990 and 2000, and Breakdown among New Workers in the United States

Time to get to work	1990 Share	2000 Share	**Share of new workers**
14 minutes and less	33%	30%	**2%**
15-29 minutes	37%	36%	**28%**
30-44 minutes	18%	19%	**29%**
45-59 minutes	6%	7%	**16%**
60-89 minutes	4%	5%	**12%**
89 minutes and more	2%	3%	**13%**
Average time	**22 minutes**	**26 minutes**	**100%**

The increase in time spent in getting to work also comes from the congestion created by the great number of vehicles on the roads. In 1999, among America's urban areas, the annual traffic delay time per vehicle stood at 36 hours and at a fuel cost of $625. The most congestion was in Los Angeles, Atlanta, Seattle, and Houston – each of those cities except Seattle posted an absolute population increase of at least one million people between 1990 and 2000. In the coming years, car and truck sales are expected to follow current growth rates, putting a greater strain on American roads. As one begins to think about non-personal transportation responses to these problems, it is important to take account of population density, which can greatly affect the utility of various strategies. An analysis of population densities in the fastest-growing metropolitan centers shows that all but two have population densities lower than 4,200 persons per square mile (see Table D-16).

Population growth will bring more traffic to American roads, and traffic congestion will force state and local governments to consider ways to ease the ever-growing congestion in big cities. Transportation officials will also need to consider the effect of the growing diversity of the American population in terms of both age and race. Programs may need to be put in place to help elderly drivers become accustomed to new auto technology, and there may be an increased demand for multilingual driving instructors for the foreign-born who come to America. This diversification of the population through age and nativity may also create new pressure for more collective transportation systems, as many immigrants may come from areas where collective transportation is more culturally expected.

Table D-16: Population Densities of Fastest-Growing Metropolitan Centers, 2000

Metropolitan Center	Population per Square Mile	Share using private vehicles
Nashville, TN	1,152	93.5%
Orlando, FL	1,998	92.7%
Charlotte, NC	2,232	93.8%
Austin, TX	2,610	90.2%
Phoenix, AZ	2,781	90.0%
San Antonio, TX	2,808	90.9%
Atlanta, GA	3,161	90.6%
Riverside, CA	3,267	91.6%
Houston, TX	3,371	91.3%
Dallas, TX	3,469	92.7%
Denver, CO	3,616	87.1%
Portland, OR	3,939	85.2%
Las Vegas, NV	4,222	89.5%
Miami, FL	10,160	90.1%

Contributors

Authors

Mr. Lance R. Grenzeback
Dr. Herbert I. London
Dr. Richard Mudge
Mr. Sergio J. Ostria
Mr. Jeffrey A. Parker
Mr. Tom Warne
Mr. Richard J. Weiland

Board of Advisors

Mr. Tom Barry
Mr. Martin Capper
Mr. Michael Doyle
Mr. Butch Eley
Mr. Michael L. Eskew
Mr. Fred M. Fehsenfeld, Sr.
Mr. Art Guzzetti
Mr. Jeffery S. Held
Mr. John Horsley
Mr. Gerald A. Huber
Mr. Michael P. Huerta
Mr. Crawford F. Jencks
Dr. Herbert I. London
Mr. Mario Marsano
Mr. Robert M. McQueen
Mr. William Millar
Mr. Charles F. Potts
Mr. Frank Provenzano
Mr. David Rader
Mr. Robert Skinner
Mr. Harry Voccola
Mr. Tom Warne
Ms. Sheryl Washington
Mr. Arnold F. Wellman
Mr. Parker F. Williams
Mr. Michael Zimmerman

We wish to acknowledge support from the following organizations:
ACS State and Local Solutions
Alstom Transport
Econolite Control Products, Inc.
Heritage Group
Infrastructure Corporation of America
Mark IV Industries, Ltd.
National Cooperative Highway Research Program
NAVTEQ
PBS&J Engineering
Quixote Corporation
Raymond James
Transit Cooperative Research Program
United Parcel Service

Participants

Mr. Tom Barry
Senior Vice President
PBS&J Engineering

Mr. Grant Belanger
Executive Director of Material Planning & Logistics
Ford Motor Company

Ms. Susan Binder
Director of Legislation and Strategic Planning
Federal Highway Administration Office of Policy

Ms. Merri Boylan
Consultant

Ms. Debra Brisk
Deputy Director
Arizona Department of Transportation

Mr. Jeffrey N. Buxbaum
Senior Associate
Cambridge Systematics, Inc.

Ms. Anne P. Canby
President
Surface Transportation Policy Project

Mr. Martin Capper
President
Mark IV IVHS

Ms. Christina S. Casgar
Technical Assistant
U.S. Department of Transportation

Mr. Lew Dale
Director of Public Policy
General Motors Corporation

Dr. William J. DeWitt
Professor
University of Maryland

Mr. Michael Doyle
CEO
Econolite Control Products, Inc.

Ms. Lisa Dumke
Vice President
ADDCO, Inc.

Mr. Butch Eley
Chief Executive Officer
Infrastructure Corporation of America

Mr. Michael L. Eskew
Chairman and Chief Executive Officer
United Parcel Service

Dr. Peter B. Everett
Professor
Pennsylvania State University

Mr. Eugene Farber

Mr. Fred M. Fehsenfeld, Sr.
Chairman of the Executive Committee
Heritage Group

Mr. Tony Furst
Director
Federal Highway Administration

Mr. Lance R. Grenzeback
Senior Vice President
Cambridge Systematics, Inc.

Mr. Art Guzzetti
Director of Policy and Advocacy
American Public Transportation Association

Mr. Justin Heet
Research Fellow
Hudson Institute

Mr. Jeffery S. Held
Vice President of Corporate Development
Quixote Corporation

Mr. Tamar Henkin
Director
Transtech Management, Inc.

Mr. Gilbert Holmes
President/CEO
Indianapolis Public Transportation Corporation

Mr. John Horsley
Executive Director
AASHTO

Mr. Gerald A. Huber
Associate Director of Research
Heritage Group

Mr. Michael P. Huerta
Senior Vice President and Managing Director
ACS State and Local Solutions

Mr. John M. Inglish
General Manager
Utah Transit Authority

Mr. Crawford F. Jencks
Manager
National Cooperative Highway Research Program

Mr. Patrick D. Jones
Executive Director
International Bridge, Tunnel and Turnpike Association

Mr. Dennis C. Judycki
Associate Administrator
Federal Highway Administration

Mr. Anthony Kane
Director of Engineering & Technical Services
AASHTO

Ms. Marci Kenney
Director of Office of Program Development
Federal Highway Administration/RD&T

Mr. Larry M. King
Deputy Secretary for Planning
Pennsylvania Department of Transportation

Mrs. Janice Susie Lahsene
Corporate Planning Manager
Port of Portland

Mr. David M. Laney, Esq.
Chairman of the Board
National Railroad Passenger Corporation

Mr. Jack F. Letteire
Commissioner
New Jersey Department of Transportation

Dr. Herbert I. London
President
Hudson Institute

Mr. Gary E. Maring
Senior Associate
Cambridge Systematics, Inc.

Mr. Mario Marsano
Senior Vice President
Raymond, James & Co.

Ms. Kathleen Marvaso
Managing Director, Government Relations Office
American Automobile Association

Mr. James W. McClellan
Senior Vice President for Planning
Norfolk Southern Corporation

Mr. Robert M. McQueen
Vice President
PBS&J Engineering

Ms. Diana C. Mendes
Vice President
DMJM + HARRIS

Ms. Lydia E. Mercado
Office of Research Analysis
Federal Transit Administration

Mr. William Millar
President
American Public Transportation Association

Ms. Debra L. Miller
Secretary of Transportation
Kansas Department of Transportation

Dr. Kam Movassaghi
Former Secretary of Transportation
Louisiana Department of Transportation & Development

Dr. Richard Mudge
Vice President
Delcan, Inc.

Mr. J. Bryan Nicol
Commissioner
Indiana Department of Transportation

Mr. John R. Njord
Executive Director
Utah Department of Transportation

Ms. Iris N. Ortiz
Senior Professional
Cambridge Systematics, Inc.

Mr. Sergio J. Ostria
Senior Vice President
ICF Consulting

Mr. Jeffrey A. Parker
President
Jeffrey A. Parker & Associates

Mr. Leo Penne
Program Director
AASHTO

Mr. Charles F. Potts
Chief Executive Officer
Heritage Group

Mr. Jerome C. Premo
Senior Vice President
DMJM + HARRIS

Mr. Gordon Proctor
Director
Ohio Department of Transportation

Mr. Frank Provenzano
Director of ITS
Econolite Control Products, Inc.

Mr. David Rader
Vice President - Administration
Infrastructure Corporation of America

Dr. Robert J. Reilly
Director, National Cooperative Highway Research Program
Transportation Research Board

Mr. Arlee T. Reno
Senior Vice President
Cambridge Systematics, Inc.

Mr. Antonio Santalucia
Senior Associate
ICF Consulting

Mr. Isaac Shafran
Senior Vice President, Ports and Airports
The Louis Berger Group, Inc.

Mr. Alvin Shultz
Delcan, Inc.

Mr. Robert Skinner
Executive Director
Transportation Research Board

Mr. William M. Spreitzer
Executive Consultant ITS
General Motors Corporation

Dr. Irwin M. Stelzer
Director of Economic Policy Studies
Hudson Institute

Mr. Harry Voccola
Senior Vice President, Industry Relations
NAVTEQ

Mr. Tom Warne
President
Tom Warne & Associates, LLC

Ms. Sheryl Washington
United Parcel Service

Mr. Richard J. Weiland
President
Weiland Consulting Company

Dr. Kenneth Weinstein
Vice President and COO
Hudson Institute

Mr. Arnold F. Wellman
Corporate Vice President, Public Affairs
United Parcel Service

Mr. Parker F. Williams
Vice President
ACS State and Local Solutions

Mr. Christopher Wornum
Principal
Cambridge Systematics, Inc.

Mr. John M. Worthington
President & CEO
TransCore

Mr. Michael Zimmerman
Executive Vice President
Mark IV IVHS

Endnotes

1. Federal Highway Administration, *2002 Status of the Nation's Highways, Bridges, and Transit: Condition and Performance, Report to Congress*, U.S. Department of Transportation, Washington, D.C., January 2003 (FHWA *C&P Report*).

2. American Association of State Highway and Transportation Officials (AASHTO), *Bottom Line Report*, Washington, D.C., 2002 (AASHTO *Bottom Line Report*).

3. In the FHWA's *C&P Report* and AASHTO's *Bottom Line Report*, an economically productive transportation investment is a project that has a benefit/cost ratio of 1.0 or higher as measured by FHWA's Highway Economic Requirements System (HERS).

4. These fees, which are legally distinct from taxes, must correspond to the impact that the new development will have on local or regional transportation performance. Although not widespread and usually used for local roadway and transit improvements only, communities in states that have reduced taxing authority (e.g., California, Texas, Florida, and Oregon) have used this source aggressively.

5. These amounts are net of bond proceeds, which amounted to $11.2 billion in 2000. Bond proceeds are not revenues; rather, they are temporary debts that must be paid off with revenues from one or more of the four categories. (Tax credit bonds might be the exception if they were funded out of general revenues that were not previously allocated to transportation.)

6. FHWA *C&P Report*, cited.

7. Department of Energy, "Annual Energy Outlook with Projections to 2025." See http://www.eia.doe.gov/oiaf/aeo/demand.html and http://www.eia.doe.gov/oiaf/aeo/aeoref_tab.html.

8. NCHRP 8-36 (23), "Review of the Potential Feasibility of Using Alternative Revenue Sources to Fund Future State Transportation Needs," 2002.

9. FHWA *C&P Report*, cited.

10. The current federal fuel tax is 18.4 cents per gallon on gasoline, of which 15.44 cents per gallon are dedicated to the Highway Account of the Highway Trust Fund. The tax on diesel is 24.4 cents per gallon, of which 21.44 cents are deposited into the Highway Account.

11. FHWA *C&P Report,* Chapter 6.
12. Proposals under discussion include amendments to the Interstate System Rehabilitation and Reconstruction Pilot Program; repeal of the existing Value Pricing Program; the Allard bill; and H.R. 1767, the Freeing Alternatives for Speedy Transportation (FAST) Act.
13. Robert W. Poole, Jr. and C. Kenneth Orski, *HOT Networks: A New Plan for Congestion Relief and Better Transit,* Policy Study 305, Reason Foundation, Los Angeles, California, February 2003. Poole and Orski propose a 3,500-mile network of HOT lanes, tolled at $0.20 per mile.
14. AASHTO, "Transportation Finance Corporation Proposal," Jack Basso, 2002.
15. William J. Ankner, *Financing Intermodal Transportation,* paper prepared for the Center for Neighborhood Technology and Reconnecting America, September 2003. Available at http://www.reconnectingamerica.org or http://www.cnt.org.
16. NCHRP Final Report 8-39, *Financing and Improving Land Access to Cargo Hubs,* Transportation Research Board, Washington, D.C., 2003.
17. Ankner, *Financing Intermodal Transportation,* cited.
18. Ibid.
19. AASHTO, *National Finance Corporation,* concept paper.
20. Cambridge Systematics, Inc., *Mid-Atlantic Rail Operations Study (MAROps): Regional Infrastructure Bank Concept,* prepared for the I-95 Corridor Coalition, presented at the Transportation Research Board Annual Meeting, Washington, D.C., January 2004.
21. Bureau of Labor, Consumer Expenditure Survey data.
22. Department of Energy data.
23. Texas Transportation Institute, *2003 Annual Mobility Report.*
24. American Association of State Highway and Transportation Officials (AASHTO), *Freight-Rail Bottom Line Report,* 2002.
25. In this context, "water" includes river barge and coastal and lake shipments.
26. Strictly speaking, shippers (i.e., the owners of the cargo), when deciding on how to best get their products from production centers to markets, look at generalized logistics costs. Simplistically, the elements of logistics costs are 1) transportation costs, 2) the costs of carrying inventory, and 3) the costs associated with product storage facilities (such as warehouses or distribution centers). Generalized logistics costs are what shippers strive to minimize given other production inputs, and total logistics costs comprise transportation, inventory, and storage (costs of warehouses, insurance, etc.). Historical data on transportation and total logistics costs show that transportation has steadily increased as a share of total logistics spending over the period since 1980—a period in which truckload trucking and rail rates were steadily falling in real terms. This illustrates the "reorganization effect" in which logistics set-ups are revamped; transportation spending is substituted for inventory cost, with reduced logistics costs per unit as a result.
27. FHWA, *Economic Effects of Transportation: The Freight Story,* January 2002. Prepared by ICF Consulting and HLB Decision-Economics.
28. "Commercial Vehicle Travel Time and Delay at U.S. Border Crossings;" Federal Highway Administration; June 2002.

29. Texas Transportation Institute, *2003 Urban Mobility Study.*
30. Calculated by the ICF Team using FHWA's Highway Statistics, 2002. The data come from volume-to-service flow ratios published in table HM-61.
31. General Accounting Office, Freight Transportation: Strategies Needed to Address Planning and Financing Limitations, December 2003.
32. Association of American Railroads, *Railroad Facts,* 2002 Edition.
33. U.S. Department of Transportation, Bureau of Transportation Statistics, National Transportation Statistics, 2002.
34. For multilane facilities, volume-service flow ratio is determined by dividing the peak traffic in the peak direction by the capacity. For all other facilities, the ratio is determined by dividing the peak traffic by the capacity. Peak traffic is estimated as AADT *K, where K is the design hour volume (30th highest hour) as a percent of AADT.
35. Highway Statistics, 2002; Federal Highway Administration (FHWA). Highways are classified as severely or significantly congested if volume-to-service flow ratios are 0.80 or higher.
36. Federal Highway Administration, Commercial Vehicle Travel Time and Delay at U.S. Border Crossings, June 2002.
37. It is important to note that motor carrier policy decisions should be based on numerous criteria that reflect the range of our relevant societal values—from economic efficiency to the public safety. For instance, in the case of size and weight and hours of service restrictions, any explicit financial burdens on the industry may be counterbalanced by long-term improvements in safety. Likewise, improvements in safety performance can lead to lower insurance rates, reduced cargo damage, and better service reliability. In general, regulatory measures that effectively remedy market failures ultimately can improve social welfare.
38. U.S. Department of Transportation, Federal Highway Administration, Comprehensive Truck Size and Weight Study, August 2000.
39. Reported in: Freight Capacity for the 21st Century, Special Report 271; National Academies of Sciences; Transportation Research Board.
40. U.S. General Accounting Office, Surface Infrastructure: Costs, Financing and Schedules for Large-Dollar Transportation Projects, 1998.
41. For a more detailed discussion of the range of issues affecting the trucking industry, please see the FHWA report (prepared by ICF Consulting) entitled Evaluation of U.S. Commercial Motor Carrier Industry Challenges and Opportunities, March 31, 2003.
42. ICF Consulting and ZETA-TECH Associates, Scheduled Railroading and the Viability of Carload Service, Executive Summary, prepared for the Federal Railroad Administration, Office of Policy, March 2004.
43. Ibid., pp. 8, 24.
44. U.S. DOT, Maritime Administration. *Intermodal Access to US Ports, Report on Survey Findings.* August 2002.
45. "Collision Brings Chaos: Main Mississippi Channel Blocked," *The Advocate,* Baton Rouge, Louisiana; February 23, 2004
46. U.S. Department of Transportation Maritime Administration, 2002 Intermodal Access to U.S. Ports Report on Survey Findings, August 2002.

47. U.S. Department of Transportation Maritime Administration, 2002 Intermodal Access to U.S. Ports Report on Survey Findings, August 2002.
48. The American Waterways Operators: http://www.americanwaterways.com/
49. Reported in *Freight Capacity for the 21st Century, Special Report 271*, National Academies of Sciences, Transportation Research Board.
50. U.S. International Trade Commission; *The Economic Effects of Significant U.S. Import Restraints*; May 1999.
51. Reported in: *Freight Capacity for the 21st Century, Special Report 271*; National Academies of Sciences; Transportation Research Board.
52. Global Insight, Inc. was formed to bring together two economic and financial information companies, DRI and WEFA.
53. FHWA, Trade: From National Markets to Global Markets (Theme Paper #1) – Global Insight Data.
54. Ibid.
55. Consider the effects of the just-in-time revolution, which are palpable and intuitive. Stiglitz shows that the average lead-time for ordering materials and supplies in advance of production has declined from 72 days in 1961 to less than 50 days by 1999. Inventories have fallen from roughly 1.6 times monthly sales in the 1970s to some 1.2 times monthly sales today. Whereas logistics costs (excluding transportation) represented 19.1 percent of U.S. GDP in 1990, these costs had fallen to less than 11 percent of GDP by the turn of the century. We know that investment in advanced logistics is self-perpetuating due to the networked inter-relatedness of firms in inter-industry supply chains. For example, Ford now requires all its major suppliers to participate in e-purchasing arrangements, automated inventory management, and just-in-time delivery under stiff late penalties. Suppliers are thus compelled to make the capital investments needed at their end to assure companies like Ford a decent return on investment in the logistics investments made at its end – investments triggered by (among other things) suitable highway transportation. Again, all firms, shippers and carriers, will not share the resulting productivity gains proportionately in such a supply chain. Yet, the overall gain is positive for the regional economy.
56. Forecasts for rail ton-miles are based on 1990 through 1998 BTS data, using damped trend exponential smoothing. Forecasts for truck ton-miles are based on two forecast models: linear trend based on 1990 through 1997 data and double (Brown) exponential smoothing based on 1960 through 1995 data in five year increments; the two forecasts are combined with equal weights. Forecasts for air ton-miles are based on two forecasting methodologies: linear trend based on 1990 through 1998 data and damped trend exponential smoothing based on 1960 through 1995 data in five year increments; the two forecasts are combined with equal weights.
57. TRANSEARCH is a proprietary freight flow database owned by Reebie Associates.
58. Again, using BTS data as a benchmark, the baseline ton-miles for all other modes appear to be lower in the AASHTO Report. Air freight shows the greatest percentage discrepancy at only 9 billion ton-miles in 2000 as compared with BTS' figure of nearly 15 billion. Additionally, freight moved by rail in 2000 was 15 percent lower than what BTS reported and water freight volumes were nearly 17 percent lower.

59. The study also provides forecast revenue.
60. These hauls are characterized by being regional in nature, with typical lengths of under 100 miles.
61. ATA's forecast accounts for the effects of security concerns on the air transport industry, which dampen somewhat the projections of the demand for air cargo.
62. We do not have an exact number for team driving as a fraction of truck-miles in intercity service. The anecdotal evidence is strong, however, that the fraction is small. Many large firms will not supply team drivers. It requires a high level of management effort to find and retain compatible partners. There are niche TL companies that specialize in team service.
63. ICF Consulting estimates based on work for FMCSA on the NAFTA EIS.
64. Growth in world trade and ongoing rationalization in the liner shipping industry are two of the principal factors that will continue to push the development and implementation of post-Panamax vessels. The introduction of post-Panamax ships already has affected the ports and terminals businesses. Shippers also are accepting more transhipment and relay type services.
65. Alan M. Field, "Headed South," *The Journal of Commerce,* April 14-20, 2003.
66. Bill Mongelluzzo, *"Maquila Meltdown," The Journal of Commerce,* April 14-20, 2003.
67. Note that the rapid pace of economic development in China (and India) is one of the major factors that has led in increased fuel prices in the United States and elsewhere. China is rapidly becoming a motorized nation, and vehicle ownership is expected to increase significantly in the coming years. This means that China will become a major energy demand nation, and given limited supply it is reasonable to expect that fuel prices will remain relatively high. This has important ramifications for the freight transportation industry in the United States since fuel cost is an integral driver of the cost structure that motor carriers operate under. As shown in Figure 6-3, changes in fuel prices are closely correlated with the number of bankruptcies in the trucking industry.
68. *National Intelligent Transportation Systems Program Plan: A Ten-Year Vision,* ITS America, January 2002, p 39
69. See part five of this book.
70. http://www.dot.gov/stratplan2008/strategic_plan.htm
71. http://www.nhtsa.dot.gov/nhtsa/announce/speeches/030310Runge/Lifesavers-Speech.pdf
72. http://mobility.tamu.edu/ums/news_release/
73. Demographics Presentation to Vision 2010, Kenneth Weinstein, Hudson Institute, September 22, 2003
74. See chapter 11 of this book.
75. See part one of this book.
76. This subject is addressed separately later in this chapter.
77. http://www.its.dot.gov/ivi/ivi.htm
78. http://www.roadwaysafety.org/chap2_2.html
79. In Europe, telematics refers to any technology that can be applied at a distance, whether related to transportation or not. "Transport telematics" was an early Europe synonym for Intelligent Transportation Systems. In the United

States, however, telematics has taken on this narrower and more specific meaning.

80. http://www.findarticles.com/cf_0/m3012/4_182/85047975/p1/article.jhtml

81. Example: As of this writing, OnStar estimates that it handles about 29,000 remote unlock calls and 800 crash notification calls per month (see http://onstar.internetpressroom.com/pressroom.cfm). This is roughly 1,000 calls per day. If an operator can handle a conservative average of five calls per hour, this is 200 person hours per day. At $20/hour fully loaded and 365 days/year, the cost is ~$1.5 million per year. Double this for plant and equipment to $3 million per year. Double again, just to estimate generously, to $6 million per year. OnStar claims over 2 million subscribers, for an *annual* cost per vehicle for these services of less than $3.00, far less for handling ACN calls only, which are 30 times less frequent than remote door unlock calls. (Note that this analysis does not explicitly include costs for communications and in-vehicle equipment.)

82. http://hraunfoss.fcc.gov/edocs_public/attachmatch/FCC-03-322A1.doc

83. http://www.roke.co.uk/download/datasheets/Galileo.pdf

84. http://www.computerworld.com/mobiletopics/mobile/story/0,10801,82464,00.html

85. In principle, three external objects are required (hence *tri*lateration),but since the vehicle knows that it is on the ground and which side of the objects it is on, two objects are sufficient in a pinch.

86. http://www.eetimes.com/story/OEG20001113S0048

87. http://www.mercedestechstore.com/pdfs/W211_advisor/219%20HO%20Networking%20(ACB-ICC)%2009-03-02.pdf

88. http://www.mostnet.de/brochure/index.php

89. http://www.firewire-1394.com/what_is_idb-1394.htm

90. http://www.gizmohighway.com/pages/technology/drive_by_wire.htm

91. http://www.quinion.com/words/turnsofphrase/tp-dri1.htm

92. Adapted from Gomi & Weiland, "Prerequisites for Probe Data Processing for Traffic and Safety Applications," *Proceedings of the Safety Conference of the 9th EAEC International Congress (2003)*

93. http://www.freep.com/money/autonews/ford27_20040227.htm

94. The request to dispatch help happens at once in any case, and does not depend on making a voice connection. However, the emergency response will be canceled if no help is wanted.

95. DSRC was and continues to be used for non-mobile applications like tagging livestock and fish.

96. "The Roadway INFOstructure: What? Why? How?: Meeting the Needs for Integrated Information of Roadway System Managers and Users." See http://gulliver.trb.org/publications/circulars/ec057.pdf

97. http://www.itsa.org/inti2003.html

98. http://www.europa.eu.int/information_society/programmes/esafety/doc/esafety_communication/ esafety_communication_vf_en.pdf

99. http://www.itsa.org/committe.nsf/0/7b416b17314286e985256212004ed6f5?OpenDocument

100. *Ibid.*
101. Delcan Inc., "Rate of Return from Highway Investment," Draft Report, (Fall 2003), NCHRP 20-24 (28)
102. James R. Robinson, "The Future of Travel Time Data: A Paradigm Shift," Discussion Paper prepared for AASHTO Subcommittee on System Operations and Management (Spring 2004).
103. These measures are only one step short of what might be the best measure of customer satisfaction – did you complete your trip on time? Safety is implied by phrase on time.
104. Although deployment and development of ITS infrastructure rapidly accelerated in the 1980s, the seeds of ITS were planted decades earlier. For example, FHWA researched Electronic Route Guidance Systems in the 1960s, and the first metered ramp was installed in Chicago in 1963. Even earlier, the General Motors pavilion at the 1939 New York World's Fair highlighted what we now call ITS and telematics.
105. Data on ITS costs from: Cheslow, Melvyn and Staples, Barbara, "Working Paper: National Costs of the Metropolitan ITS Infrastructure: Updated with 2002 Deployment Data." Mitretek Center for Telecommunications and Advanced Technology, October 2003.
106. Some assumptions within the full build-out proposal include: all ramps metered, CCTV at every mile of freeway, loop detectors placed at half-mile spacing across all freeway lanes and every approach lane of a signalized intersection, and call boxes placed at half-mile intervals in each direction.
107. The constraint on the amount of roads where data can be collected relates to the fraction of vehicles equipped as probes. The time required to collect these data depends in part on the form of communication used and the density of data needed to assure statistical significance for any speed or travel time reports.
108. Systems to collect travel times using user fee tags are in place or under construction in the New York metropolitan area; the San Francisco Bay area; San Antonio, Texas; and Houston, Texas.
109. http://www.nhi.fhwa.dot.gov/coursedesc.asp?coursenum=1130
110. The autonomous ACC (AACC) system was intended to represent a typical first-generation product such as those now entering the market.
111. For example, most DOTs have adjusted the standard capacity of a lane in recent years from 1800 vehicles per lane per hour to 2000 or more after observing the ability of new models to reduce headways because of more powerful engines and better braking systems.
112. *State Route-60 Automated Truck Facility Study*; Sarakki Associates for California Department of Transportation; Working Draft; September, 2003
113. Adapted from Table F-16 in *A Guide to Best Practices for Achieving Context Sensitive Solutions (CSS)* NCHRP Report 480; Section F: Ensuring Safe and Feasible Solutions.
114. *2002 Status of the Nation's Highways, Bridges and Transit: Conditions and Performance, Executive Summary*, USDOT, Washington, DC, page ES-13.
115. Statement by William W. Millar, *Department of Homeland Security Directives Require Funding*, May 20 2004, American Public Transportation Association, Washington, D.C.

116. *The Bottom Line,* 2002, AASHTO, Washington, D.C., pages 44-45
117. *TEA-21 Reauthorization Recommendations, An Investment in America*; American Public Transportation Association, Washington, D.C., 2002, page 36
118. *Two Cents Makes Sense,* Testimony before the Subcommittee on Highways and Transit, Committee on Transportation and Infrastructure, Washington, D.C., July 16, 2002, page 8
119. This chapter is adapted from *The Benefits of TEA-21 Funding Guarantees,* Jeffrey A. Parker & Associates Inc., for the American Pubic Transportation Association, December 2002.
120. *National Transit Data Base,* 2000 Data, Federal Transit Administration, Washington, D.C.
121. Ibid.
122. *Energy Prices and Taxes,* International Energy Agency, 1st Quarter 2004, p. xxxiv
123. *International Fuel Prices,* Gerhard P. Metschies, German Federal Ministry for Economic Cooperation and Development, May 2003, p. 59.
124. *Energy Prices and Taxes*
125. *International Fuel Prices,* p. 58
126. "Livable Cities – Will Transportation Professionals Answer the Challenge?" *TR News,* "Point of View" article by Vukan R. Vuchic, Transportation Research Board, Washington, D.C., December 2003, page 23
127. *TCRP Report No. 95* – "Road Value Pricing, Traveler Response to Transportation System Changes": Chapter 14; Transportation Research Board; John E. Evans IV, Kiran U. Bhatt, and Katherine F. Turnbull; Washington, D.C., 2003, page 14-5
128. *Value Pricing Experience,* http://www.fhwa.dot.gov/policy/otps/projdesc.htm FHWA January 12, 2004
129. *TCRP Report No 95* – Chapter 14, page 5
130. *Congestion Charging: 6 Months On,* Transport for London, October 2003, Item 3.64
131. Ibid., Item 3.77
132. Ibid., Item 3.78
133. Ibid., Item 3.75
134. *An Exploration of Motor Vehicle Congestion Pricing in New York;* Regional Plan Association; Jeffrey M. Zupan and Alexis Perrotta, New York, NY, November 2003, page 30
135. Ibid., page 35
136. *2003 Public Transportation Fact Book*; American Public Transportation Association, Washington, D.C., p. 34. Heavy rail cities in the United States are Atlanta, Baltimore, Boston, Chicago, Cleveland, Los Angeles, Miami, New York, Philadelphia, San Francisco Bay Area, and Washington, D.C.
137. *Transit Needs Synthesis Report*; American Public Transportation Association, Washington, D.C. 2002 pages 1 and 5.
138. *Value Pricing Experience*
139. *Value Pricing Experience*
140. *Interstate 15 FasTrak Fact Sheet,* SANDAG, San Diego, CA, October 2003, page 2

141. *Managed Lanes – More Efficient Use of the Freeway System*; Report No 4160-5-P1 Texas Transportation Institute; Tina Collier and Ginger Daniels Goodin, College Station, TX, 2002, page 7
142. *Houston Value Pricing Pilot Program Fact Sheet,* Texas Transportation Institute, College Station, TX, 2003
143. *TCRP Report No. 97: Emerging New Paradigms, A Guide to Fundamental Change in Local Public Transportation Programs,* Robert G. Stanley, Matthew Coogan et al., Transportation Research Board; Washington, D.C., 2003
144. *TCRP Research Results Digest No. 55: Support for Fundamental Change in Public Transportation,* Transportation Research Board, Washington, D.C., December 2002, page 7.
145. *Mobility Management and Market Oriented Local Transportation,* DOT-T-92-07, Jeffrey A. Parker & Associates Inc., Office of Technical Assistance and Safety, Federal Transit Administration, Washington, D.C., 1991
146. Parker, *Mobility Management,* Executive Summary
147. Parker, pages 21-23
148. *TCRP Report No. 21 – Strategies to Assist Local Transportation Agencies in Becoming Mobility Managers*; Transportation Research Board; Crain & Associates, Inc.; Washington, D.C., 1997
149. *Running Public Transit in New York City Like a Business,* Institute for Transportation Systems, City University of New York; Jeffrey Parker, New York, NY, 1988
150. *Running Public Transit in New York City Like a Business,* Institute for Transportation Systems, City University of New York, Jeffrey Parker, 1988, pages V-10 & 11
151. *The Public Sector in Public Transportation in New York City, A Policy Perspective*; Institute for Transportation Systems, City University of New York, E.S. Savas, Sigurd Grava, Roy Sparrow; New York, NY, January 1991
152. Hancock, Kathleen L., "Freight Transportation Data," *TRB Millennium Papers,* Transportation Research Board, National Research Council, Washington, D.C., (1999)
153. Harrison, Robert, "International Trade and Transport," *TRB Millennium Papers,* Transportation Research Board, National Research Council, Washington, D.C., (1999)
154. DeWitt, William, Jennifer Clinger, "Intermodal Freight Transportation," *TRB Millennium Papers,* Transportation Research Board, National Research Council, Washington, D.C., (1999)
155. Regan, Amelia, et.al., "Freight Transportation Planning and Logistics," *TRB Millennium Papers,* Transportation Research Board, Washington, D.C., (1999)
156. Regan, op. cit.
157. DeWitt, op. cit.
158. Clarke, David B., "Local and Regional Rail Freight Transport," *TRB Millennium Papers,* Transportation Research Board, National Research Council, Washington, D.C., (1999)
159. Skinner, R.E., "Transportation in the 21st Century," *Public Roads,* Federal Highway Administration, Vol. 64, Issue 2, September (2000)

160. Fletcher, David R., "Geographic Information Systems for Transportation: A Look Forward," *TRB Millennium Papers,* Transportation Research Board, National Research Council, Washington, D.C., (1999)
161. Morehouse, James, "Vision for the Future," *Global Intermodal Freight: State of Readiness for the 21st Century,* Conference Proceedings 25, Transportation Research Board, National Research Council, Long Beach, CA, February 23-26, (2000)
162. Hynes-Cherin, Brigid, "Institutions in Flux," *TRB Millennium Papers,* Transportation Research Board, National Research Council, Washington, D.C., (1999)
163. Pisarski, A, "Trends We Cannot Afford to Miss," *Public Works Management & Policy,* American Public Works Associates, Vol. 8, Issue 1, July (2003)
164. Christopher, Richard, et. al., "Environmental Issues in Transportation Law," *TRB Millennium Papers,* Transportation Research Board, National Research Council, Washington, D.C., (1999)
165. Judy, Richard W., Carol D'Amico, *Workforce 2020: Work and Workers in the 21st Century,* Hudson Institute, Indianapolis, Indiana (1997)
166. Heet, Justin, *Vision 2010 and Beyond: The Future of Transportation,* presented at the 2010 and Beyond Board of Advisors Meeting, Washington, D.C. (January 9, 2004), p. 2
167. Friedman, Thomas L., *The Lexus and the Olive Tree: Understanding Globalization,* Farrar, Straus and Giroux, New York, 1999
168. Goodman, Peter S., Phillip P. Pan, "Chinese Workers Pay for Walmart's Low Prices; Retailer Squeezes Its Asian Suppliers to Cut Cost: [Final Edition]" *Washington Post,* Washington, D.C., February 8, 2004
169. Grogan, Jim, "Steel Price Crisis," *Engineering News Record,* McGraw-Hill Construction, March 22, 2004, p. 26
170. *"Making the Nation Safer, The Role of Science and Technology in Countering Terrorism,"* Transportation Research Board, National Research Council, Washington, D.C., 2002, pp. 212-213
171. Bickel, Richard G., "Key Issues Confronting Public Transportation Planning and Development," *TRB Millennium Papers,* Transportation Research Board, National Research Council, Washington, D.C., (1999). See also Boyle, Daniel, K., Peter J. Foote, Karla H. Karash, "Public Transportation Marketing and Fare Policy," *TRB Millennium Papers,* Transportation Research Board, National Research Council, Washington, D.C., (1999).
172. Harrison, John A., "Intercity Passenger Rail," *TRB Millennium Papers,* Transportation Research Board, National Research Council, Washington, D.C., (1999)
173. Boyle et al., op. cit.
174. Suen, S. Ling, C.G.B. Mitchell, "Accessible Transportation and Mobility," *TRB Millennium Papers,* Transportation Research Board, National Research Council, Washington, D.C., (1999).
175. Bickel, op. cit.
176. Ross, Nancy, *Transportation: Invest in America, The Bottom Line*
177. Ross, op. cit., p. 2

178. U.S. Freight Transportation Forecast To 2014, American Trucking Associations, Inc., 2003.
179. Marine Transportation: Federal Financing and a Framework for Infrastructure Investments, U.S. General Accounting Office, September 2002, p.3.
180. "Amid FCC Decency Push, Satellite Radio Is Poised to Grow," Wall St. Journal, March 1, 2004, p. B1
181. This table uses the latest projections available from the Census Bureau. This means a Middle Series that reflects the 2000 Census but a High Series that reflects only the 1990 Census.
182. For consistency, this figure uses the projections based on the 1990 Census for all series. However, in a general sense it has little effect on the shape of the data. The most recent Middle Series projections adjust expectations about net migration from the earlier projections by taking a weighted basket of the product of 0.938 and the earlier Middle Series assumptions and the product of 0.062 and the earlier High Series assumptions.